DEER HUNTERS
ALMANAC

From the publishers of
DEER & DEER HUNTING MAGAZINE

2004 EDITION

© 2003 by
Krause Publications

All rights reserved. No portion of this publication may be reproduced or transmitted in any form or by any means, electronic or mechanical, including photocopy, recording, or any information stored in a retrieval system, without permission in writing from the publisher, except by a reviewer who may quote brief passages in a critical article or review to be printed in a magazine or newspaper, or electronically transmitted on radio or television.

Deer & Deer Hunting is a registered trademark of Krause Publications Inc.

Published by

Krause Publications
700 E. State St. • Iola, WI 54990-0001
Telephone: 715/445-2214   fax: 715/445-4087
World Wide Web: www.deeranddeerhunting.com

Please call or write for our free catalog of outdoor publications.
Our toll-free number to place an order or obtain a free catalog is 800-258-0929.

Library of Congress Catalog Number: 92-74255

ISBN: 0-87349-330-3
Printed in the United States of America

Front cover photo by Charles J. Alsheimer.
Back cover photos by Jim Schlender.

DEER HUNTERS' ALMANAC – 2004 EDITION, VOLUME 13

CONTENTS

Editor's Note 4

CHAPTER 1: VITAL CONCERNS FOR TODAY'S HUNTERS 7
Buck Fawn Harvests............... 7
The Disappearing Hunter......... 17
The Antlerless Hunt 21
QDM: Are You Doing it Right? 27
A Brief History of QDM........... 29
Day Marks Sportsmens' Efforts 31

Almanac Insights
   Ordinance Limits Bow-Hunting........ 9
   DVCs Kill Many People............. 12
   Pittsboro, N.C. Seeks Bow-Hunt...... 13
   Wildlife Recreation = Big Bucks 14
   IBO Dontates to U.S.S.A. 15
   Employees Can Donate to FHFH..... 24
   Pittman-Robertson Act History....... 25
   Consequences of High Deer Numbers. 30

Whitetail Classroom
   Carrying Capacity.................. 12
   Deer Density...................... 22
   Recruitment 25
   Sustainable Harvest 30

CHAPTER 2: CWD STRIKES THE EAST 33
Wis., Ill., Join the Infamous List 33
CWD Timeline 34
What's the Human Risk? 35
2003 State CWD Testing 36
CWD is Just One of Many Diseases 38
CWD FAQs..................... 39
N.M. Gives Incentive for Testing.... 41
Livestock Diseases............... 43
Pathway of a Prion 44
The Race is On 47
Studies Link Bacteria, Copper 50
Venison Not Linked to Human Death 51
Colorado Isn't Worried 52

Almanac Insights
   Trucker Hauled Illegal Deer 35
   Are You Worried Aboud CJD? 42

CHAPTER 3: THE BIG BUCKS OF NORTH AMERICA 55
Man Awaits 20-Pointer............ 55

Hunter Bags Drop Tine Buck 56
Wyo. Produces Buck of a Lifetime... 57
Hunter Finds 18-Pointer........... 58
Hunter Uses Release to Call in Buck. 59
Southern Hunt Produces Best Buck . 60
N.J. Hunter Kills 11th-Hour Buck.... 61
How to Age White-Tailed Deer 62
Bow-Hunting Gets Boost From P&Y . 64
Will Your Buck Make the Books? ... 64
B&C Score Sheet................ 65

CHAPTER 4: ADVANCED BOW-HUNTING TIPS & TACTICS 67
Archery Accessories: Details Make A Difference................ 67
11 Tips to Becoming a Better Archer 73
Urban Areas Seek Solutions....... 77
Drop-Away Arrow Rests 79
Don't Lose Your Deer! 80
Diffraction: Why to Hate It 82
Martin Inducted Into Archery HOF .. 85
Carbon Arrows: The Future is Now.. 87
How to Select Fletchings 88
Silence That Bow! 89
Selecting Accurate Broadheads ... 90
Paper-Tuning Instructions 90
Photos Reveal Fletching Integrity ... 91
Proper Broadhead Tuning 92
Are Expandibles Right for You?..... 92
Today's Hot New Bows 93
Try the Winter Challenge! 95
The Buck at 4 Yards 97

Almanac Insights
   Antis Interfere with Pa. Hunt......... 68
   Bow-Hunting is Effective Urban Tool.. 71
   U.S. Army Uses Modified Arrow 81
   Bow-Hunters are Self-Taught 98

Archery Insights
   Setting Up a Clinometer............ 76
   Fall-Away Range-Finders 78
   Be Stealthy 84
   Eight Tips for Accuracy............. 98
   Tips for Cold Weather.............. 99

CHAPTER 5: INSIGHTS FOR RIFLE AND SHOTGUN HUNTERS 101

Choosing the Best Bullets 101
Break In Your New Rifle.......... 103
Revive a 'Shot-Out' Rifle......... 103
The History of Semi-Automatic Rifles 104
Barnes' Rules for Reloading Ammo 105
How to Mount a Riflescope 108
Use a Partner to Sight-In Your Rifle . 109
Find Gun-Hunting Gear on the Web 110
Today's Hot New Deer Rifles 111
Remington Unveils Beefy New Slug 113
Firearms Cleaning 114
Today's Hot New Shotguns 115
Accessories: Endless Possibilities.. 117
Into the Fog 123
Disposing of Smokeless Powder .. 124
Muzzleloader Supplies 126
Mossy Oak Blind-Hunting Tips.... 127
Keep Your Muzzleloader Clean ... 128
Prepare for Long Shots 128
Today's Hot New Muzzleloaders .. 129
Sight-In Your New Muzzleloader ... 130
Pyrodex Pellets are Consistent .. 131
Muzzleloading Projectiles........ 132
Muzzleloader Ballistics Chart..... 133

Almanac Insights
Aldo Leopold Quote 125
Bucktail Facts................... 127

CHAPTER 6: THE WEIRD WORLD OF THE WHITETAIL 135

Hunter Kills Mule Deer in Minnesota 135
Toy Tire Deforms Oklahoma Buck .. 136
Mich. Hunter Shoots 'Basket Rack' . 137
First Big Buck Has Deformed Rack . 138
Odd Racks Have All Shapes, Sizes. 139
Technology Detects Lyme Faster... 140
Peanut Butter Fails to Deter Deer .. 140

CHAPTER 7: NATIONAL WHITETAIL TRENDS .. 143

All-Time High Whitetail Harvests..... 143
Single-Season Record Harvests..... 143
Average Annual Deer Harvests...... 145

STATE-BY-STATE INFORMATION:
Alabama 146
Arizona 147
Arkansas 148
Colorado 149
Connecticut..................... 150
Delaware 151
Florida......................... 152
Georgia 153
Idaho 154
Illinois......................... 155
Indiana......................... 156
Iowa........................... 157
Kansas......................... 158
Kentucky 159
Louisiana....................... 160
Maine.......................... 161
Maryland 162
Massachusetts.................. 163
Michigan 164
Minnesota 165
Mississippi..................... 166
Missouri....................... 167
Montana....................... 168
Nebraska...................... 169
New Hampshire................. 170
New Jersey 171
New York 172
North Carolina.................. 173
North Dakota................... 174
Ohio........................... 175
Oklahoma 176
Oregon......................... 177
Pennsylvania................... 178
Rhode Island 179
South Carolina................. 180
South Dakota................... 181
Tennessee..................... 182
Texas.......................... 183
Vermont....................... 184
Virginia......................... 185
Washington 186
West Virginia 187
Wisconsin 188
Wyoming 189

CHAPTER 8: WHITETAIL FACTS.. 191

Insights Into Deer Behavior 191
Peak Rut Predictor 193
Full Moon Dates................ 194
Plan Hunts By the Rutting Moon ... 194
Standard Time Differences 195
Sunrise/Sunset Timetable 195
10 Steps to Safe Venison......... 196
Mossy Oak Food Plot Guide 200
Hunting Gear Web Sites 201
QDMA Record Kill Map 202
QDMA Deer Density Map 203
Hunting Organization Directory 204

Whitetail Classroom
Albino Deer/Body Size 192

Editor's Note

By Joe Shead

Almanac Reminds Us of Forgotten Tips and Tricks

I think it's safe to say there are few publications out there like the *Deer Hunters Almanac*.

When you open the pages of this publication, you won't find pictures of world-record bucks or articles that make you think you need to spend your life savings to enjoy deer hunting.

The *Deer Hunters Almanac* steps back from the headlines and hype we too often hear about deer hunting and gets back to the basics. Let's say you've hunted with "Ol' Trusty" for a decade or so, but this year you decided you need a new rifle. However, it's been so long since you've mounted a scope atop a new tack-driver that you need a little refresher. Turn to Page 108 and we've got you covered.

Maybe you're curious about those drop-away arrow rests you've been hearing so much about, but you really have no idea how they work. "Drop-Away Arrow Rests" on Page 79 should clear things up a bit.

Or maybe all the talk about chronic wasting disease has you leery of meat processors, and this year you're going to butcher your own deer. "10 Tips to Safe Venison" on Page 196 will walk you through the process.

These types of stories, I think, are the real beauty of the *Deer Hunters Almanac*. These articles give new hunters the instruction they need to take up the sport, and help veterans brush up on their hunting skills. The *Almanac* covers things most deer hunting publications don't take the time to cover, yet this information is something we all use.

Faithful *Deer and Deer Hunting* readers may recognize a few reprints from that magazine. These stories are some of our most popular pieces from that magazine, and the demand for them gives them new life here in the *Almanac*.

But mounting new scopes and butchering deer isn't all you'll learn about in the *Almanac*. We tackle hard-hitting stories such as "Buck Fawn Harvests" on Page 7 and "The Disappearing Hunter" on Page 17. Whether it's arguments over the impact of buck fawn harvests during antlerless hunts or low new-hunter recruitment, these are some of the issues hunters face now and in the future.

You'll also find articles on choosing the best hunting bullets, dealing with diffraction on your bow sight and insights into deer behavior. And of course, the *Almanac* wouldn't be complete without Deer Browse and a few big-buck stories. Plus, we've thrown in a few "mood" pieces, simply for your reading pleasure.

So I guess you could say the *Almanac* is a lot of useful information floating around inside a book to be drawn upon for quick reference.

Huh. Kinda sounds like the random thoughts floating around in my head as I sit on my deer stand.

Enjoy!

Practical Advice for Today's Hunters

The Little Book of Big Bucks
From the Publishers of *Deer & Deer Hunting*
The only thing little about *The Little Book of Big Bucks* is its trim size! Arranged in eight easy-to-digest chapters, this comprehensive guide provides insight into all of the important elements of deer hunting, including possible second chances at mature bucks and chasing whitetails across America. Chapters such as "For the Record," "Beginner's Luck," and "Worth the Wait" contain amazing photographs and tales of recent record-class bucks taken in North America. Complete coverage includes references with state-by-state agency information, Web sites for hunting gear manufacturers and hunting organizations, and tips for airline travel.
Softcover • 5¼x8 • 208 pages
130 b&w photos
Item# LBBB • $12.99

Modern Whitetail Hunting
by Michael Hanback
Don't rely on luck to harvest a big deer this fall. With advice from one of the foremost hunting writers in the world today, learn where mature bucks live and what triggers their movements, best early and late-season strategies, up-to-date tree stand, rattling, calling, and scent tricks, how to hunt huge deer on small lands, and much more. Get the advice of Mossy Oak's top big-buck hunters. More than 100 photographs and illustrations set into motion today's latest and greatest whitetail strategies!
Softcover • 6x9 • 216 pages
100 b&w photos • 8-page color section
Item# MWH • $19.99

Mapping Trophy Bucks
Using Topographic Maps to Find Deer
by Brad Herndon
Remain one step ahead of the competition! The next time out in the field, the odds will be in your favor if you have a topographical map. With this new guide, you will learn the basic concepts of topographical maps and implementing sound terrain hunting strategies. From inside corners and double inside corners to the perfect funnel and mastering the wind, get a better concept of using the wind and understanding topographical maps. Illustrations show details of how deer move, where to place your stand, and how to use the wind to ensure a successful whitetail hunt.
Softcover • 8¼x10⅞ • 192 pages • 150 color photos
Item# TRTT • $24.99

To order call
800-258-0929 Offer OTB3

Krause Publications, Offer OTB3
P.O. Box 5009, Iola WI 54945-5009
www.krausebooks.com

Please add $4.00 for the first book and $2.25 each additional for shipping & handling to U.S. addresses. Non-U.S. addresses please add $20.95 for the first book and $5.95 each additional.
Residents of CA, IA, IL, KS, NJ, PA, SD, TN, WI please add appropriate sales tax.

MANY CRITICS of antlerless-only deer hunts believe hunters kill a disproportionate number of buck fawns during these hunts. However, the facts show the buck fawn harvest during antlerless-only hunts is similar to those during regular gun-hunts, and will not adversely affect adult buck numbers.

1

Vital Concerns For Today's Hunters
Buck Fawn Harvests
Tragic Loss or Necessary Evil?

As my truck slowed to a stop across the street from the small-town cafe, my friend spoke up.

"Look at the 'puppy dogs' on that car," he said, pointing his finger and scowling at a pair of orange-clad hunters across the street, strapping two buck fawns to the roof of their vehicle. "I hope they're happy they've killed two of next year's bucks."

I shrugged my shoulders and walked into the cafe for breakfast without saying a word. It was late October 2000, during Wisconsin's early antlerless firearms season, and as I sat down at the cafe's counter, I was bombarded with the sounds of angry hunters trading complaints about the hunt's effect on buck populations.

Along with gripes claiming the state's Department of Natural Resources was decimating the deer herd, the DNR was criticized by some self-proclaimed quality deer management participants for killing a disproportionate number of buck fawns, undermining QDM principles and decreasing adult buck numbers down the road.

The situation wasn't unusual. In fact, similar scenes play out across the Midwest and other states that have adopted specialized antlerless-only seasons or have issued more doe tags to combat rapidly expanding deer populations.

Dispelling Misconceptions

At a glance, it's easy to understand how hunters reach such conclusions. Reason suggests increased hunting pressure on antlerless deer will increase buck fawn kills. Fewer buck fawns, of course, mean fewer bucks. And that means disappointed hunters.

However, deer biology, decades of detailed harvest records, and Pope and Young and Boone and Crockett trends simply do not support this reasoning.

Despite "eyewitness accounts" of trailers filled with dead buck fawns headed home from deer camps, harvest records from several leading whitetail states clearly show that concerns about antlerless seasons decimating buck populations are unfounded.

RYAN GILLIGAN

Mississippi Deer Harvest Breakdown*

Year	Antlered Bucks	Does	Buck Fawns	Buck Fawns in Antlerless Harvest (percent)
1991	17,478	17,329	1,312	7
1992	17,884	17,768	1,555	8
1993	18,792	20,278	1,415	7
1994	18,264	22,927	1,588	7
1995	14,292	26,133	1,243	5
1996	15,042	23,410	1,308	5
1997	13,397	21,763	1,008	4
1998	12,481	17,601	797	4
1999	11,596	16,288	740	4
2000	10,763	15,228	566	4

* This information was collected from lands enrolled in Mississippi's Deer Management Assistance Program, not the entire state. However, the figures are generally consistent with deer harvests across Mississippi.

Missouri Deer Harvest Breakdown

Year	Antlered Bucks	Does	Buck Fawns	Buck Fawns in Antlerless Harvest (percent)
1992	69,439	60,387	21,047	26
1993	70,035	64,197	22,128	26
1994	76,017	63,928	23,100	27
1995	89,142	74,170	23,811	24
1996	83,974	79,781	25,130	24
1997	80,943	86,157	28,707	25
1998	89,225	84,006	29,448	26
1999	88,121	80,311	24,005	23
2000	96,023	94,839	28,452	23
2001	104,649	98,994	30,372	23

Georgia Deer Harvest Breakdown

Year	Antlered Bucks	Does	Buck Fawns	Buck Fawns in Antlerless Harvest (percent)
1987	73,548	26,194	6,650	20
1988	66,272	34,383	9,552	22
1989	68,262	34,563	10,254	23
1990	65,805	19,809	5,296	21
1991	74,753	28,135	8,008	22

For example, in Wisconsin's 2000 early antlerless-only firearms season, hunters killed 66,417 deer. Of those, about 53 percent were adult does, 24 percent were doe fawns and 23 percent — about 15,275 — were buck fawns. Although that might seem like a lot, those kills were spread across 16.25 million acres of deer habitat. In other words, on average, only one buck fawn died per 1,064 acres — about 1.5 square miles — of deer range.

Admittedly, those buck fawn kills weren't spread evenly throughout that range, nor does that figure reflect how much of a given area's buck fawn population was eliminated by the hunt. However, it refutes the idea that antlerless-only hunts decimate buck populations.

And that figure was no fluke. In fact, in the 40 years the Wisconsin DNR has been aging and sexing antlerless deer kills, the percentage of buck fawns has averaged only 21.6 percent of the antlerless harvest.

Harvest Figures Remain Constant

Other states' data reflect similar harvest structures. From 1990 to 2000, the percentage of buck fawns in the antlerless harvests in Minnesota, Illinois and Indiana averaged 19.7 percent, 26.7 percent and 24.8 percent, respectively.

New York data mirror those statistics. Since 1982, buck fawns averaged 23 percent of the Empire State's antlerless harvest. What's more, the buck fawn harvest averaged less than 21 percent of the antlerless harvest within the past five years — a period in which New York hunters achieved record antlerless harvests three out of five seasons. Even more telling, New York's adult buck harvests during those seasons were the highest in state history, averaging 126,867 bucks.

These buck fawn kill rates aren't unique to Northern states, either. Despite the fact Georgia — like most Southern states — kills far more antlerless deer than antlered bucks, buck fawns account for less than 22 percent of the state's antlerless harvest.

And on Mississippi's Deer Management Assistance Program lands, buck fawns averaged less than 6 percent of the antlerless harvest from 1991 to 2000.

ALMANAC INSIGHTS

➤ **AN ORDINANCE** being considered by the Cromwell Board of Selectmen would ban the discharge of a bow within city limits without a permit. The ordinance places the control of discharging a bow and, potentially, all bow-hunting, solely in the hands of the police chief.

The Cromwell Board of Selectmen will meet to discuss the ordinance. It is vague and shortsighted. Perhaps the current chief of police supports hunting and archery and is willing to issue permits, but what happens if his replacement does not? The ordinance does not require the chief to issue a permit in a timely fashion, nor does it set parameters under which he must approve or reject a permit request.

Such ordinances have been introduced in other states. They stem from unfounded safety fears and anti-hunting sentiment.

— U.S. Sportsmen's Alliance

Missouri has experienced similar trends. In 2001, Missouri hunters killed 257,910 deer — 116,015 adult bucks, 89,100 adult does, 22,808 doe fawns and 34,212 buck fawns. That means buck fawns made up only about 24 percent of the antlerless harvest and just 13 percent of the overall harvest.

Missouri's harvest information also dispels the common misconception that specialized antlerless seasons take a higher percentage of buck fawns because they occur when newly dispersed juvenile bucks are disoriented. However, Missouri's special antlerless season harvest is just 19 percent buck fawns — compared to 24 percent killed during the state's traditional gun season.

The same principle holds true in Wisconsin, where the special antlerless-season buck fawn harvest has averaged 22 percent since the

New York Deer Harvest Breakdown

Year	Antlered Bucks	Does	Buck Fawns	Buck Fawns in Antlerless Harvest (percent)
1982	78,460	82,559	24,436	23
1983	79,746	67,621	20,082	23
1984	77,596	71,038	21,676	23
1985	80,732	51,184	17,167	25
1986	90,719	66,372	21,622	25
1987	97,595	81,237	25,833	24
1988	92,987	76,673	23,804	24
1989	99,589	61,690	20,600	25
1990	103,258	67,208	20,314	23
1991	110,701	77,606	24,326	24
1992	117,984	86,903	28,257	25
1993	102,431	91,449	26,408	22
1994	89,328	57,895	18,460	24
1995	113,566	58,048	16,670	22
1996	104,689	75,295	22,781	23
1997	119,090	75,935	21,811	22
1998	121,911	85,195	23,652	22
1999	125,392	104,262	26,305	20
2000	140,857	123,685	31,317	20
2001	127,084	123,372	31,414	20

Arkansas Deer Harvest Breakdown

Year	Antlered Bucks	Does	Buck Fawns	Buck Fawns in Antlerless Harvest (percent)
1987	73,548	26,194	6,650	20
1988	66,272	34,383	9,552	22
1989	68,262	34,563	10,254	23
1990	65,805	19,809	5,296	21
1991	74,753	28,135	8,008	22
1992	74,900	27,362	8,139	23
1993	79,354	33,513	9,196	22
1994	76,537	34,622	9,332	21
1995	98,283	53,999	11,642	18
1996	94,050	48,400	10,010	17
1997	92,896	61,770	12,639	17
1998	55,117	100,461	23,647	19
1999	70,313	102,101	22,273	18
2000	72,408	88,996	20,728	19

season's 1996 inception. Despite claims that the hunt's late October and mid-December timing catches buck fawns at their most vulnerable periods, this is almost identical to the state's traditional firearms-season harvest, in which buck fawns have averaged 21.6 percent of the antlerless harvest since 1964.

Wisconsin biologists also stress that if the state's antlerless season was claiming a disproportionate

Wisconsin Deer Harvest Breakdown

Year	Antlered Bucks	Does	Buck Fawns	Buck Fawns in Antlerless Harvest (percent)
1990	166,989	183,597	48,268	21
1991	149,748	205,681	63,759	24
1992	141,468	166,154	41,415	20
1993	147,168	93,109	30142	25
1994	172,346	150,310	51,054	25
1995	211,270	197,465	57,171	23
1996	172,247	230,631	58,604	20
1997	157,862	157,219	44,341	22
1998	193,485	164,719	49,233	23
1999	204,858	222,893	66,548	23
2000	212,332	313,997	88,773	22
2001	182,845	200,889	60,588	23

number of buck fawns, it would be reflected by a lower buck fawn kill during the state's regular firearms season. However, that simply hasn't happened.

Collateral Damage?

Like Wisconsin, Missouri accomplishes a significant portion of its antlerless harvest during a four-day, late-season antlerless-only hunt. The hunt receives criticism similar to Wisconsin's antlerless hunts, and Missouri wildlife research biologist Lonnie Hansen offers a simple rebuttal to such concerns.

"You don't want to kill buck fawns when you're trying to kill does, but that's an unfortunate consequence of controlling and managing deer herds," he said.

Furthermore, retired Wisconsin deer biologist Keith McCaffery said hunters in areas experiencing heavy antlerless harvests should face the facts. Regardless of how many buck fawns antlerless hunts remove, hunters should expect to see fewer deer of all ages and sexes — that's the point of increased antlerless quotas. They're *supposed* to lower deer populations.

Buck-Fawn Biology

To understand buck-fawn harvest dynamics, you first need to understand natural buck fawn birth and mortality rates.

According to Bill Mytton, Wisconsin's chief deer ecologist, does usually give birth to more buck fawns than doe fawns, and those buck fawns typically die — from various natural causes — at a higher rate than doe fawns. Therefore, "sparing" them accomplishes little.

When antlerless-season critics are faced with harvest figures showing buck fawn kills are constant and make up a relatively small percentage of the overall deer harvest, they commonly contest that such figures gloss over the fact many of those bucks were killed in relatively small areas, resulting in "holes" in buck ranges. However, yearling buck dispersal behavior disproves this argument.

According to *Deer & Deer Hunting's* Research Editor John Ozoga, domination by female relatives causes most bucks to disperse

ALMANAC INSIGHTS

▶ **ACCORDING TO** the *Wall Street Journal*, each year, auto accidents involving deer kill more people than plane, train and bus crashes combined.

In addition, those accidents kill 1.8 million whitetails per year — about four times North America's entire deer population in 1900.

WHITETAIL CLASSROOM

Biological Carrying Capacity: The maximum number of deer that can be supported on a given range during average weather and habitat conditions.

Social Carrying Capacity: The number of deer people will tolerate.

from their birth range by age 1. This prevents bucks from eventually breeding their mothers and sisters.

(See "Here Today, Gone Tomorrow: When and Why Young Bucks Must Find New Homes," in the March 2002 issue of *D&DH*.)

In scientific studies from Illinois, Minnesota, Michigan and Georgia, yearling bucks dispersed three miles to 100 miles, depending on habitat, deer populations and herd structures, Ozoga wrote. Regardless of the distance, such dispersal prevents "empty spots" of buck range.

Hansen agrees. In studies he conducted on deer movement in eastern Illinois and northern Missouri, 70 percent of bucks dispersed from their birth range by age 1½. In eastern Illinois, dispersal averaged 24 miles. In Missouri, bucks dispersed shorter distances, averaging nine miles. However, as Ozoga found, some of the bucks in Hansen's studies dispersed more than 100 miles.

In any case, unless you own at least several thousand acres of prime deer habitat, a buck you see on your property as a fawn stands little chance of ranging on your property as an adult.

"Buck fawns are big dispersers," Hansen said. "If you want to produce larger age classes on your property, buck fawns are the most expendable animals."

Record Books Don't Lie

It stands to reason if states with high antlerless harvests were actually killing excessive buck fawns, those states would yield proportionately fewer record-class bucks. However, B&C and P&Y record-book entries from the past 10 years refute this.

For example, despite years of relatively high antlerless harvests, 24 Wisconsin counties rank among the top 50 P&Y-producing counties nationwide. Six of those counties rank among the top 10, and all of them — Buffalo, Dane, Waukesha, Columbia, Sauk, Trempealeau and Waupaca counties — have had intense antlerless-only hunts during at least one season since 1996.

These counties are not exceptions. In fact, about 90 percent of Wisconsin's counties each accounted for more than 31 record-class bucks between 1991 and 2000. That alone is impressive, but it's even more incredible, considering the same period saw state hunters rack up some of the highest antlerless harvests recorded in North America.

The same is true for Minnesota, Illinois and Indiana, where buck fawns average 19 percent to 25 percent of the antlerless harvest. All of these states ranked within the top 10 B&C- and P&Y-producing states from 1991 to 2000.

Admittedly, record-books aren't as

dependable as harvest figures. Many hunters who shoot record-class bucks don't have their bucks scored. Furthermore, an area's genetics, nutrition and other factors affect its ability to produce record-class bucks. Still, P&Y and B&C records clearly show heavy antlerless harvests — and the buck fawn kills that go with them — do not decimate adult buck populations.

A Justified Cost

The miniscule loss of buck fawns through antlerless hunting is a small price to pay to control bulging deer herds. For example, in 2000, Wisconsin hunters killed about 313,997 does and doe fawns, which — based on a statewide average of adult doe and doe fawn productivity — would have given birth to about .85 fawns each in Spring 2001.

Therefore, the hunt prevented the birth of more than 266,897 deer the following spring, for a net population reduction of about 580,894 deer! All this at an "expense" of 88,773 buck fawns — less than 24 percent of the pre-hunt buck fawn population.

Population reductions like these are even more important with the spread of fatal illnesses like bovine tuberculosis and chronic wasting disease, which was discovered in wild Wisconsin whitetails in Spring 2002.

Yearling Harvests: The Real Culprit?

The facts regarding buck fawn kills are hard to deny. Comprehensive harvest data clearly show buck fawns make up relatively insignificant portions of each state's antlerless harvest. What's more, high recruitment of buck fawns ensures many

ALMANAC INSIGHTS

➤ **DO YOU THINK** of animal-rights groups when you hear about terrorism? The FBI does. In fact, the FBI recently identified the Animal Liberation Front and Earth Liberation Front as two of the country's greatest domestic terrorist threats.
— *U.S. Sportsmen's Alliance*

➤ **AN EXPLODING** deer population in a North Carolina town has led residents to seek an urban bow-hunt. Bow-hunting is a safe and effective form of deer population control, but anti-hunting residents are working to stop the proposal.

Residents of Fearrington Village in Pittsboro, N.C., will decide if a group of skilled hunters will be permitted to bow-hunt on unpopulated land around the village. Residents supporting the hunt want to try to control the escalating deer population, but anti-hunters are spreading their emotional rhetoric to prevent the hunt.

A local anti-hunter contacted the Humane Society of the United States to obtain anti-bow-hunting propaganda. She later distributed the information at a private homeowners association meeting.

"They want to do the same thing to the deer that this country has done to the Native Americans," said anti-hunter Robert Leopold. "I think it's a terrible thing. I just hope I'm not around when the first arrow hits a person."

Leopold has little to fear.

Bow-hunting is one of the safest forms of outdoor recreation in this country. According to figures collected by the International Hunter Education Association, while there were 6 million bow-hunters in 1999, only four injuries and one fatality were reported.

In addition, sportsmen have been the driving force behind wildlife conservation over the past century. In fact, their funding of conservation programs — over $2 billion annually — is the primary reason many wildlife species are more abundant in more areas of the country today than at any time during the last 100 years.
— *U.S. Sportsmen's Alliance*

ALMANAC INSIGHTS

➤ **WILDLIFE-RELATED** recreation is far more than just an American tradition. With more than 82 million active participants age 16 and older in 2001, sportsmen and women and wildlife watchers play a critical role in the nation's economy from rural towns to the bottom-line of Fortune 500 companies. Most importantly, people who participate in wildlife-associated recreation have proven to be a demographic group that transcends age, gender, race and income levels.

If sportsmen were a corporation, they would rank No. 11 on the Fortune 500 list with revenues of $70 billion — ahead of corporate giants Coca-Cola, Microsoft and AT&T.

Wildlife Watchers spent $40 billion in 2001 — more than the combined receipts for the performing arts, motion pictures and spectator sports ($27.3 billion).

The 13 million hunters in America could fill every NFL stadium, combined — six times over.

The 50 million anglers in America support one million jobs — more than Exxon-Mobil, General Motors and Ford employ combined.
— *U.S. Sportsmen's Alliance*

➤ **A CANADIAN CHAPTER** of the Sierra Club wants to ban hunting and trapping in Canada's wildlife reserves.

According to the *Montreal Gazette*, the Quebec Group of the Eastern Canada Chapter of the Sierra Club of Canada launched a campaign to denounce Quebec's wildlife conservation policies and begin a movement to ban hunting and trapping on reserves.

A spokesperson for the group told reporters that hunting and trapping devastate biodiversity and have no place in conservation.

Of course, nothing could be further from the truth. Trapping, hunting and fishing are regulated to prevent declines in wildlife and habitat deterioration. In fact, hunter-tallied records of deer and moose numbers help gauge the condition of wildlife populations.
— *U.S. Sportsmen's Alliance*

enter the 1½-year-old age class — despite normal losses during antlerless hunts.

But, the data tell another tale. Although hunters in most states harvest only 20 percent to 25 percent of the buck fawn population each fall, 1½-year-old bucks in many of those states are killed at much higher rates, giving QDM proponents legitimate reasons to worry.

In fact, according to data published by the Quality Deer Management Association, buck harvests in leading whitetail states like New York, Missouri, New Jersey, Michigan and Wisconsin are routinely 60 percent to 70 percent 1½-year-old bucks.

Pennsylvania is an even more extreme example.

"In many areas of Pennsylvania, we kill up to 90 percent of the buck population," said Jerry Feaser of the Pennsylvania Game Commission. "Less than one in 100 deer reach their fourth birthday."

Although Missouri experiences a much lower yearling buck kill, Hansen believes the state's 1½-year-old buck harvest — not its buck fawn harvest — is the primary cause for reduced adult buck numbers.

"At most, we're shooting 10 percent to 15 percent of our buck fawns," Hansen said.

In Missouri, about 60 percent of the antlered buck harvest — about 70,000 deer in 2001 — are yearlings. Compare that figure to the 10 percent to 15 percent buck fawn harvest, and it's easy to see the primary culprit in reducing mature buck numbers is inflated yearling buck harvests.

"Killing 70,000 yearling bucks

has a much greater effect on future buck production compared to killing 34,000 button bucks," Hansen said.

Conclusion

In a perfect world, hunters would kill at least 25 percent more does and doe fawns and would refrain from killing buck fawns. If that happened, more bucks would reach maturity, herds would have more balanced adult-doe-to-antlered-buck ratios and deer numbers would be better suited with the habitat's ability to support them. However, as harvest records in several states have proven, that's a tall — if not impossible — order.

Hunters almost always shoot too few deer, and their hesitation to shoot antlerless deer out of fear of killing buck fawns invariably decreases antlerless harvests. As a result, deer herds swell even larger, increasing disease risks, damaging deer range and hurting sex and age ratios.

Fortunately, the facts show the buck fawn kills that unavoidably accompany heavy antlerless harvests aren't nearly as high as commonly thought, and do little or no harm to hunting prospects, QDM agendas and adult buck populations.

Considering these facts, the message seems clear: Deer herds don't require pampering to produce adequate numbers of adult bucks. The best way to control growing deer herds is to kill antlerless deer, and lots of them. Yes, buck fawns will die, but ultimately, it will benefit white-tailed deer herds.

ALMANAC INSIGHTS

►**THE INTERNATIONAL BOW-HUNTING ORGANIZATION** (IBO), a longtime supporter of conservation issues and sportsmen's rights, has contributed $10,000 to the U.S. Sportsmen's Alliance as it works to defeat the anti-hunting movement.

The IBO's generous contribution will help fund efforts by the U.S. Sportsmen's Alliance to facilitate the introduction of two important model bills in state legislatures. One bill contains proposed language to limit birth-control projects for wildlife, while the other was created to protect those who are targeted by animal-rights terrorists.

The first bill would limit unrestricted use of birth control on wildlife. The use of birth-control drugs on deer is promoted and funded by animal-rights groups that seek to eliminate hunting as a means of controlling wildlife populations. Legislators in Ohio and West Virginia are poised to introduce the bill in 2003.

The second bill, The Animal and Ecological Terrorism Act, will protect individuals and companies engaging in legitimate medical, biomedical, agricultural and research activities and aid in the arrest and punishment of those supporting and carrying out animal rights or eco-terror acts.

"Both of these bills would be of great benefit to bow-hunters, and all sportsmen," said Ken Watkins, IBO president. "Anti-hunting groups continue to mislead the public and the media with unsubstantiated claims about deer birth control. It's time states put the brakes on this unregulated, so-called science."

Since 1990, the IBO has contributed in excess of $180,000 to the U.S. Sportsmen's Alliance to defend bow-hunting, further pro-hunting legislation and preserve hunters' rights.

This year's contribution was made possible by the IBO Bowhunter Defense Fund, which is generated through the efforts of IBO affiliate clubs, special donations and the shooting participation of members at IBO Bowhunter Defense ranges during IBO Triple Crown and World Championship 3-D tournaments.

— *U.S. Sportsmen's Alliance*

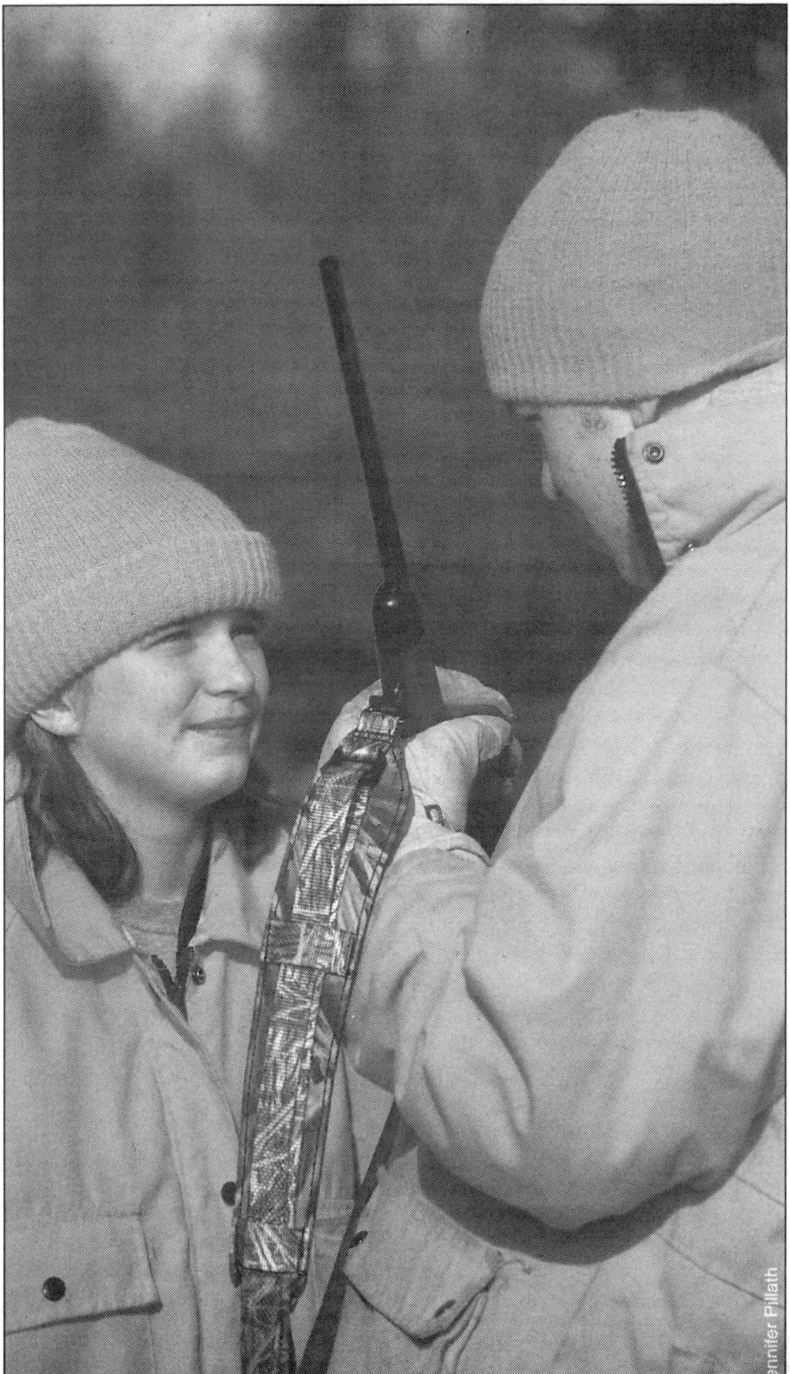
Jennifer Pillath

The Disappearing Hunter

Deer hunters have never had it better in terms of the number of deer and the hunting opportunities available. But it won't last — in part *because* of so many deer.

Deer management will have to change in the near future, as swelling deer populations collide with a shrinking pool of hunters. More deer and fewer hunters will require game agencies to target does (the best way to keep herd numbers in check) at the expense of buck hunting. Translation? In the next two to three decades it's possible a basic deer license will only let people hunt does — any chance at antlers will necessitate a buck tag, likely awarded through a drawing. Some game departments are already experimenting with changes to put hunting pressure on does and take it off bucks.

Blame demographics for the upcoming drop in hunter numbers. In 1997, the U.S. Fish and Wildlife Service counted 14 million hunters over the age of 16. Of these, about 47 percent were from the baby boomer generation born from the end of World War II to roughly 1960. Today, people in this group range from about 40 years old to the mid-50s. That's significant, said Gerry Lavigne, deer biologist with Maine Fisheries and Wildlife, because all the studies show that "for baby boomers, 50 is the age at which a lot of deer hunters begin dropping out."

The USFWS also found that 18 percent of hunters were ages 55 and older. Add these to the baby boomers, and a staggering two-thirds of America's hunters are 40 years old and older. Unfortunately, the recruitment of younger people is far too low to offset hunters who drop out.

Meanwhile, the general public is clamoring for fewer deer, and not without reason. In 1998, according to the Insurance Information Institute, America had 25 million deer and a half-million deer-vehicle collisions. Average cost: $2,000 each. Human costs? Thousands of injuries and more than 100 deaths. The Centers for Disease control found that Lyme disease, usually transmitted by deer ticks, jumped 25 percent nationwide in 1998 to 15,984 cases. And farmers are tired of hungry deer ravaging hundreds of millions of dollars worth of their crops.

A Steady Decline

Two decades ago, New York boasted 750,000 deer hunters. Today, there are 650,000, and according to state biologist Mike Matthews, current projections estimate only 300,000 hunters by 2010, as aging boomers leave the sport. Can New York manage deer populations with less than half of its present hunter base? No one is sure, Matthews admitted, though he predicts no radical changes for the immediate future. However, if the projection proves accurate, a system where "a license

BRIAN McCOMBIE

More Young Hunters?

As a group, Generation X, which immediately followed the baby boomers, isn't terribly interested in hunting. The U.S. Fish and Wildlife Service 1997 hunter survey found only about 20 percent of all hunters are Gen-Xers. Today's youngsters, though, show more promise. In 1998, Oklahoma saw a 17 percent increase in people completing its hunter certification course, most under 16 years old. J.D. Peer, hunter education coordinator, thinks the promotion of deer hunting has brought more young people into hunting. The Wildlife Conservation Department (WCD), for example, publicizes higher bag limits and longer seasons created by increasing deer numbers. Kids also find this information on WCD's Web site (www.state.ok.us/odwc/). To make that first outing even more memorable, earlier youth hunts give juniors "a higher chance of success than adult hunters," said Peer.
— Brian McCombie

gets you a doe, and a buck (permit) goes through a lottery system, is not out of the question," Matthews said.

The story is similar elsewhere. Vermont fielded 140,000 deer hunters 20 years ago. In 1998, only 95,000 partook in the hunt, and biologists think another 25,000 will drop out by 2050. Over the past 15 years, Mississippi has lost between 6 percent and 8 percent of its deer hunters, while Virginia has seen 70,000 exit during the past quarter-decade alone. Maine, Tennessee and Georgia report similar problems.

Raw statistics, though, don't tell the whole story. While some 220,000 deer hunters have called Alabama home the past two decades, deer project leader Chris Cook noted, "The average age of our hunters continues to go up. We haven't seen (a drop in hunter numbers) yet. But it's inevitable.

Wisconsin grapples with a different predicament. Though it has seen a steady 670,000 deer hunters since 1980, the November firearms hunt was once an unofficial nine-day vacation. Today, former deer biologist Bill Mytton estimates the average hunter only spends $1^{1}/_{2}$ days afield.

"We have more product than demand," Mytton said. "We're trying to figure out how to get hunters to harvest these excess deer."

Do's and Does

Then there's the issue of killing does. Vermont and Michigan saw 40 percent and 50 percent, respectively, of their 1998 harvests in antlerless deer. Other states show favorable doe percentages, too. But for many hunters, it's antlers or nothing.

Brian Murphy, executive director of the Quality Deer Management Association, remembers when QDMA began in South Carolina in the late 1980s, and "there was a petition floating around to make doe harvesting illegal." That's not surprising. Many states entered the 20th century nearly devoid of deer. To restore herds, hunts were bucks-only. By the time deer rebounded in the 1970s and '80s, three generations of sportsmen had had "bucks-only" driven into their hunting psyches.

The Wisconsin Department of Natural Resources discovered this lingering resistance to does in 1996 when it initiated its "earn-a-buck" program. In severely overpopulated management units, hunters had to kill an antlerless deer (during the regular season or a special antlerless hunt in October) before they killed a buck. "Many people were very critical of it because it forced them to do something they didn't want to," Mytton said. "Take a doe."

In Fall 1999, Wisconsin again saw too many deer: 1.5 million, in fact. Accordingly, the DNR upped the number of either-sex and antlerless permits; some units saw three to four times the number of available permits versus the previous year. Mytton knew not all these permits would be taken. But the distribution identifies a baseline of hunters willing to harvest does. Thus, the DNR can adjust seasons and regulations in the future, depending on deer numbers. Earn-a-buck? If there's not enough voluntary demand for does, "I'm sure we'll use it again down the road," Mytton said.

Planning for the Future

As the QDMA's Brian Murphy explains, a buck's antlers essentially double in size between ages 1^1/$_2$ and 2^1/$_2$, and nearly do it again in another year. However, QDMA data show 60 percent to 90 percent of the bucks killed in most states are yearlings.

"In most areas, literally only one in 100 bucks makes it to maturity (4-plus years)," Murphy said.

By working to increase doe harvests, game agencies reflect a key component of QDM: Kill does, let bucks grow bigger. Of course, deer biologists knew long ago that higher doe harvests help manage herds and produce more mature bucks. But in past years, biologists had more hunters to work with, so a larger percentage of bucks could be harvested.

Not so in future decades, as aging boomers leave the sport. Still, there are things we can do now to lessen future impacts on deer hunting.

First, ease off the bucks-only mindset. That's easier said than done, of course. Yet what's the option when wildlife managers have to cull more does? Voluntarily killing a doe, say every other season, might diminish the need to limit buck hunting.

Second, be open to modified seasons and bag limits, too. Wisconsin is tinkering with special early seasons. As Mytton said, "When it's warm, hunters stay out until they get a deer."

Other regulations are changing, too. Mississippi went to bucks of 4 points or better during its 1995-96 season. Since then, doe harvests and age of bucks have increased. In 1998, 26 percent of the bucks taken were 3^1/$_2$ years old — twice that of the 1991 season.

Third, and most important, keep hunting. "Those people who continue to be involved in recreational sport hunting should have better hunting opportunities," said Matthews. True, it might be does more often than not. But despite fewer opportunities to hunt them, tomorrow's bucks should carry heftier racks.

In a perfect world, this isn't the worst deal for hunters.

The author originally had a version of this article published in Field and Stream *magazine.*

ANTLERLESS HUNTS bring out the best in deer hunters: Camaraderie, teamwork and meat for the freezer, without thoughts of jealousy or greed over antlers.

The Antlerless Hunt

Antlerless deer hunts bring out the best in hunters. The hunts center on the most altruistic reasons for hunting deer: procuring venison and camaraderie. Absent are any notions of greed over shooting the biggest buck or other negative actions associated with hunting. Antlerless hunting, simply put, is deer hunting at its best.

This idea was driven home to me during Wisconsin's 2001 Zone T hunt. Myself and three friends decided to hunt a backwater area of the Wisconsin River that we hoped would receive little hunting pressure. It didn't matter that one of us had just returned from Alaska or that one was running on little sleep because he worked second shift; the four of us simply love to hunt deer, and we were all wide awake and ready to go when we rendezvoused at 4:30 a.m.

Right away it was apparent it would be a unique hunt. The wind was howling, which makes hunting difficult enough, as deer are often reluctant to move in windy conditions. However, our hunt would be extra difficult, as we had to canoe to our hunting spot through the blustery winds. With three guys in one canoe and another in a smaller canoe, we made it to the island without incident.

We exited our canoes and hiked into the woods. The night was so dark that when any one of my companions stopped moving, he was lost in the night. After a short walk, Ryan stopped.

"This is where we'll put you," he explained to Andy.

Andy had never shot a deer before, and we all hoped that the first spot would be the best one. With directions on where the rest of us would be and a few encouraging words, we left him.

I was the next to be dropped off. I wasn't far from Andy — maybe 100 yards or so. None of us, for that matter, would be far apart. The plan was to string out so we could intercept deer walking east and west. As Ryan and Chico walked off into the darkness, I saw them shine their flashlight in the air. They hadn't turned it on before, and I assumed they turned it on to show me where they were going.

With Ryan and Chico gone, I was left alone with my thoughts. It was 5:56 a.m. It would be more than an hour until legal shooting time. I leaned against a large white oak and tried to stay out of the wind. I moved occasionally from one side of the tree to the other, trying to find the spot that offered the best shelter from the unrelenting gusts. Within a half-hour I'd worn a circle around the base of the trunk. Still groggy, I buried my head inside my jacket and thought about drifting off

JOE SHEAD

> ## WHITETAIL CLASSROOM
>
> **Deer Density:** This concept seems basic, however, most hunters misunderstand deer density when they hear numbers from their state's wildlife agency. Aside from unique circumstances, deer densities published by state deer biologists are an expression of the number of deer per square mile of deer range — not total land. Although this distinction might sound like splitting hairs, it makes all the difference when expressing deer numbers.
>
> When calculating deer densities, wildlife managers divide the deer population over a given area by square miles of forests, brush-covered land, marsh and a 330-foot margin of agricultural fields bordering these areas. Biologists do not include areas like cities, lakes, large fields and isolated patches of deer range smaller than 10 acres.
>
> For example, a deer density of 35 deer per square mile might give the impression that deer are standing behind every tree. However, in heavily agricultural areas with few woodlots and other forms of habitat, hunters must remember that the square-mile of habitat holding those 35 deer might be spread out over several square miles of actual land.
>
> **Sex-Age-Kill (SAK) Formula:** A formula used by deer managers to determine the pre-hunt deer population.

to sleep, but I was too excited for the hunt.

It was quarter to seven before I realized why the guys had shone the flashlight. A startled "putt" grabbed my attention, and as I looked skyward, I saw a hen turkey in the tree directly above me. As I looked around the area, I could make out four more black blobs in the limited light. It was also then that I noticed that there was snow on the ground. It had been so dark I hadn't been able to see the scattered accumulation.

Fifteen minutes till shooting time. Excitement clutched me as I loaded my rifle. A flock of wood ducks buzzed by. It was already a memorable hunt.

The first shot of the season rang out 200 yards behind me. I knew it wasn't someone from my bunch, but I excitedly turned in the shot's direction, thinking maybe a deer would come running, but I saw nothing.

My eyes swiveled back and forth as I waited, not knowing which direction a deer might come from, if at all. I longed to find out if the other guys had seen anything, but I decided that the lack of shooting was a silent indication that no one had seen a deer.

At 8:09 a.m., a shot came from my right. Then another a few seconds later. It sounded like an initial shot, followed by a killing shot. At least I hoped so. I knew either Chico or Ryan had shot, and I could hardly contain my excitement. I tried to guess in my mind who shot, but I knew I'd have to wait. The plan was to wait 10 minutes after a shot before we met up.

But so much for the plan. Andy was coming my way, and we quickly headed toward Ryan and Chico. Ryan had told Andy over the radio that Chico had killed a deer.

Soon we could see Chico and Ryan standing around a deer. To get to them we had to cross a small ditch.

As we tried to find a crossing point, a deer jumped up and ran straight away from us. We quietly pursued it, and after about 50 yards, it ran back toward us. It stopped, broadside, at about 70 yards, right

THE AUTHOR'S FRIEND Chico canoes his doe fawn back to the mainland after a successful antlerless deer hunt.

in the open. Andy dropped to one knee and shouldered his rifle. He was directly between me and the deer, so I couldn't pull up my gun. The deer stood frozen, staring at us. Andy was motionless as well as he looked at the deer through the scope. I could only stand and watch the drama unfold. After a few seconds, the deer took off. It was running through the woods and didn't present a shot. Seconds later, a large buck with a wide, sweeping rack and lots of points sprinted after the doe. Never in my life have I seen an animal run that fast.

Andy and I stared in disbelief. It was a sight I know we'll never forget.

Andy was disappointed that he hadn't shot the doe and wished he could have the opportunity back. I guarantee that I wanted him to have that opportunity back twice as much as he ever will, but such is deer hunting.

We joined Chico and Ryan and congratulated Chico on a job well done. He'd shot a doe fawn. Of course, we ribbed him a little because the deer was pretty small, but each one of us would have shot that deer given the same chance, and we were happy he'd shot it. It was meat for the table made even more special by the bond of friends hunting deer.

We took pictures, dressed the deer, then carried it back to the canoes on a pole. We made some deer drives, always putting Andy in the places we hoped the deer would run. We saw several deer, but somehow or another they never gave us a shot or ran in the direction we hoped they would.

By that time it was well after noon. We canoed back to our vehicles, registered the deer and ate a late lunch. Chico called it a day. He'd been in Alaska for months and had spent little time with his girlfriend, so we let it slide. The rest of us headed back out.

It was a quiet afternoon sit for me. By now the lack of sleep was

> **ALMANAC INSIGHTS**

> ➤ **FARMERS AND HUNTERS FEEDING THE HUNGRY** is now listed in the Combined Federal Charity Campaign (CFC).
>
> Federal employees can now donate to FHFH via their payroll-deduction plan. FHFH is listed as No. 1334 under "National/International Organizations."
>
> FHFH is a national campaign that donates venison to the hungry. Hunters can donate their deer to the program, and FHFH picks up the butchering fee and distributes the meat to food pantries.
>
> To date, FHFH has donated more than 1,400 tons of venison, equating to about 12 million meals.
> — *Farmers and Hunters Feeding the Hungry*

catching up to me and I fought to stay awake. I passed the time without seeing a deer.

Just as I stepped out from under the red oak I'd called my stand, I heard a distant shot. It was so windy that I couldn't tell which direction it had come from. When I didn't see Andy on his stand, I became confused. Remembering that I now carried a radio, I asked Ryan where Andy was. Ryan said that Andy was with him.

"Did you shoot?" I asked Ryan.

"Yes."

"Did you get him?

"I think I might have."

That was all I needed to hear. Ryan is an expert marksman and I hurried to where he'd taken a stand in a deadfall.

It was now dusk and past shooting hours. We had to hurry our search to find the deer to utilize the light that remained.

Ryan quickly related the story how he'd watched six or seven deer, including a 6-pointer "eating acorns like pigs." Just minutes before season closed, he was able to determine for sure that one of the deer that separated from the herd had no antlers. He found the deer in his 2X scope and the .30-30 roared.

Ryan gave us excellent directions to where the deer had been standing when he fired. It was only 70 yards from Ryan, but it was so windy we needed the radios to maintain contact. Just as we reached the spot, I noticed a light-colored spot on the ground 30 yards away. I raced over to it and found Ryan's deer.

"You got him, Ryan," I yelled back to him.

He and Andy raced over to admire Ryan's buck fawn.

We repeated the process we'd performed on Chico's deer, then canoed the deer back to the trucks. I must say, you have not truly hunted until you've experienced canoeing with a deer in the moonlight.

Friends came and went, pitching in intermittently the following day on the butchering, and by that night, both deer were completely taken care of.

Two nights later we threw a feast, with fresh vegetables, elk shot in Idaho the week before, halibut caught in Alaska the previous summer, rice and, of course, fresh deer heart. As we sat down to enjoy the meal, I was surrounded by good food, good friends and good memories.

Crop Damage Programs Cost States Millions

High deer numbers do more than degrade ecosystems, decrease herd health and increase vehicle-deer collisions — they cost state wildlife agencies millions of dollars.

For example, since starting its crop damage abatement and compensation program in 1982, the Wisconsin Department of Natural Resources has spent more than $23 million, most of which was used to compensate landowners who experienced crop depredation.

— *Wisconsin Department of Natural Resources*

Everybody Out of the Pool!

Although hunting often gets a bad rap for being dangerous, other seemingly safe sports are much more deadly.

For example, according to the National Safety Council, about 1,500 people died while swimming in 1997. Those fatalities were spread among about 57 million participants.

On the other hand, the International Hunter Education Association reported that the nation's 14 million hunters were involved in only 93 fatal hunting accidents that year.

Comparing these figures suggests that people are four times as likely to die while swimming as while hunting.

— *U.S. Sportsmen's Alliance*

WHITETAIL CLASSROOM

Recruitment: The number of fawns born in spring that survive to hunting season. Most hunters don't realize overall deer numbers affect recruitment rates. For example, recruitment declines as deer populations increase. In fact, more adult deer are available in herds maintained at 50 percent to 60 percent of their biological carrying capacity.

ALMANAC INSIGHTS

➤ **THE FEDERAL AID** in Wildlife Restoration Act, or Pittman-Robertson Act, was approved by Congress Sept. 2, 1937, and took effect July 1, 1938. The Act provides funding for the selection, restoration, rehabilitation and improvement of wildlife habitat, wildlife management research and the distribution of information provided by the projects.

This funding comes from an 11 percent federal excise tax on sporting guns, ammunition and archery equipment, and a 10 percent excise tax on handguns. Funds are collected by the Department of the Treasury, then allocated to the states based on a formula that considers the total area of the state and the number of licensed hunters. States then are reimbursed with this federal money for 75 percent of their project costs.

The Act was amended Oct. 23, 1970, to include funding for hunter training programs and the development, operation and maintenance of public target ranges. Funding for these projects comes from half of the tax money from handgun and archery equipment sales.

— *U.S. Fish and Wildlife Service*

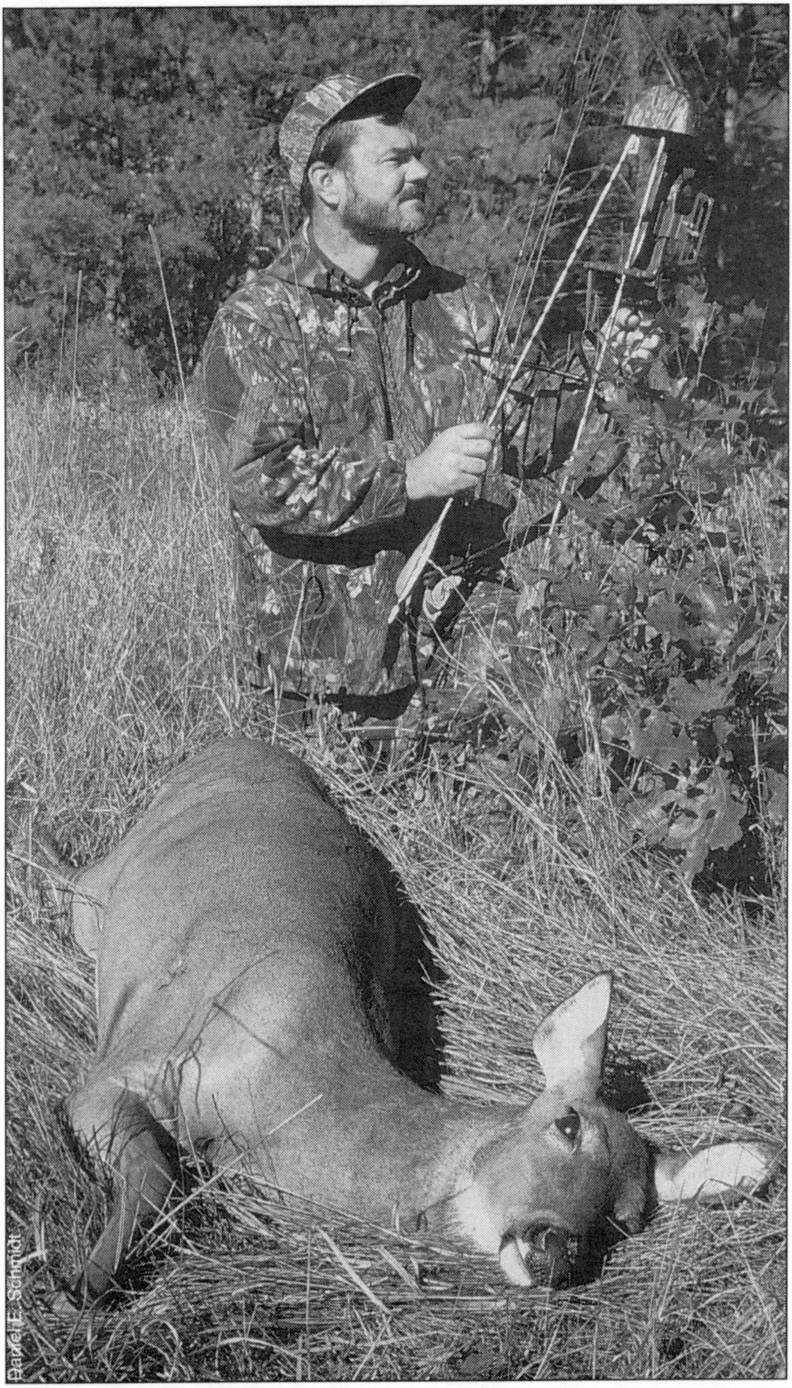
Daniel E. Schmidt

Quality Deer Management: Are You Doing it Right?

At the turn of the 20th century, deer hunters and managers faced a looming tragedy. After more than two centuries of unregulated hunting and habitat loss, North America's whitetail population — not to mention those of most other wildlife — was at its all-time low.

Drastic times called for drastic measures, so wildlife managers closed or tightly restricted deer hunting. So began the era of restoration. With hunting seasons closed or limited to bucks, and deer range sprouting nutritious second-growth vegetation, deer populations slowly recovered.

The results have been nothing short of miraculous. Deer populations are booming across North America, and hunters have never had such good prospects of filling their freezers. However, that has caused yet another change. The question on many hunters' minds has shifted from "Will I kill a deer this year," to "How many deer will I kill, and how big will they be?"

And with that, selective harvest entered the picture. Hunters realized they could often affect the size, age and number of deer they saw on their properties by regulating the age and number of deer they killed. Instead of killing the first deer that presented a shot, hunters began passing up smaller, younger animals in hopes of killing mature bucks.

In the Southeast, an area with out-of-control herds, suffering habitat and poor antler and body growth, that idea quickly evolved into quality deer management, a concept that has forever changed deer hunting and management. Today, hunters across whitetail country use QDM to produce larger whitetails, improve habitat and increase rutting activity on their properties.

However, although most professional biologists believe the QDM concept is sound, not all hunters follow many of the plan's fundamental tenets, namely killing enough antlerless deer. That "pick-and-choose" brand of QDM has spawned deer management headaches every bit as threatening as those caused by overhunting and habitat loss in the 1800s.

Take, for example, Spring 2002, when three bucks killed near Madison, Wis., during the 2001 firearms season were diagnosed with chronic wasting disease.

As part of a massive effort to determine the extent of the disease, biologists began intensive population surveys of 63-square-mile blocks around the sections where the diseased bucks were killed. What they found was almost more shocking than CWD: Many sections within the area held more than 100 deer per square mile!

This was especially alarming,

RYAN GILLIGAN

considering most of these population hot spots were on or immediately adjacent to properties supposedly enrolled in QDM.

Although Brian Murphy, wildlife biologist and executive director of the Quality Deer Management Association, believes most QDM participants do an excellent job of controlling deer numbers on their properties, a few — like some of those in southern Wisconsin — simply aren't seeing the big picture.

"If they (certain Wisconsin landowners) aren't harvesting adequate numbers of antlerless deer, they aren't practicing QDM," Murphy said. "Since the QDMA was established 15 years ago, we've continuously stressed that the most important part of QDM is harvesting does. All we can do is keep repeating this message and hope the hunting public eventually listens."

"It's (QDM) like giving someone a cake recipe, after which the recipient picks and chooses which of the ingredients they will use. At some point, the end product can no longer be called a cake."

The QDM "cake" has four basic building blocks: herd management, habitat management, hunter management and herd monitoring.

In short, herd management means maintaining an adequate harvest of antlerless deer to keep the habitat at or below carrying capacity. Of course, because carrying capacities vary from property to property, from year to year, there is no hard and fast formula for determining how many deer should be harvested from a given property.

Understandably, this is where some QDM programs go astray, causing excessive deer densities and habitat damage. To prevent this, it's vital to consult a professional deer biologist to assess how many deer are on your property and how many must be killed to maintain the balance. Furthermore, hunters need the dedication and willingness to carry out these recommendations, by killing does when given the opportunity, rather than passing up does in hopes of killing a buck.

Another better-known, aspect of QDM is letting more bucks reach older age classes. As most QDM programs begin, this involves passing up just yearling bucks. However, many QDM landowners soon begin sparing older bucks, too.

Of course, none of this is possible if hunters can't estimate the approximate age of bucks they see. Therefore, it's important to educate hunters on body and antler characteristics that indicate maturity. However, hunters should realize there is no magic formula for estimating a deer's age without looking at its jawbone. In fact, professional biologists often have difficulty aging deer by antler and body characteristics alone.

Tracking harvest data of the age, sex, weight, antler size and overall number and condition of deer killed on your property is also vital. The better records you keep, the more able you'll be to formulate harvest quotas, adequately lower the deer population and produce larger, healthier deer — the right way!

For more information on QDM, contact the QDMA: Box 227, Watkinsville, GA 30677, call (800) 209-3337 or visit www.QDMA.com.

A Brief History of the QDMA

In the late 1960s and early 1970s, two Texas wildlife biologists, Al Brothers and Murphy E. Ray, Jr., began to question the traditional deer-management methods. They formalized their thoughts in the early 1970s and, in 1975, published *Producing Quality Whitetails*, which put quality deer management concepts on paper for the first time.

South Carolina biologists Joe Hamilton and Gerald Moore invited Brothers to be the keynote speaker at the 1982 Southeast Deer Study Group in Charleston, S.C. — the nation's largest annual meeting of deer biologists. Brothers accepted the invitation on the condition that for every biologist in the crowd there would be one hunter. His request was honored and the meeting was packed with hunters and biologists eager to learn.

After Brothers' address, many landowners and private hunt clubs in South Carolina embraced QDM.

The next meeting of the original hunter/managers is considered the beginning of the Quality Deer Management Association. It was here that the first funds were generated, the logo was created, a newsletter was developed and the name was selected.

In October 1988, the South Carolina QDMA was officially formed. In addition to the core group of supporters present at previous meetings, South Carolina Deer Project Leader Derrell Shipes also attended. The group decided to elect Andrew Harper as president, and officially did so a few months later at a QDM seminar for area landowners, hunters, and managers hosted by Heyward Simmons at Cedar Knoll Hunt Club.

Harper operated out of his outdoor clothier shop in Estill, S.C., covering nearly all of the association's operating funds. Then, in March 1989, Robert Manning approached Hamilton to learn more about the group. Manning, an avid hunter and landowner from Greenwood, S.C., was informed about the purpose of the association and the need for a concerted effort to increase the awareness and interest in the SCQDMA. He organized a branch of the SCQDMA in Greenwood and was elected president.

In May 1990, Manning agreed to relieve Harper. Manning and his wife, Kathy, spread information on QDM. They contacted timber companies for hunters' names and addresses and invited them to meetings. Two additional branches, in Greenville and Columbia, were organized. Membership grew quickly and soon the SCQDMA needed a computer to track membership. Before this rapid increase, records had been kept by hand and stored in a filing cabinet.

Grant Woods bought a computer and loaned it to the SCQDMA. The Mannings' attic served as the SCQDMA office. All other office equipment was provided by the Mannings, as well as the necessary out-of-pocket donations.

In Summer 1989, Joe Hamilton produced the first issue of *The Signpost* newsletter. It was hand-collated, folded and stapled by SCQDMA members and friends. *The Signpost* was enthusiastically received and is still widely quoted in deer management literature.

By Fall 1990, membership increased to more than 1,000, and six SCQDMA branches had been established.

To better reflect the distribution of the membership, the SCQDMA was officially changed to the North American QDMA and became incorporated under that name on Aug. 6, 1990. A Board of Directors was formed to assist the Mannings with the increasing number of decisions. This board was comprised of presidents of all branches. Several wildlife biologists and university professors also worked with the Mannings to direct the association.

The QDM message has spread, even to several foreign countries. On May 22, 1991, the name was officially changed to the Quality Deer Management Association.

— *Quality Deer Management Association*

WHITETAIL CLASSROOM

Sustainable Harvest: A harvest rate that matches the recruitment rate. Maintaining harvests at this level ensures that recruited fawns annually replace deer killed during hunting season.

ALMANAC INSIGHTS

➤ **WHAT HAPPENS** when deer numbers grow too high?

Because of their voracious appetites for browse, whitetails are among the few wildlife species that can adversely affect their environment on a large scale.

Here's a few examples of how excessive deer numbers affect habitat and other wildlife.

✓ The abundance and diversity of herbaceous plants decreases as deer numbers exceed 12 to 15 deer per square mile. Particularly vulnerable species include trillium, Indian cucumber, showy lady-slipper and white-fringed orchid.

✓ Tree species like pines, white cedar, hemlock, oaks and Canada yew become less prevalent as deer numbers rise above 20 to 25 deer per square mile.

✓ Small mammals like the red-backed vole decrease as deer numbers exceed 25 deer per square mile. These species require the ample forest floor vegetation overpopulated deer consume.

✓ Bird numbers and species diversity decrease as deer numbers rise from 15 to more than 35 deer per square mile. Intense browsing by overpopulated whitetails extremely limits ground-level vegetation, shrub layer and tree species composition.

✓ In Northern areas, moose might be excluded from suitable habitat if deer densities exceed 12 to 15 deer per square mile. That's because deer often carry brainworm. Although the parasite is harmless to whitetails, it's often fatal to moose.

— *Wisconsin Department of Natural Resources*

FHFH Seeks Members

Farmers and Hunters Feeding the Hungry is based in more than half the states and has more than 40 chapters.

In the program's first six years, it provided more than 1,400 tons of venison (nearly 12 million servings) to soup kitchens and pantries across the country.

Supporting members of FHFH receive hunting gear and FHFH apparel valued at more than the cost of their donation. For example, a $25 donation yields more than $40 worth of gear. There are seven donation levels. Gear items include knives, muzzleloaders, tree stands, hats, T-shirts and more.

Supporting members are also entered for the Grand Prize drawing — a filmed deer hunt.

Hunters Spend $1,581 Each Annually, Survey Says

The U.S. Fish and Wildlife Service announced that the average hunter spent $1,581 annually in its latest five-year survey of animal-related activities.

The survey revealed that in 2001, 13 million Americans hunted, spending $20.6 billion on the sport. Most expenditures were for equipment. Expenditures from hunters, anglers and wildlife watchers made up 1.1 percent of the U.S. gross domestic product, and made a strong statement that wildlife is not only ecologically important, but financially important, too.

Although the number of participants in these three activities was down slightly from 1991, 39 percent of Americans partook in these activities.

Special Day Marks Sportsmens' Efforts

What began more than 30 years ago as a fledgling promotion has developed into a national celebration. National Hunting and Fishing Day introduces millions of Americans to the outdoors annually.

At thousands of NHFD events each year, the focus is not just ensuring the future of the outdoor sports, but also recognizing past conservation efforts and achievements of American sportsmen.

Hunters and anglers were the earliest and most vocal supporters of conservation and wildlife management. They were the first to recognize that development and the unregulated use of wildlife threatened the future of many species.

Led by President Theodore Roosevelt, these early conservationists sought to outlaw market hunting and provide funds to state wildlife agencies through hunting and fishing licenses and taxes on sporting equipment. Hunters and anglers today provide more than 75 percent of the funding for these agencies.

During the past century, sportsmen have also worked countless hours to protect and improve millions of acres of vital wildlife habitat — lands also available for the use and enjoyment of everyone.

The environmental awareness that developed in America during the 1960s was embraced by hunters and anglers, but many were discouraged by the lack of awareness of the crucial role they had played — and continued to play — in the conservation movement. Many felt the time had come for the public to recognize their efforts, which had restored many species to levels of abundance not seen in a century.

Ira Joffe, owner of Joffe's Gun Shop in Upper Darby, Pa., first put forward the idea for an official day of thanks to sportsmen. An ardent outdoor enthusiast, Joffe's goal was nothing less than a coast-to-coast celebration of the outdoor sports.

In 1970, Joffe's concept was adopted by Pennsylvania Gov. Raymond Shafer, who proclaimed "Outdoor Sportsman's Day" in his state. Rising interest carried the idea to the U.S. Senate, where in June 1971, Sen. Thomas McIntyre of New Hampshire introduced Joint Resolution 117, asking President Nixon to declare the fourth Saturday in September as National Hunting and Fishing Day. The following month, Rep. Bob Sikes of Florida introduced an identical resolution to the House.

The job of promoting National Hunting and Fishing Day at the national level was taken up by the National Shooting Sports Foundation (NSSF), a non-profit organization formed to promote a better understanding of and a more active participation in the shooting sports. The NSSF soon won the support and assistance of more than 40 national conservation and sportsmen's organizations, including the National Wildlife Federation, the Izaak Walton League and The Wildlife Society. NSSF advertisements and mailings informed leaders of thousands of sportsmen's clubs and millions of individuals of the National Hunting and Fishing Day observance.

— *National Shooting Sports Foundation*

32

A DEPARTMENT OF NATURAL RESOURCES worker saws the head off a doe for chronic wasting disease testing. Wisconsin tested more than 41,000 deer for CWD in 2002-2003.

2

Chronic Wasting Disease Strikes The East
Wisconsin, Illinois Join The Infamous List

Just a few years ago, most Eastern hunters had probably never heard of chronic wasting disease. Those who had likely associated it with elk and mule deer in Colorado.

No more.

In February 2002, three deer killed during Wisconsin's 2001 gun-deer season tested positive for CWD. It was the first time the disease was discovered east of the Mississippi River.

The Wisconsin Department of Natural Resources took quick action to slow the spread of CWD. The DNR created an Eradication Zone of approximately 411 square miles, extending in a 4½-square mile radius around each documented case of CWD. (The area has since more than doubled after more CWD-positive deer were found in new areas.) The DNR also established an Intensive Harvest Zone buffer and a CWD Management Zone, which extends 40 miles from the location CWD was first identified. These areas hosted an extended gun-season in an effort to kill additional deer.

Four week-long summer hunts were held in the Eradication Zone in 2002 to kill as many deer as possible. The state also put a temporary ban on deer feeding and baiting in an effort to stop nose-to-nose contact among deer, which may spread the disease.

The DNR also set a goal of testing 500 deer from each county for CWD during the 2002 gun-hunt. Overall, more than 41,000 deer were tested for CWD, with the only positives coming from Dane, Iowa, Richland and Sauk counties. In this area, 207 deer have tested CWD-positive since the disease was first discovered.

The temporary feeding and baiting ban has since expired, but the Natural Resources Board has approved a permanent ban, pending legislative approval.

The DNR plans to hold an extended gun-hunt in these areas again this year, running from late October to early January.

CWD Appears in Illinois

Illinois joined the infamous list when CWD was found in a Winnebago

JOE SHEAD

Chronic Wasting Disease Timeline

1967 — Mule deer at a Fort Collins, Colo., wildlife research facility become thin and listless, and then die. Biologists are uncertain of the cause.

1978 — Beth Williams, now with the Wyoming State Veterinary Laboratory, finds evidence that the disease affects the brain. She observes tiny holes in nerve cells that create a sponge-like appearance.

1980 — Chronic wasting disease is identified.

1981 — First wild elk with CWD detected in Colorado.

1983 — Surveillance for CWD in free-ranging deer begins in Colorado and Wyoming.

1985 — "Mad cow" disease, also a brain spongiform disease, is first reported.

1986 — Wyoming elk diagnosed with CWD. It's the first free-ranging case in the state.

1990 — Hunter-harvest surveillance for CWD begins in Colorado.

1997 — First captive elk herds test positive in South Dakota. Extensive surveillance of CWD in farmed elk begins nationwide.

1999 — Wisconsin begins precautionary testing for CWD in wild white-tailed deer herd.

1999 — Montana and Colorado begin depopulating wild herds.

November 2000 — Nebraska records its first wild mule deer with CWD. In December, elk from a ranch test positive.

April 2001 — CWD moves to Saskatchewan's wild deer. Two wild mule deer test positive.

September 2001 — CWD is found on several Colorado game farms, which are quarantined.

February 2002 — South Dakota reports its first wild case of CWD. Wisconsin reports CWD in its wild deer herd. It's the first time CWD has been found east of the Mississippi River.

March 2002 — Illinois creates a task force to deal with CWD possibilities. Alberta reports its first case of CWD in a captive elk.

April 2002 — CWD reported west of the Continental Divide.

August 2002 — An elk in a Minnesota game farm tests positive for CWD.

October 2002 — A wild white-tailed doe was diagnosed with CWD in Illinois.

May 2003 — Illinois has discovered 14 CWD-positive deer. Wisconsin has discovered 207 positives since the disease's discovery.
— *Jennifer Pillath*

County doe last October. A landowner noticed the deer's unusual behavior, killed it, then notified the Illinois DNR.

The IDNR subsequently tested about 4,100 deer across 36 counties during the state's shotgun seasons and discovered six more CWD-positive deer. Sharpshooters killed about 400 additional deer in late winter, of which five more tested positive for CWD. Two more animals, which were killed because of their unusual behavior, also were CWD-positive, bringing Illinois' tally to 14 CWD cases as of May 2003. The diseased deer were killed in Winnebago, McHenry and

ALMANAC INSIGHTS

➤ **WILDLIFE BIOLOGISTS** were shocked when a former deer hauler testified to illegally transporting deer and elk.

The captive deer trade is driven largely by the desire for record-book bucks, which fetch up to $50,000 in canned hunts. However, legally transported deer sport shaved necks and ear tags — telltale signs of game farm upbringing that make the animals ineligible for entry into the record books.

The trucker said wild deer were trapped in Ontario, then transported to many states with the help of veterinarians who created false papers for a share in the profit.

Boone counties in the northern part of the state. IDNR plans to sample a similar number of deer in new counties in the state in 2003 and may increase firearm quotas in the three counties where CWD has been found to help control the spread of the disease.

CWD Appears in Captive Minnesota Elk

With CWD-positive wild deer found in surrounding South Dakota and Wisconsin, Minnesota has been fortunate that the disease hasn't been found in wild deer within its borders. However, two Minnesota captive elk have tested positive for CWD.

The first elk was found in an Aitkin County game farm in August 2002, and the second was found in a Stearns County game farm soon after. Both captive herds have been euthanized.

Sharpshooters, archers and landowners killed 69 deer in Aitkin County near the game farm where the diseased elk was found, but no deer were found to be CWD-positive. During Minnesota's gun-season, about 4,500 deer were sampled statewide, but no evidence of CWD in wild deer was found.

Editor's Note: *With chronic wasting disease's recent spread to wild whitetails in Wisconsin and Illinois, many hunters are wondering about the health and safety of their state's deer herd. Check out the state-by-state rundown of what biologists have done to monitor and control CWD nationwide on the accompanying pages.*

What's the Human Risk?

Despite the recent public concern regarding if CWD is transmissible to humans, most signs indicate venison — even from CWD areas — is safe to eat.

For example, in Colorado and Wyoming, where CWD has been present in wild and captive deer and elk for almost 40 years, researchers have found no apparent transmission of the disease to humans. What's more, Creutzfeldt-Jakob disease, a similar illness, has occurred in those states at the typical rate of about 1 case per 1 million people. Even more telling, that figure was obtained from a sample of people including individuals who handled deer and elk, such as researchers and butchers.

The same has held true in Wisconsin. Despite the state's CWD status, CJD occurs there at a rate of about one case per 1 million people — the worldwide average. In fact, CJD's frequency in Wisconsin was even lower from 1991 to 2000, when the state averaged 4.3 CJD cases per year among its 5 million inhabitants. In 2000, only one Wisconsinite contracted CJD.

2003 State by State CWD Testing Measures

Alabama: testing 400 to 500 whitetails. Reinforced long-standing ban on import of cervids. Increased fines and penalties.

Arkansas: testing 1,600 to 1,750 deer. Banned the import of live cervids. Any cervid mortality in an inclosure must be tested for CWD.

Arizona: testing 1,500 to 1,800 deer/elk. Permanent ban of import of all live cervids.

California: testing 590 mule and blacktails. No cervid spinal or brain tissue is allowed to be imported into the state.

Colorado: testing 27,000 deer and elk. Only the following can be taken out of the CWD area: cut and wrapped, deboned meat with no head or spinal cord; hides; antlers with clean skull caps; canine teeth; taxidermy mounts. Upon death, all captive deer and elk must be tested for CWD. No imports of live cervids allowed unless they come from areas free of CWD for at least five years. All moose imported must be checked for CWD.

**Connecticut: Targeted surveillance. Banned the import of live cervids. Might test deer statewide this year; definitely will test in 2003.

Delaware: testing 300 whitetails. Nothing yet, but expecting to create captive cervid regulations by 2004.

Florida: testing at least 500 whitetails. Banned import of cervids from herds not certified CWD-free for five years.

Georgia: testing 600 whitetails. Stepping up enforcement of current law that prohibits transport of deer. Closing borders to transport of other cervids.

Idaho: testing 1,000 deer and elk. Banned import of captive cervids; exports must be from CWD-free herds.

Illinois: testing 4,000 to 5,000 whitetails. Ban on wild deer feeding; Ban on import of cervid carcasses.

Indiana: testing 2,100 whitetails. Ban on cervid imports. Mandatory testing of captive deer that die.

Iowa: testing 4,000 whitetails. Mandatory testing of captive deer. Banned import on cervids from CWD infected areas. CWD task force formed.

Kansas: testing 2,400 to 3,000 whitetails. Intensive statewide monitoring. Has also banned the import of all cervids.

Kentucky: testing 2,500 whitetails. Banned import of cervids. Monitoring required of cervid farmers.

Louisiana: testing 1,000 whitetails. Banned import of deer. Will not issue any more game-breeder licenses.

Maine: testing 800 whitetails. Banned import of all live cervids.

Maryland: testing 500 whitetails. Limits on possession, import/export and transport of live cervids.

Massachusetts: testing 238 whitetails. Ban on all live cervid imports.

Michigan: testing 3,600 whitetails. Strict baiting restrictions (no more than 2 gallons of feed at a time). One-year ban on all deer and elk imports.

Minnesota: testing 12,000 whitetails. Banned importation of whole cervid carcasses.

Mississippi: testing 1,300 whitetails. Permanent ban on the import and movement of all live cervids.

Missouri: testing 6,000 whitetails. All captive deer and elk must come from certified CWD-free herds.

Montana: testing 1,000+ whitetails. Stricter regulations on import of all cervids and cervid carcasses. Does not allow baiting or feeding.

Nebraska: testing 3,500 whitetails. Cervids must come from herds CWD-free for five years. Hunting over bait no longer allowed.

New Hampshire: testing 400 whitetails. Ban on all cervid imports. Strict restrictions on cervid carcass imports.

New Jersey: Targeted surveillance. Banned imports of all live cervids.

New Mexico: testing 1,000 deer and elk. Banned import of live cervids. Special regulations on units where CWD is found.

New York: testing 800 whitetails. Banned import on live cervids. Permanently banned feeding of wild deer.

North Carolina: testing 1,000 -1,200 deer. Banned import of live cervids. Limited transportation within the state.

North Dakota: testing 1,500 whitetails. Ban on the import of whole cervid carcasses.

Ohio: testing 500 to 600 whitetails. Import of cervids only allowed from a CWD-free herd.

Oklahoma: testing 1,000 whitetails. Ban on import of cervids from states with free ranging populations.

Oregon: testing 1,000 deer/all species. Ban on the import of all cervids. Similiar regulations to Colorado.

Pennsylvania: testing 500 whitetails. All cervid imports must enroll in a CWD testing program for three years (five if from a CWD-positive state).

South Carolina: testing 400+ whitetails. Restrictions on import of cervid parts.

South Dakota: testing 2,500 deer and elk. Monitoring occurrences of CWD. Stricter regulations on transportation of captive deer and elk.

**Tennessee: testing 1,000 whitetails. Banned cervid imports from CWD endemic areas. Imported cervids must be from herds CWD-free for at least 18 months.

Texas: testing 5,000 whitetails. Import of all live cervids under strict regulations.

Utah: testing 2,200 deer/all species. Imports from CWD areas limited to hides, mounts, meat with no spinal cord, and antlers with clean skull caps.

Vermont: testing 400 whitetails. Reconfirmed ban on cervid importation. Only boned meat, capes, antlers and antlers attached to clean skull caps will be allowed across state lines.

Virginia: Targeted surveillance. Banned import of all cervids into state. Stricter restrictions placed on captive deer.

Washington: testing 1,000 deer/all species. Reconfirmed 1993 ban on cervid imports.

West Virginia: testing 460 whitetails. Ban on import of all live cervids from outside of West Virginia.

**Wisconsin: testing 25,000 in hot zone. Holding eradication hunts in CWD zone. Banned feeding and baiting of wild deer. 30,000 in rest of state. Essentially banned the import and export of captive deer and elk.

Wyoming: testing 6,000 deer — all species. CWD testing stations expanded.

** Indicates 2002 CWD measures.

Nature's Wrath
CWD is Just One of Many Deer Diseases

It's easy to forget that diseases besides CWD — many of which most hunters have never heard of — claim untold numbers of whitetails every year. And, although the discovery of CWD in wild Wisconsin whitetails has attracted much attention from hunters nationwide, it has also taken attention away from other pressing deer-health issues.

Here's a look at some of the many other dangers facing today's whitetail herds.

Hemorrhagic Disease

A major, and long-misunderstood killer of wild whitetails is hemorrhagic disease. Deer & Deer Hunting magazine recently addressed the ailment in its September 2001 issue with Walt Hampton's article, "Epizootic Hemorrhagic Disease and Whitetails: When Nature's Plans Ruin Yours."

What is collectively referred to as hemorrhagic disease is actually two similar diseases — epizootic hemorrhagic disease and bluetongue virus. Both illnesses are spread by biting midges, commonly referred to as no-see-ums. Midges transmit the virus after taking a blood meal from an HD-infected deer, then biting another deer. Because the midges require warm weather to survive, HD is most prevalent in the Southeast, but it afflicts whitetails through much of their range from late summer through fall.

The disease occurs in acute and chronic forms. In the acute, late-summer form, deer weaken and often die soon after transmission. An infected deer's head and tongue swell, and its organs hemorrhage, especially the lungs. Infected deer are weak, disoriented, and run a high fever. As a result, they often seek water.

In the chronic form, which typically afflicts deer during fall and winter, deer lose weight and their hoofs become sloughed. The pain caused by this condition often causes HD-infected deer to crawl on their elbow joints rather than walk on their hoofs. As Hampton reported, deer surviving this variety of the disease often have decreased reproductive success and lowered milk production among does, possibly causing fawn starvation in subsequent years.

During severe outbreaks, the disease can significantly lower deer populations across a large area. In 1976, for example, EHD killed 30 percent to 40 percent of Nebraska's deer population. And in the 1940s and '50s, the disease, which was then known only as "Killer X," killed untold numbers of deer throughout the Southeast.

RYAN GILLIGAN

Although HD was once thought isolated from Wisconsin, that changed in September 2002, when 18 deer were found dead near Arena in Iowa County. Although all but one of the carcasses were too decomposed for necropsies, that deer, a 2½-year-old doe, tested positive for EHD.

According to Kerry Beheler, wildlife health specialist with the Wisconsin DNR, the disease's appearance in southern Wisconsin is likely linked to recent unseasonably warm weather. Illinois, Iowa and Indiana are dealing with EHD outbreaks, and warm weather apparently let EHD-carrying gnats expand their range into Wisconsin.

The phenomenon might carry deadly consequences for Wisconsin whitetails.

"We expect high mortality (from EHD) because we have a immunilogically naive population," Beheler said.

Aside from whitetails, HD also affects mule deer, pronghorn antelope and bighorn sheep, although at lower rates. Humans cannot contract the disease.

Bovine Tuberculosis

Bovine tuberculosis is another feared deer disease — especially in the Upper Midwest. This, the most infectious type of tuberculosis, affects almost all warm-blooded mammals, including deer and humans. TB has been diagnosed in captive elk herds in several states, including Wisconsin. Michigan has been diagnosing TB in its wild deer herd since 1994.

In its advanced stages, TB

Most Commonly Asked Questions About CWD

■ **Can I contract CWD?**
Probably not. However, because CWD, "mad cow" disease and Creutzfeldt-Jakob disease are all brain spongiform diseases, and because the latter two can infect humans, it is only logical that people fear CWD. Because two spongiform diseases have been transmitted to humans, no one can say with certainty that CWD will never infect humans.

Another point to remember is the odds of contracting a spongiform disease like mad cow or CJD are nearly astronomical. It's true that about 100 people contracted mad cow disease in Great Britain, but it's estimated that 80 million people might have been exposed to it.

■ **Should I worry about eating deer?**
That can be answered with a qualified "no." The World Health Organization has said there is no scientific evidence the disease can infect humans. However, the agency says no part of a deer or elk with evidence of the disease should be eaten by people or other animals.

Bad prions congregate in nervous tissue and lymph nodes. Therefore, boning out meat — without cutting into the brain or spine — and discarding blood vessels and internal organs should protect you even if the animal is infected.

■ **How does a deer get CWD?**
According to the Agricultural Research Service, "the natural route of transmission of these diseases (i.e., spongiforms, including CWD) in ruminant animals is unknown, but oral exposure to contaminated feeds, bedding or tissues is presumed to be a major source of infection."

■ **Can prions infect the ground?**
Although this has not been proven, some studies indicate CWD-causing prions can remain active in soil for years.

■ **Will CWD infect my hunting area?**
CWD could pop up anywhere deer or elk live. However, it seems prevalent in high-density herds.

attacks a deer's respiratory system, causing weight loss and breathing difficulty. Infected deer often have pea-sized nodules on the inside of their rib cage, lungs and sometimes other organs, although such symptoms often manifest themselves only in the advanced stages of the disease.

However, TB isn't as lethal, nor does it have the same potential for spreading as CWD. In fact, despite it's bad reputation, TB is unlikely to affect deer and deer hunting on a large scale. Unlike CWD, TB is a chronic illness and isn't necessarily fatal to otherwise healthy deer.

"If a deer has a good immune system, they can confine the disease and keep it latent," said Dan O'Brien, wildlife veterinarian with the Michigan Department of Natural Resources. "When the animal becomes stressed or debilitated, the disease might manifest itself and actually make the animal ill."

According to O'Brien, the occurrence of TB varies within an infected herd like Lower Michigan's. For example, in that state's TB core area, the rate of infection hovers at a bit more than 2 percent. In the surrounding counties, the infection rate is about .5 percent.

Because of it's limited spread within wild whitetails and chronic, rather than immediately fatal, effects, O'Brien doubts TB will ever cause the large-scale deer die-offs anticipated with CWD.

"(With TB) you could see significant effects on a population if conditions were right, but it would probably be limited to a small area. TB isn't likely to affect herds like CWD," said O'Brien. "TB is never going to cause deer to just drop dead like flies."

Furthermore, although humans can transmit bovine TB, it is highly unlikely a person would contract the disease from field dressing or eating the meat of an infected deer, as proper cooking kills TB-causing bacteria.

"Thus far, there is no case of bovine TB (in humans) that has been definitively linked to deer," said O'Brien.

Then why do hunters and wildlife managers hear so much about TB? The answer has more to do with agricultural economics than whitetails. Although TB primarily affects deer on a limited scale, it can have much more devastating effects on beef and dairy cattle. Therefore, controlling TB in whitetails is vital for protecting agricultural interests and the economy.

Anthrax

Although usually associated with domestic livestock and humans, anthrax also affects whitetails. In fact, the disease has quietly caused significant die-offs among whitetails across North America.

However, anthrax doesn't occur everywhere. According to the Southeastern Cooperative Wildlife Disease Study, anthrax usually occurs in areas with highly organic, alkaline soils that experience drought conditions after receiving heavy rains. Unlike CWD and EHD, anthrax is caused by a bacterial infection. Deer primarily contract anthrax spores by ingesting contaminated food or water.

Anthrax-infected deer develop a fever, have difficulty breathing, appear disoriented and quickly die. After dying, deer bloat rapidly. Because these carcasses contain millions of anthrax spores, they are a prime means for spreading the disease, especially because the spores resist heat, chemicals and dry conditions, letting them persist in the soil for years after being deposited.

Perhaps most alarming, humans can contract anthrax while handling infected deer carcasses or byproducts.

Cranial Abscessation Syndrome

Whitetails are also occasionally burdened by cranial abscessation syndrome. This condition is caused when Actinomyces pyogenes bacteria enter a wound in velvet-clad antlers or head skin and penetrate the skull, causing a brain abscess.

Bucks with CAS look clumsy, and are sometimes unusually aggressive or unwary. Bucks with CAS often have foot sores, swollen eyes and ankles, and soft antlers. In addition, infected bucks often weep pus from their pedicles and eyes. Biologists estimate CAS might cause up to 6 percent of natural buck mortality.

As far as human health risks are concerned, hunters have little to worry about regarding CAS, as proper cooking kills the Actinomyces pyogenes bacteria.

New Mexico Gives Incentive for CWD Testing

New Mexico has unveiled an interesting program to encourage its hunters to have their deer or elk tested for chronic wasting disease. Hunters who brought a fresh head from a legally killed deer or elk to a Game & Fish Department collection station in 2002 were entered in a drawing for one Valle Vidal bull elk license and one oryx license for the 2003 season. If they desired, the winners could sell their authorization, barter it or transfer it to another hunter.

Parasites

Although they aren't technically diseases, dozens of parasites also take their toll on wild whitetails. According to Beheler, the two parasites most associated with Wisconsin whitetails are the giant liver fluke and lungworm, both of which kill deer during heavy infestations.

Parasitism in general becomes more common and takes a greater toll on whitetail herds when deer numbers grow too large and stress the habitat. Therefore, keeping populations in check through aggressive antlerless hunting is vital for maintaining herd health.

Human-Caused Illnesses

Not all deer sicknesses are caused by natural means, either. Ironically, people trying to help deer often make them sick.

Grain overload, or lactic acidosis, is a perfect example. According to Beheler, this ailment, which usually occurs when deer have access to bait piles or supplemental feeding stations, often afflicts Wisconsin

Putting Health Risks In Perspective

➤ **ARE YOU WORRIED** about contracting Creutzfeld-Jakob disease from eating venison? If so, the following statistics might change your mind.

Driving to deer camp? Be careful. The lifetime odds of dying in a car wreck are 12,346 times higher than that of getting CJD.

■ Keep an eye on the weather. The odds of freezing to death or getting hit by lighting are 119 and 17 times higher than that of CJD, respectively.

■ Don't get lost. The odds of dying from hunger, thirst, exposure or neglect are 72 times that of CJD.

■ Chew carefully. The odds of choking to death are 326 times greater than those of CJD.

■ Be careful with knives and arrows. The odds of being killed by cutting and piercing instruments are 34 times that of CJD.

■ Review firearm-safety rules. The odds of being killed by a hunting rifle are 14 times that of CJD.

■ Wear a safety harness while climbing to and while in your tree stand. The odds of dying by falling from a ladder are 100 times that of CJD.

■ Double-check the cabin's stove, wood burner and electric wiring. The odds of dying in a fire are 924 times that of CJD.

■ Finally, choose your hunting partners carefully. The odds of being murdered by someone using a hunting rifle are 40 times that of CJD.

This short list of activities collectively carries a risk of death much higher than CJD. However, even that might be giving CJD too much credit. After all, there's never been a case of a human prion disease linked to consumption of CWD-infected venison.

— Compiled with data from the National Safety Council

whitetails. Some deer are simply incapable of digesting the high carbohydrate diet supplied by these artificial feeding areas, and often die as a result.

"Grain overload is a common source of mortality," Beheler said. "It results from an overload of sugars in high-carbohydrate feed. Their (whitetails') digestive system can't handle it all at once, and it causes a metabolic shutdown."

O'Brien also stressed that baiting and supplemental feeding can cause deer more harm than good.

According to O'Brien, deer are not ideal carriers of TB, which explains why the disease occurs at such low rates within affected herds. Ordinarily, this prevents the disease from being self-sustaining. However, Michigan's rampant baiting practices and high deer densities gave the disease a unique opportunity.

"The use of supplemental feed and high deer densities were likely contributing to keeping the disease self-sustaining, where it hasn't been elsewhere," O'Brien said.

Keeping Things in Perspective

CWD isn't the only or likely the last disease-related threat to face whitetail herds. In fact, North America's deer herds are virtually plagued with deadly, often contagious diseases — not to mention parasites, bacterial infections and human-caused dietary problems. But is this reason to panic for the future of deer and deer hunting?

Probably not.

According to Bob Zaiglin,

D&DH's Southern field editor, hunters and the general public must keep such disease concerns in perspective.

Zaiglin stressed that CWD isn't the first seemingly devastating disease to hit North America's whitetail population, and likely won't be the last.

When hemorrhagic disease first appeared on a large scale in the Southeast, biologists and hunters were as baffled and afraid as they are today when facing CWD. However, although hemorrhagic disease did and still does take a toll on whitetails throughout much of North America, it's not the species-killer hunters and biologists feared it might be when they discovered it.

And despite diseases like CWD — not to mention pollution, predators, poaching, habitat loss and deer-vehicle collisions — deer herds are booming.

As far as human health risks are concerned, Zaiglin again emphasized that people must look at CWD in context with other wildlife diseases. For example, even within CWD endemic areas, such as Colorado and southern Wisconsin, no human death or illness has been scientifically linked to CWD. In fact, Creutzfeld-Jakob disease, the so-called human equivalent of CWD, afflicts only about one in a million people worldwide — and that ratio is consistent in CWD-endemic areas. For perspective, rabies infects 30,000 to 40,000 people per year, while attracting little media attention or fear from hunters.

Livestock Diseases

Although Veterinarians and deer biologists believe transmission of livestock diseases is extremely rare in wild whitetails, deer can contract some diseases commonly thought reserved to domestic stock.

For example, brucellosis can affect whitetails. The disease, which is characterized by decreased milk production and increased abortion of fetuses, is transmitted primarily through ingesting infected bodily discharges.

Deer are also susceptible to Johne's disease (pronounced yo-knees), also known as paratuberculosis. Although the disease usually affects domestic cattle, it can infect most ruminants. Animals usually contract Johne's disease during their first year of life, often by nursing on their mothers' manure-tainted udder. After initial infection, the disease might take as long as two years to manifest symptoms, which primarily include rapid weight loss and diarrhea.

Like CWD-causing prions, Johne's bacteria are extremely hard to destroy. The bacterium's thick cell wall protects it from light, heat, cold, sunlight and disinfectants, while letting it persist in soil and water for more than a year after contamination, which usually occurs through defecation by infected animals.
— *Ryan Gilligan*

Still, experts like Beheler stress that hunters shouldn't be nonchalant. If you kill a deer with lesions, or one that is hemorrhaging or displaying other symptoms of disease, immediately contact a warden or state game biologist. Do not eat the meat. By doing this and using common-sense safety precautions while handling deer carcasses, you virtually eliminate disease-transmission risks.

Pathway of a Prion

Chronic wasting disease is an always-fatal brain disease found in deer and elk. Like scrapie in sheep, mad cow disease in bovines and Creutzfeld-Jakob disease in humans, scientists believe CWD is transmitted and caused by abnormal prions, which are naturally occurring proteins.

And as with all prion diseases, no one knows exactly how CWD reaches the brain. However, we do know that prions accumulate in certain areas of the body.

Studies on scrapie prions, headed by Adriano Aguzzi of the University of Zurich, Austria, indicate that prions move from the digestive system to the lymphatic system before invading the central nervous system.

Scientists believe that after ingestion, abnormal prions enter the bloodstream where they are filtered by the lymphatic system, which includes the spleen, marrow, tonsils, lymph nodes and several other organs.

The lymph nodes act like a drain trap to stop harmful microorganisms. In your body, major lymph nodes are located in your neck, groin and armpits. When your body fights an infection, you've probably noticed that the lymph nodes swell in defense. Because invaders, like abnormal prions, accumulate in the lymphatic system, you should avoid handling and eating the affected organs.

From the lymphatic system, Aguzzi's study suggests that the abnormal prions move to the peripheral nervous system. Because the eyes include hundreds of nerve endings that are closely associated with the brain, prions likely accumulate there.

The final stop for abnormal prions is the central nervous system, which includes the brain, brain stem and spinal cord. Here, the prions begin their devastating work

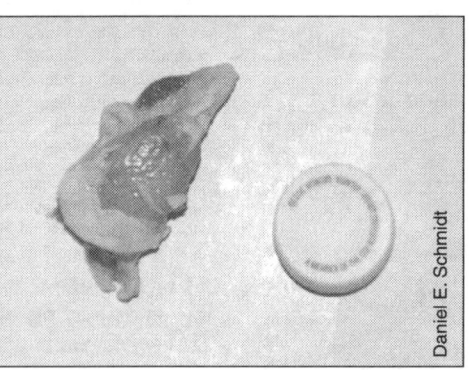

FIELD DRESSING removes most lymph nodes, but some are found within the meat. This node was located near the hip joint in the hindquarter. The item on the right is the cap to a 20-ounce plastic bottle.

Daniel E. Schmidt

JENNIFER A. PILLATH

ORGANS TO BE AVOIDED AND DISCARDED

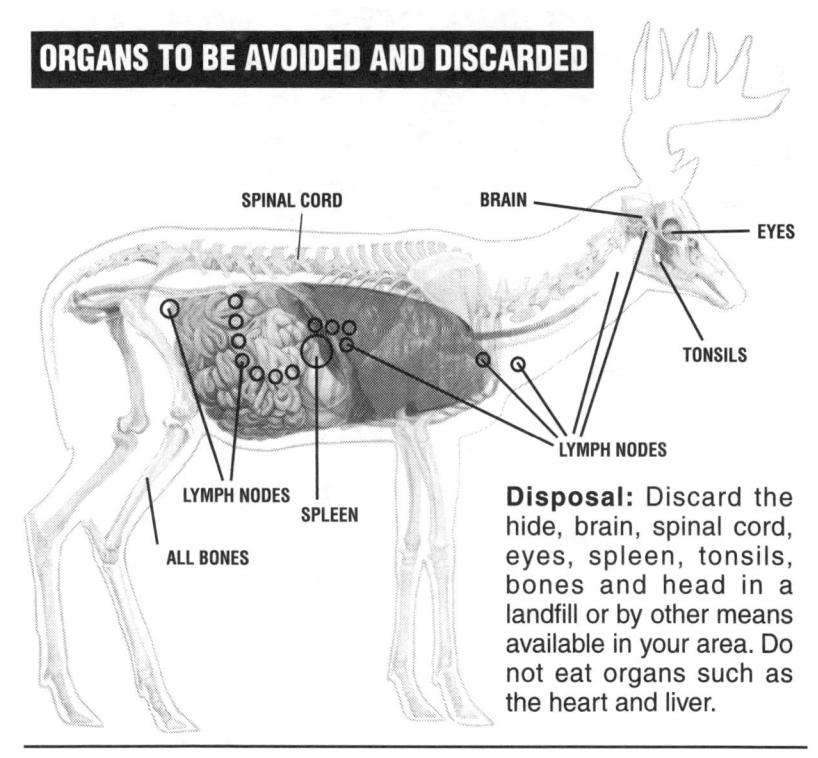

- SPINAL CORD
- BRAIN
- EYES
- TONSILS
- LYMPH NODES
- SPLEEN
- LYMPH NODES
- ALL BONES

Disposal: Discard the hide, brain, spinal cord, eyes, spleen, tonsils, bones and head in a landfill or by other means available in your area. Do not eat organs such as the heart and liver.

---

by pairing up with normal prions and converting them to "bad" prions, which results in a sponge-like appearance of the brain.

The most obvious and consistent clinical sign of CWD is weight loss. Behavioral changes, listlessness, lowering of the head and walking in repetitive patterns are also signs of the disease.

Removing Affected Organs

Most prion-infected organs are removed during normal field dressing. Others, such as the lymph nodes along the legs, can be removed as you skin your deer. The lymph nodes are a creamy-tan color similar to an oyster. They are large enough to see, and are located just under the skin but before the muscle.

Bone the meat out instead of cutting through bones. If you remove the head for a mount, make sure to use a separate saw blade.

The Good News

According to the World Health Organization, there is no evidence that CWD can be passed to humans. Also, there is no evidence that the abnormal prions exist in muscle tissues.

With that said, safety precautions are never a bad thing. We hope you take this advice into the woods and into your home this fall. Enjoy deer season, but keep it safe.

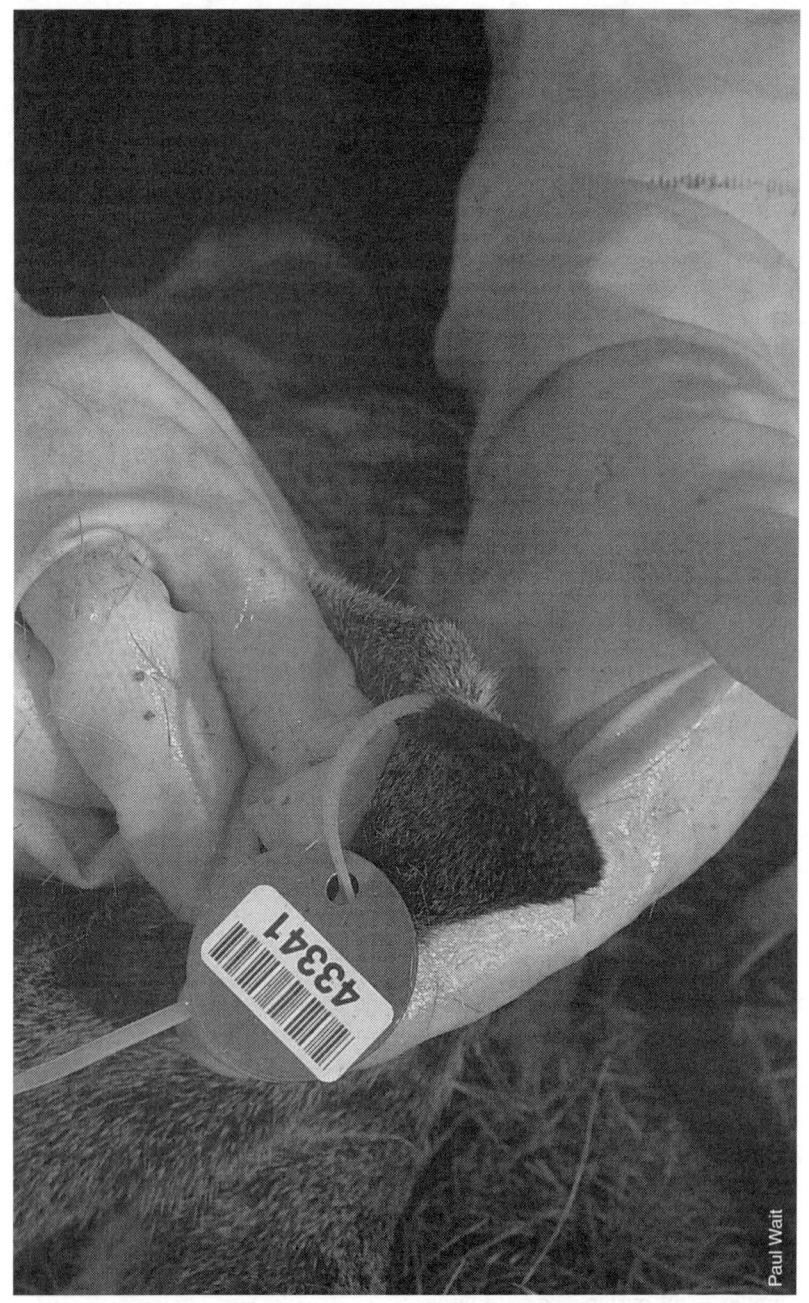

A WISCONSIN DEPARTMENT OF NATURAL RESOURCES employee affixes an ear tag to a head collected for CWD testing. Hunters could track their deer's testing results online.

The Race is On

With the discovery of chronic wasting disease in Wisconsin early in 2002, hunters east of the Mississippi realized the disease was not simply someone else's problem. It was no longer some faraway game-farm problem, a Colorado problem or a Western problem. CWD was spreading, and the mystery lent an eerie resonance to any mention of the disease.

Along with the uncomfortable reality that CWD had infiltrated one of the country's largest deer herds came the baggage that usually accompanies bad news: scientific speculation, media sensationalism and public hysteria. Without a doubt, CWD is the most intensely publicized wildlife malady in history.

CWD has given a new sense of purpose to some of the country's top conservation organizations. Along with habitat projects and fundraisers, these groups are now in the information business. Setting the record straight on CWD has become part of their everyday agenda.

Getting the Message Out

It's a painful irony that the first incidence of CWD east of the Mississippi was found in Whitetails Unlimited's home state. WTU, a national group with 65,000 members in more than 300 chapters, is headquartered in Sturgeon Bay, Wis. WTU is taking the initiative to educate hunters and, ultimately, eradicate this frustrating problem.

With an overpopulated herd estimated at 1.6 million deer, Wisconsin faced plenty of challenges before CWD entered the picture. WTU wants people to know that if CWD scares hunters into not participating, the problems associated with high deer densities could get worse.

"The deer herd is at a record-high level, and needs to be reduced for a number of reasons, including the threat of CWD," said WTU executive director Peter J. Gerl. "Wildlife biologists believe the optimum pre-hunt population should be no larger than 1 million animals. The DNR has reported early license sales are down, and that worries us."

The group immediately took on the monumental task of educating hunters about CWD in an effort to keep them from quitting the hunt.

"Hunters need information, not hysteria," Gerl said.

To that end, WTU mailed a CWD information package to 550,000 Wisconsin hunters. To offset costs and raise money to combat CWD, the mailing included an attractive raffle package.

WTU is now extending its campaign with a message encouraging hunters to get informed, and then get out and hunt.

"We're setting up a billboard campaign with the goal of 100

JIM SCHLENDER

boards across Wisconsin," Gerl said.

"The message is to get out and hunt, and that message will be repeated everywhere we can get it. We are working with retailers to set up in-store seminars to educate hunters about CWD. We also have corporations who want to get involved. The important thing is that wherever hunters go, they will see the same, consistent message."

Gerl said it's ironic that at a time when it's essential to reduce the deer herd, some hunters are considering not hunting.

"Hunters are leading conservationists, and the white-tailed deer is the wildlife species in which citizens have the greatest interest. The hunting tradition is an important and strongly held, family-oriented value in Wisconsin, and we believe in continuing this tradition. If we don't protect our tradition, no one else will," Gerl said. "Every health expert has said that there is no evidence of transmission of CWD to humans, and even in the eradication zone, 97 percent of the deer are not infected. It is essential to the health of the deer herd that as many hunters as possible get out and hunt this fall."

Gerl noted that Colorado set a record for 2002 deer and elk license sales, even though CWD has been a problem there for more than 30 years.

"We encourage deer hunters to educate themselves about CWD, new recommendations about handling deer and what the risks really are. Proper wildlife population management will reduce the chance of CWD and other diseases impacting the deer population," Gerl said.

CWD Research

Another project, still in its infancy, will perhaps further aid researchers in understanding how CWD spreads. The organization has purchased two trucks, a trailer, radio telemetry equipment, box traps and other equipment to be used in a 5-year buck-dispersal study.

"It's welcome help," said Tim Van Deelen, a Wisconsin Department of Natural Resources research scientist. He said WTU's response might be "the only positive story coming out of the whole CWD crisis ... It's a great example of a deer hunter group stepping up to the plate to fight CWD."

Other activities WTU has undertaken since the discovery of CWD in Wisconsin include setting up a $100,000 cost-share fund to be used for CWD research; sponsoring the national CWD symposium in Denver; and urging states where CWD has not been identified to take a proactive approach by developing random surveillance testing programs.

Forming the CWD Alliance

People who didn't hear about CWD until it crossed the Mississippi might not be aware that the disease has been around since 1967, when it was first discovered in mule deer at a wildlife research facility in northern Colorado. It was detected in free-ranging deer and elk in northeastern Colorado and southeastern Wyoming in the mid-1980s.

Conservation organizations in the West had each been addressing the CWD issue separately. Yet, the question remained of what a conservation group's role in combating such a threat should be. For example, a Rocky Mountain Elk Foundation statement explained:

"The Rocky Mountain Elk Foundation recognizes CWD as a threat to elk. However, the Foundation's involvement in CWD issues must be carefully measured and balanced against an even more significant and long-term threat to elk — habitat loss. Leaders believe the Elk Foundation must be a part of the CWD solution while retaining its primary emphasis on permanent land protection and habitat stewardship."

The solution to balancing traditional goals with a search for the CWD solution came when three conservation groups formed an alliance in early 2002. RMEF, the Boone and Crockett Club and the Mule Deer Foundation chartered the formation of the CWD Alliance.

The Alliance's mission states: "The mission of the CWD Alliance is to promote responsible and accurate communication regarding CWD, and to support strategies that effectively control CWD to minimize its impact on wild, free-ranging deer and elk populations."

Soon, the Pope and Young Club and the Quality Deer Management Association joined the charter partners, and sporting goods retailer Cabela's joined as a supporter.

"The object is to pool resources," explained Gary Wolfe, the CWD Alliance project leader. "This is a collaborative project. I feel confident there will be more organizations participating, as well as additional corporate support as more people become aware of our efforts."

Furthering Education

Perhaps the most notable and visible project the Alliance has undertaken in its short existence is the development of its comprehensive CWD Web site: www.cwd-info.org. It provides a central point for hunters to learn about the latest CWD findings.

"There is so much misinformation out there," said Rich Lane, RMEF president and CEO. "Everyone from Washington D.C. lawmakers to sportsmen planning fall hunting trips is thinking about CWD — and reacting based on bad information is worse than not reacting at all."

Other Alliance activities include:

✓ Co-sponsorship of the National CWD Symposium in Denver, Colo., in August 2002.

✓ Consideration of grant requests for specific CWD research and management projects.

✓ Working with state and federal agencies to develop policies for the management and eradication of CWD.

✓ Providing expert testimony to select decision-makers such as state wildlife commissions, state legislatures and the U.S. Congress.

✓ Supporting legislative actions that provide positive measures for the control and eradication of CWD.

Conclusion

The hunting community has a long history of pulling together for the long-term benefit of wildlife. The proactive, can-do attitude of these prominent conservation organizations provides comforting hope that CWD will someday be nothing more than a bad memory.

Studies Link Bacteria, Copper to Diseases

Chronic wasting disease may be the most mysterious and least understood transmissable spongiform encephalopathy disease (sometimes called TSEs or "prion diseases").

The "spongiform" name comes from the fact these diseases give the brain a spongy appearance. The four TSEs we hear most about are scrapie in sheep, "mad cow" disease in cows, Creutzfeldt-Jakob disease in humans and CWD in deer and elk.

Much research has been done on the other spongiform diseases, and some decade-old studies might shed light on CWD. Recently, research and speculation led to two prion-based theories on a cause for CWD. Both theories have supporters and detractors in the scientific community.

One theory centers on spiroplasma bacteria. The key proponent and researcher of this theory is Frank Bastian, a research professor of pathology at Tulane University. Bastian has shown that injecting spiroplasma in rodents induces spongiform encephalopathy in the brain, similar to what is seen with CWD in deer. Bastian believes bad prions are a reaction to spiroplasma in the brain, whereby the "bacteria may coat itself with this host protein (prions) to hide from the immune system."

Research also shows spiroplasmas can be transmitted by insects to mice. No one has speculated that insects might transmit spiroplasmas to deer and, therefore, cause CWD. If spiroplasmas can cause CWD, researchers must determine how to stop or slow that source.

A second theory states CWD is caused or spread when animals become copper deficient. Copper is a naturally occurring mineral vital to proper brain functions.

The basis for this theory is healthy prions contain copper, but copper is stripped away when animals ingest organophosphate insecticides. Some researchers believe heavy insecticide use played a role in the spread of mad cow disease in Great Britain.

An alternate theory suggests deer become copper deficient when they live on crowded range where copper sources — found mostly in browse — are depleted.

Dr. Michael McDonnell, a private consultant from Nebraska, believes low copper levels in soil causes low levels in the diets of deer and elk and, therefore, contribute to CWD. McDonnell said one study of game-farmed elk in Nebraska indicates a link between CWD and copper.

In the study, researchers examined the diets of pen-raised elk. Of the elk that did not receive supplemental copper in their diets, 25 percent to 55 percent contracted CWD. Of the elk receiving copper sulfate supplements, 5 percent to 7.5 percent tested positive for CWD. The third group of elk were given the recommended daily allowance of copper, and none of those animals contracted CWD.

"The concept that manganese in the environment could initiate the start of TSE is interesting," McDonnell wrote in a report highlighting several scientific studies. "The soils in Iceland, Slovakia and Colorado are low in copper and higher in manganese, which may explain the clusters of scrapie, CJD and CWD in these locations."

How could a copper imbalance cause a TSE? McDonnell offers this explanation:

"Imagine a prion is like a screen-door spring — long length with a curling structure like DNA. On each end of the prion are two hooks. These hooks carry copper to various body tissues. The prion then 'goes' to the liver to pick up more copper. When copper is low or manganese is high, manganese gets stuck on these hooks. Manganese has a different shape than copper, causing the screen door spring to bend with both ends coming together.

"Most human CJD is of this type," McDonnell continued. "After the first rouge prion is formed, it continues to bend. The prion becomes proteinase resistant (the proof of being a TSE rouge prion). As the prion bends, the intracellular bonds break and stick out of the prion. These 'fishhooks' stick into normal prions and knock off copper ions. Manganese replaces the copper, and the cycle starts again. The fishhooks latch onto each other and form chains. These chains with the fishhooks sticking out tear holes in the brain tissue. This is how the holes in the brain occur."

Finding cures for brain spongiform diseases has been challenging because the chemistry and pathology are so difficult to understand. The same is true for chronic wasting disease. Finding the cause will be extremely difficult. That's why culling huge numbers of deer in infected areas is the only choice at this time.

It's important to note that although spiroplasmas and copper deficiencies have been linked to other diseases, they have not been proven to cause CWD. The possibility, however, gives researchers many avenues to investigate while racing for answers.

— *Dave Samuel and Daniel E. Schmidt*

Venison Not Linked To Three Human Deaths

The case of three hunters who attended wild game feeds in Wisconsin and died of unusual causes was not linked to eating venison after a four-month investigation.

The story of these men caused quite a stir when it first hit the media in 2002.

Wayne Waterhouse of Chetek, Wis.; Roger Marten of Mondovi, Wis.; and James Botts of Minneapolis, Minn., regularly attended wild game feeds at Waterhouse's cabin in northern Wisconsin.

It had been suggested that the men had died of Creutzfeldt-Jakob disease — a neurological disorder caused by prions. Prions are what cause chonic wasting disease in deer and elk.

Mad cow disease has caused a variant form of Creutzfeldt-Jakob disease in about 130 people, mostly in Great Britain. The disease is always fatal. When news of CWD in Wisconsin deer was announced, many people tried to link the death of the three men to the wild game feeds and the venison the men consumed. In the United States, CJD infects about 1 person per million.

Pathologists ran new tests on Waterhouse, who died in 1993 of an unknown brain disorder, but found no evidence of a prion-related illness.

Marten also showed no sign of the disease. The test confirmed that Botts did die of CJD.

Since speculation about a connection between the men's deaths arose, more than half of the approximately 75 people who attended the wild game feeds have been contacted, and none of them have evidence of a brain disease.

— *Joe Shead*

Colorado Isn't Worried

Chronic wasting disease has been present in Colorado deer and elk for decades, but that hasn't stopped hunters. Colorado hunters purchased a record number of permits for deer and elk in 2002.

The fatal brain disease was first documented in a captive mule deer at a Colorado Department of Wildlife lab near Fort Collins in 1967. In 1981, the first CWD case in the wild was found in a free-ranging elk in northeastern Colorado.

So why then, did many Wisconsin hunters discard venison and consider swearing off killing deer, while hunters flock to the fields and hills of Colorado to kill whitetails, mule deer and elk?

Because unlike Wisconsin, Colorado has a secret weapon: an inexpensive CWD test that is available to all hunters.

Colorado hunters can drop off deer and elk heads at 60 locations throughout the state, fill out a survey tag and attach it to the head. For $17, the state's department of wildlife will test the animal for CWD and notify the hunter of the results.

Because Colorado hunters have a safeguard, most are not afraid of CWD, despite an onslaught of media attention and the discovery that the disease has expanded its range, according to Marvin Miller, a long-time hunter from Boulder, Colo.

"CWD areas are well-known," he said. "I have no doubt there are people who won't go hunting this year because of it, but of the people I know, it wouldn't even be one out of 10."

Miller expects fewer people will hunt in areas known to be infested with CWD. However, fewer hunters in those areas increases trophy potential, so hunters seeking heavy-antlered animals might choose those management units, hoping for less hunting competition.

But Miller, like most Colorado hunters, will hunt in areas where CWD has not been detected.

"I'll hunt where I've always hunted," he said. "But I wouldn't eat a deer this year without having it tested, even though where I hunt is supposed to be a disease-free area. I'll kill a deer and have it tested. I don't mind $17."

In cooperation with Colorado State University's Veterinary Diagnostic Laboratory, the DOW is preparing to collect and test as many as 50,000 deer and elk heads for CWD. The state's Department of Agriculture, Veterinary Medical Association and outfitters and guides will help conduct the tests.

"This year, we're making it faster and easier for hunters," said Todd Malmsbury, chief of information for the DOW. "They can take a deer or elk head to any DOW office and find out results on our Web site or by calling the DOW. If the animal tests positive, we will call the hunter to notify them."

Testing is mandatory for deer and

PAUL WAIT

elk killed in 19 management units known to harbor CWD. In these units, testing is free.

If a deer or elk killed in a non-mandatory testing unit is positive for CWD, the hunter's $17 fee is refunded and any preference points used to draw the tag are restored.

Deer and elk hunting are big business in Colorado, generating an estimated $500 million annually. By offering a test, the DOW is helping alleviate hunters' fears about contracting CWD by eating meat from an infected animal. At the same time, the DOW is ensuring that hunter revenues keep flowing in.

"There's a demand from hunters to make the testing easier," Malmsbury said. "Also, this is going to be surveillance for us. We're hoping hunters from around the state will submit heads for testing."

State officials expect hunters to kill 100,000 deer and elk this year. And although CWD testing has been available to hunters for seven years, this is the first year the DOW expects to test more than 20,000 animals.

"The number we've tested in the past was usually around 1,000," Malmsbury said. "This is the first year (2002) we're going to test a lot of deer."

Notification of results should take no longer than three weeks, he said.

"It's important to note there's no guarantee that this test is 100 percent accurate — no test is — but it is a very reliable test," Malmsbury said.

Ted Hall, a deer and elk hunter from Pleasanton, Neb., has traveled to Colorado 15 times since 1982 to hunt elk. Hall said he has killed seven elk, including one in 2002, in Unit 18, an area thought to be CWD-free even though it borders three units where the disease has been discovered.

Hall chose not to have his elk tested for CWD.

"I thought about it," he said. "Maybe I should be more concerned about it, but I'm not."

Hall said many Colorado hunters accept that CWD is present in the herd and don't worry about it.

"Until they prove people can get it, people will go hunting," he said. "I hunted with a guy from Wisconsin this year who owns land bordering the CWD hot zone there. He ate back straps from the elk I shot."

Hall and Miller had read a July 21, 2002, Milwaukee Journal/Sentinel article chronicling how three men who attended wild game feasts in northern Wisconsin died from brain diseases.

"I heard all about that," Miller said. "Good news sometimes takes 15 seconds to reach us, but bad news is instantaneous."

Miller said that article certainly made some Colorado hunters nervous about CWD, and expects many more hunters to have their animals tested.

"The information age has gotten the word out, and that's what has caused this panic about CWD," Hall said. "But it hasn't changed the way I hunt."

Editor's note: *Since the Milwaukee Journal/Sentinel published its article, researchers tested brain samples of the three men who died in the 1990s. See the sidebar on Page 51.*

ADAM TAYLOR of Cambridge, Ohio, bagged this 20-point buck after watching it and two other impressive bucks for four months. The drop tine buck scored 183 3/8 nontypical.

3
THE BIG BUCKS OF NORTH AMERICA

Man Passes Dozens Awaiting 20-Pointer

Adam Taylor of Cambridge, Ohio, noticed three big bucks that stood out from the rest of their bachelor group in early summer 2002.

Taylor followed these bucks for three months, trying to decide which one to hunt. Two of the bucks made the decision for him when they suddenly left one day a month before bow-season.

The remaining buck looked to be a 13-pointer, and Taylor didn't think it looked overly big in his low-quality binoculars. Still, he decided to hunt it.

On Taylor's first bow-hunt of the season, he saw 14 bucks, but he didn't see the 13-pointer he'd watched the last few months.

The second evening was more of the same.

On the third evening, the big boy came right underneath Taylor's stand, but it was after shooting hours.

Each night Taylor moved closer to where he saw the buck come out the third night, hoping to catch it during shooting hours.

On Oct. 16, everything came together on his sixth hunt.

Taylor was late getting to his tree stand. About a half-hour after he got to his stand, Taylor saw the big buck running about 45 yards away. The buck turned and was walking out of sight when Taylor grunted.

The buck turned and approached, then stopped broadside about 35 yards away.

When Taylor drew, his arrow fell off his rest. There was nothing he could do, because he didn't want to spook the buck, so he held at full-draw for what seemed like forever.

When the buck finally looked away, Taylor grabbed the arrow with his teeth, flopped it onto the rest, and let it fly.

The arrow caught the buck in the spine and dropped it instantly. A quick follow-up shot finished the buck.

Fearing ground shrinkage, Taylor was afraid to look at his buck.

However, he couldn't believe it when he counted 20 points, including two drop tines. The trophy scored $183^{3}/_{8}$ nontypical, and Taylor was ecstatic.

Four months of watching the buck had paid off. With all the time Taylor spends scouting, it might be time for new binoculars.

NORTHEAST

Prophetic Hunter Bags Drop-Tine Buck

David Lange of Newfane, N.Y., didn't have as much time to bowhunt as usual during the 2001 bow season, due to the birth of his daughter. However, he made up for lost hunting time in a big way when he managed to get out a bit during the firearms season.

On Nov. 27, he got home from work early and decided to go hunting. He told his family he was going to get "the big one" as he walked out the door. Although his family laughed at him, his words proved prophetic.

Armed with his scoped .30-30 pistol, he walked into the woods toward his stand on a wood pile. On the way, he saw movement in a field. Two does in the field saw him and ran into the woods, followed by a monster buck.

After spooking the deer, Lange quickly changed his plans and sneaked down a logging road to a food plot downwind of the deer. He decided to sit there until dark.

Fifteen minutes later two does and a small buck entered the food plot. Lange was about to shoot the small buck when he caught movement in some adjacent pines. It was the big buck!

The buck was nervous, but it saw the other deer and cautiously fed toward them.

Lange was shaking so bad he couldn't hold his gun up. He crept to a big tree for a rest.

The big buck was now about 120 yards away. Lange told himself to take his time and squeeze the trigger. When he had the cross hairs on the buck's shoulder, he touched off a round. The buck dropped.

Lange thanked the Lord, then ran to the fallen buck, which was still kicking. A second shot finished the deer.

Lange called home and explained that he would be late because he shot "the big one." His family was doubtful, having heard that story before. But when he got home, Lange's family was impressed with the buck and the fact that he'd killed a big buck, just as he said he would.

The buck sported an 18-inch spread and an 8-inch drop tine. It weighed 168 pounds field dressed and is Lange's biggest buck in 16 years of hunting.

DAVID LANGE of Newfane, N.Y., shot "the big one" on Nov. 27, 2001. His drop-tine buck had an 18-inch spread and an 8-inch drop tine.

WEST

Wyoming Hunt Produces Buck of a Lifetime

Lester Arnold of Jonestown, Pa., and his son have hunted whitetails together for almost 20 years. Over the years, each hunter had shot several bucks and does, and both enjoy each other's company while hunting. But something was always missing from their hunts: a once-in-a-lifetime trophy buck.

To fill the void, Arnold and his son, Brent, began going on out-of-state hunting trips in pursuit of a wall-hanger buck. However, each hunt only resulted in disappointment.

In 2000, they got serious about setting up their dream hunt.

They researched outfitters and sought recommendations. After poring over their findings, they booked a hunt in Wyoming for the 2001 season.

Lester and Brent had plenty of time to prepare for the hunt, and they gathered their gear, shot a lot of targets and did everything they could to ensure success on their hunt.

When the trip finally arrived, they flew from Harrisburg, Pa., to Rapid City, S.D., and went to Mt. Rushmore, Devil's Tower and Spearfish Canyon before traveling to Wyoming for their five-day hunt.

The first morning both hunters saw several average and large bucks, but they were too far to shoot. In the afternoon, Lester went with the guide, and Brent hunted by himself. Brent saw

LESTER ARNOLD shot this Wyoming buck in 2001. It is the only "trophy" buck he has killed in many years of hunting.

seven bucks that evening, but didn't fire a shot. When darkness overcame him, he could do nothing but wait for the guide to pick him up.

After waiting for an hour after dark in minus 10-degree weather, the guide and Lester finally arrived. When the truck pulled up, Brent saw a huge set of antlers in the box!

Lester had bagged a 13-point whitetail with three sticker points — his best buck ever. It brought the kid out of the 57-year-old hunter, and the Arnolds threw a major celebration.

They are now planning a caribou hunting adventure. No matter what the outcome of their trips, they always enjoy the time spent together and the memories of their hunts.

MIDWEST

Hunter Sneaks Up Hill, Finds 18-Pointer On Top

Dec. 5, 2002 — the first day of Illinois' second 2002 shotgun season — was cold and snowy, however, it's a day Mike Robards of Homer, Ill., will not soon forget.

Robards spent the day hunting on a Clark County farm.

Two inches of snow had fallen the night before, and the temperature was only 5 degrees for the morning hunt. But the bitterly cold December weather didn't deter Robards from his plan. He hoped to find an active buck.

In the morning, Robards hunted in a deep draw with a cut soybean field above it. He only saw one small buck, which he passed up.

For his afternoon hunt, Robards set up where he'd seen the buck in the morning.

By 4:00, he'd seen only a pair of does, so Robards decided to sneak up the side of the draw to take a peek at the picked soybean field. He hoped deer might feed early because of the weather.

When he reached the top of the draw, he saw a large-bodied deer with its head down just 50 yards away. Robards shouldered his shotgun and scoped the deer.

When the deer raised its head, Robards saw that it was a buck with an enormous rack, and

MIKE ROBARDS of Homer, Ill., shot his biggest buck — this 18-pointer — with his shotgun during Illinois' second 2002 shotgun season after sneaking up a draw. The buck field dressed at 200 pounds and grossed about 180 inches.

Robards immediately knew this was the buck he'd been waiting for.

However, before Robards could shoot, the buck bolted. In his haste to shoot, Robards missed the deer on his first shot, but but his slug connected with the fleeing whitetail on his second shot.

Robards' large-bodied 18-point buck is the largest he's ever shot. The buck grossed about 180 inches and field dressed at 200 pounds.

Amazingly, no one in Robards' hunting party had ever seen the heavy-racked 18-point buck before.

MIDWEST

Hunter Calls In Buck With His String Release

I could hear heavy footsteps 70 yards to the south. I lifted my binoculars, but saw nothing. But then a tree shaking violently tipped me off. I could hear the buck's antlers, as the bark slid between the points, making a very distinctive sound — one that made my heart skip a beat. Earlier three bucks had passed out of range. I needed to try something to bring the buck into range.

I had nothing to lose. I took the head of my release and scraped it against the tree. The release sounded very much like an antler. I stopped and listened intently. I heard sticks and leaves flying as the buck pawed the ground. I let out a snort-wheeze and raked my release again. The buck tore up the scrape it was working with even greater determination. I snort-wheezed again and raked more aggressively. The buck went ballistic and rushed toward me.

I looked intently in the direction of the sound and finally saw the buck on a path that would take him to the scrape I'd made 20 yards south of my position.

I peered through my binoculars and could tell he was a very respectable buck. As he approached I looked at my release to make sure no bark was wedged in a critical area. After flipping a piece of bark from a small crevice, I clicked onto the string and drew when the buck passed behind a few trees. The buck stopped at my mock scrape, and I shot as he lifted his head into the overhanging branches.

JIM SCHERER called in this 10-point Illinois whitetail by scraping his string release on a tree, imitating a buck rubbing its antlers.

I never saw the arrow, but I knew where the pin was when the arrow left the bow. The buck turned and headed in the direction he had come from, but he only made it 60 yards before falling.

I sat and watched the buck through shaking binoculars. The rush of adrenaline had done me in as I sat trying to calm down before I descended my trusty white oak.

The buck was a very nice $3\frac{1}{2}$-year-old 10-pointer with an 18-inch inside spread. One tine looks as if it had broken while still in the velvet. It had partially healed and grew into a mushroom shape. The buck also had a tiny hole from fighting just above his right eye.

— *Jim Scherer*

SOUTH

Southern Hunting Trip Produces Biggest Buck

Anthony Vaccarelli of Mahopac, N.Y., takes a hunting trip every year with his partner, Charlie. They have traveled to Wyoming and Canada to hunt whitetails, but decided to try something different in 2002.

Vaccarelli and Charlie met an outfitter from South Carolina at the Harrisburg, Pa., Outdoorsman's Show and were impressed by the description of his hunting operation.

In November 2002, they traveled to South Carolina for their annual deer hunt. They were hoping to experience some warm weather instead of the cold they often encountered on their hunts at home and out of state. The only problem was, Vaccarelli thought Southern deer had small antlers. He had a lot to learn!

The first day of the hunt, Vaccarelli entered his tower stand overlooking a large food plot at 6 a.m. Charlie was hunting about 400 yards away.

Every hour the hunting partners radioed each other to learn of any deer sightings. Things were pretty slow. Charlie saw three does at 9:30 and Vaccarelli saw one at 10:30. They decided to meet on a logging road halfway between their stands at noon for lunch.

ANTHONY VACCARELLI of Mahopac, N.Y., shot this wide-racked 9-pointer in South Carolina. Vaccarelli thought southern deer had small antlers, but after bagging his biggest buck in 22 years, he says he'll be back!

However, as mid-day neared, something told Vaccarelli that he should stay on stand a little longer. Instead of meeting Charlie, Vaccarelli ate his lunch in his stand, then took a 20-minute nap in the warm, sunny, 55-degree weather.

When Vaccarelli awoke at 12:30, he learned that his hunch to stay put was dead on. Vaccarelli saw a huge 9-pointer about 120 yards away.

Vaccarelli shouldered his .270, aimed, and fired. The 9-pointer stumbled and fell to the ground.

The 130-class 9-pointer is Vaccarelli's best in 22 years of hunting. Vaccarelli intends to hunt the South's whitetails again on future hunts.

CANADA

N.J. Hunter Kills 11th-Hour Whitetail

Leonard Didonato of Princeton, N.J., celebrated his 72nd birthday, but his sons got the present.

Didonato has hunted whitetails for 55 years in several states and in Canada. For his birthday in 2002, he took his sons with him on a deer hunt in Saskatchewan.

Didonato saw several deer during his week-long hunt, and four of the six hunters in camp had killed nice bucks, but on the last morning, Didonato's tag remained unfilled.

On Nov. 11, Didonato only had until noon to hunt before heading for home. A foot of snow lay on the ground and the trees were covered like a winter wonderland. It was a picturesque setting for his last day of hunting, if nothing else.

Didonato had used his grunt tube several times that morning with no luck. At 11:00, he produced one final grunt.

Five minutes later, a big 8-pointer appeared over Didonato's left shoulder.

Didonato let the buck walk past him, as he was out of position for a shot. Didonato carefully reached for his 7 mm as the buck passed, but the scope pinged on the icy tree stand.

The buck spun around and

LEONARD DIDONATO killed this big Saskatchewan 8-pointer during the last hour of his Canadian hunt. It is the largest he's killed in more than a half-century of deer hunting.

looked right at Didonato, then bolted toward thick brush.

Didonato knew he had little time to shoot before the buck disappeared. Didonato shouldered the rifle, swung hard and pulled the trigger.

The bullet nailed the big 8-pointer in the spine, and the buck slid to the ground.

The 8-pointer grossed 136 inches and its longest tine is $12^{1/8}$ inches. It weighed 287 pounds.

Didonato got a birthday present afterall, as the buck is the largest he's killed in more than a half-century of hunting.

How to Age a White-tailed Deer

Biologists and deer researchers agree that analysis of tooth replacement and wear — though not perfect — is the most handy and reliable field method for aging whitetails. That's because, regardless of where they live, whitetails lose their baby "milk" teeth and wear out their permanent teeth on a fairly predictable schedule.

At birth, white-tailed fawns have four teeth. Adult deer have 32 teeth — 12 premolars, 12 molars, six incisors and two canines.

Aging analysis often is based on the wear of the molars, which lose about 1 millimeter of height per year. It takes a deer about $10^{1}/_{2}$ years to wear its teeth down to the gum line. Therefore, it's difficult to determine the age of a deer that's older than $10^{1}/_{2}$ years.

Most importantly, the ability to estimate a deer's age based on the wear of its teeth is something most hunters can learn with a little study and practice.

To order a full-color poster of our complete guide to tooth aging, call (888) 457-2873.

Instructions: Cut one side of the deer's jaw all the way to its socket. Prop open the jaws and compare the lower jaw to these photos to estimate the deer's age.

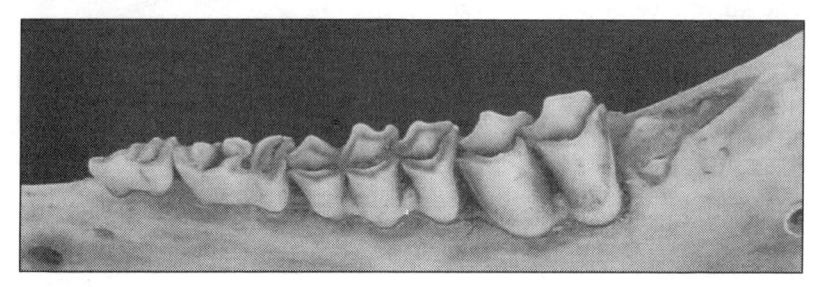

Fawn

Few hunters have difficulty aging a white-tailed fawn, whose short snout and small body are usually obvious when viewed up close. If there is doubt, simply count the teeth in the deer's lower jaw. If the jaw has less than six teeth, the deer is a fawn.

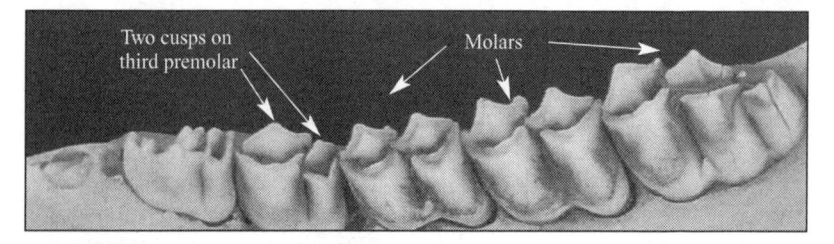

Yearling: At Least 19 Months

About 1 year, 7 months, most deer have all three permanent premolars. The new teeth are white in contrast to pigmentation on older teeth. They have a smooth, chalk-white appearance and show no wear. The third molar is partially erupted.

$2^1/_2$ Years

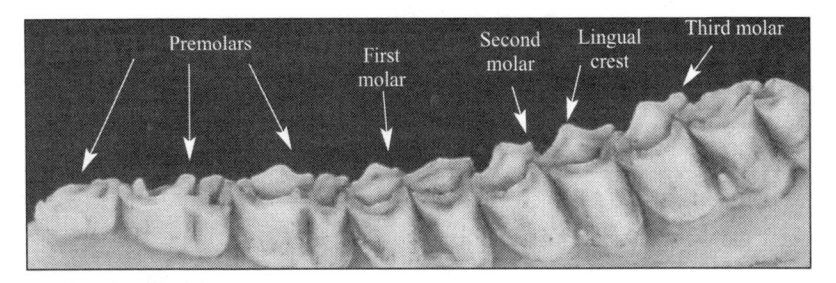

The lingual crests of the first molar are sharp, with the enamel rising well above the narrow dentine (the dark layer below the enamel) of the crest. Crests on the first molar are as sharp as those on the second and third molar. Wear on the posterior cusp of the third molar is slight, and the gum line is often not retracted enough to expose the full height of this cusp.

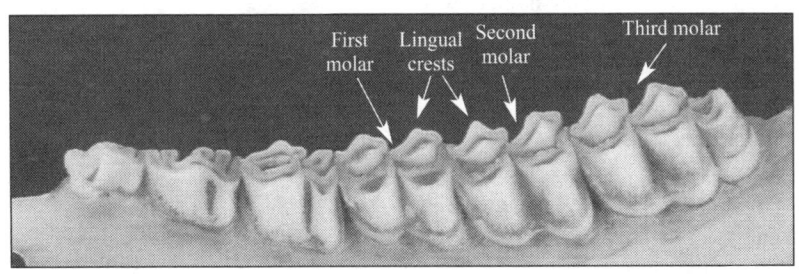

$3^1/_2$ Years

The lingual crests (inside, next to tongue) of the first molar are blunted, and the dentine of the crests on this tooth is as wide or wider than the enamel. Compare it to the second molar. The dentine on the second molar is not wider than the enamel, which means this deer is probably $3^1/_2$ years old. Also, the posterior cusp of the third molar is flattened by wear, forming a definite concavity on the biting surface of the teeth.

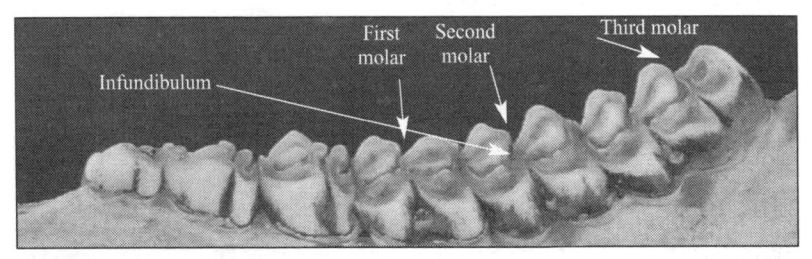

$4^1/_2$ to $5^1/_2$ Years

At this point, it's often hard to distinguish between the two age classes. The lingual crests of the first molar are almost worn away. The posterior cusp of the third molar is worn at the cusp's edge so the biting surface slopes downward. Wear has spread to the second molar, making the dentine wider than the enamel on first and second molars. By age $5^1/_2$ wear has usually spread to all six teeth, making the dentine wider than the enamel on all teeth. Because the first molar is the oldest, it wears out first. Also, by $5^1/_2$, there might be no lingual crests on the first and second molars, although rounded edges might appear like crests. A line drawn from lingual to outside edges of first and second molars generally touches the enamel on both sides of the infundibulum.

Bow-Hunting Receives Boost from Pope and Young Club

The formation of the Pope and Young Club arose from a need to show the world the bow was an effective, viable hunting tool. Most hunters and state game agencies of the 1940s and 1950s believed the bow was little more than a toy, and few recognized it as a hunting weapon.

It was Glenn St. Charles and a group of dedicated bow-hunters who conceived the idea of pulling together all the nationwide bow-hunting successes they could document. Their idea was to bring all of the information together and show it to those who believed bow-hunting was ineffective.

Today, the bow is accepted nationwide.

Although few people in the non-hunting world think of the hunter as a conservationist, the hunter has always been one. Aldo Leopold, the father of the modern conservation ethic, was a bow-hunter and advocate of land stewardship. It was Theodore Roosevelt — an avid hunter — who conceived the idea of the Boone and Crockett Club, of which P&Y is modeled after.

— *Reprinted courtesy of the Pope and Young Club*

Will Your Big Buck Make The Books?

The Boone and Crockett scoring system, with few changes, is essentially the same one developed by a committee of Boone and Crockett Club members and staff in 1950. The system was developed in the 1940s with valuable additions by Grancel Fitz. It was Fitz, who had his own scoring system, that emphasized antler symmetry in the rack's final score.

A B&C score chart for typical-antlered bucks is included on the facing page.

For B&C record-keeping purposes, official scores can be disputed, even years after the original measurement. Repeat measurements are allowed because of the enduring nature of white-tailed deer antlers.

Scoring a rack begins with careful reading of the official score charts reproduced in this book. Be sure to follow the instructions carefully. After taking a rough measurement, the owner must contact a volunteer B&C measurer to get an official measurement for the records program.

An official measurement cannot be made until the rack has dried 60 days after the date of kill. A drying period is necessary to allow for normal shrinkage. The drying period also ensures shrinkage will be relatively the same for all trophies, an impossible condition if "green" scores were allowed.

Where to Write

For more information on white-tailed deer records, contact:

Boone and Crockett Club
The Old Milwaukee Depot
250 Station Drive
Missoula, MT 59801
Phone: (406) 542-1888

Pope and Young Club
15 E. Second St., Box 548
Chatfield, MN 55923
Phone: (507) 867-4144

Boone and Crockett Score Sheet

OFFICIAL SCORING SYSTEM FOR NORTH AMERICAN BIG GAME TROPHIES

Records of North American Big Game

BOONE AND CROCKETT CLUB®

250 Station Drive
Missoula, MT 59801
(406) 542-1888

Minimum Score:	Awards	All-time
whitetail	160	170
Coues'	100	110

TYPICAL
WHITETAIL AND COUES' DEER

Kind of Deer: _____

Abnormal Points	
Right Antler	Left Antler
Subtotals	
Total to E	

SEE OTHER SIDE FOR INSTRUCTIONS

				Column 1 Spread Credit	Column 2 Right Antler	Column 3 Left Antler	Column 4 Difference
A. No. Points on Right Antler		No. Points on Left Antler					
B. Tip to Tip Spread		C. Greatest Spread					
D. Inside Spread of Main Beams		(Credit May Equal But Not Exceed Longer Antler)					
E. Total of Lengths of Abnormal Points							
F. Length of Main Beam							
G-1. Length of First Point							
G-2. Length of Second Point							
G-3. Length of Third Point							
G-4. Length of Fourth Point, If Present							
G-5. Length of Fifth Point, If Present							
G-6. Length of Sixth Point, If Present							
G-7. Length of Seventh Point, If Present							
H-1. Circumference at Smallest Place Between Burr and First Point							
H-2. Circumference at Smallest Place Between First and Second Points							
H-3. Circumference at Smallest Place Between Second and Third Points							
H-4. Circumference at Smallest Place Between Third and Fourth Points							
		TOTALS					

ADD	Column 1		Exact Locality Where Killed:
	Column 2		Date Killed: Hunter:
	Column 3		Owner: Telephone #:
	Subtotal		Owner's Address:
SUBTRACT Column 4			Guide's Name and Address:
	FINAL SCORE		Remarks: (Mention Any Abnormalities or Unique Qualities)

Copyright © 1997 by Boone and Crockett Club®

(Sample — Not for Official Use)

Joe Sheed

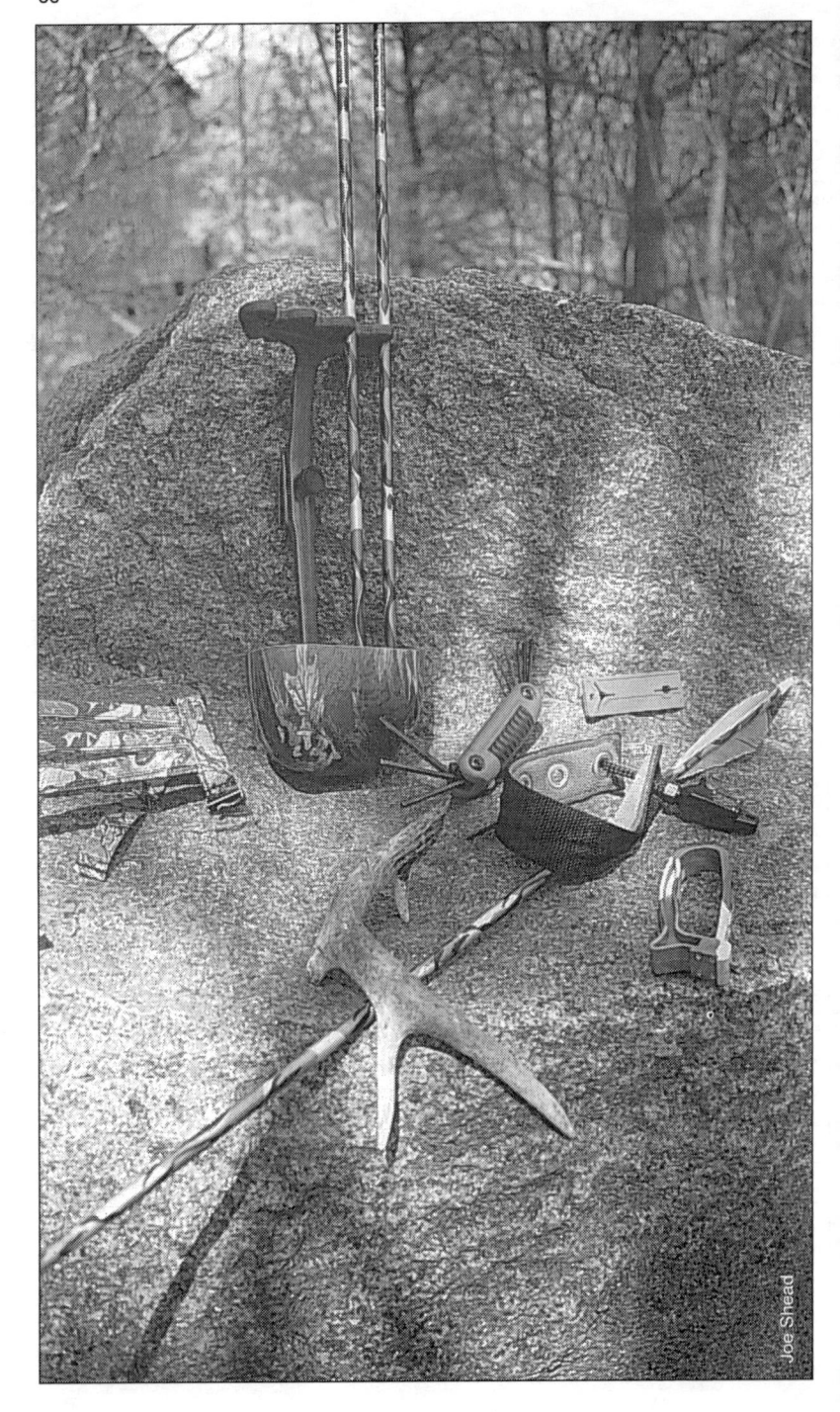

4

ADVANCED BOW-HUNTING TIPS & TACTICS

Archery Accessories:
Details Make a Difference

Ask seasoned bow-hunters and they will probably tell you they were attracted to archery by its beautiful simplicity. Indeed, the challenge of killing a white-tailed deer with a bow, arrow and broadhead is perhaps the most difficult challenge in hunting.

While today's bow-hunters still enjoy the challenge, archery has grown a bit more complicated, especially when it comes to equipment. Hunters must still possess skill and strength to shoot a bow accurately, but they also must know how to use high-tech equipment to achieve the same goal.

That's where today's abundant archery accessories come into play. From arrow rests to bow sights, high-tech accessories help modern high-performance bows fling arrows at incredible speeds while keeping them on target, shot after shot.

What follows are some of the hottest new archery accessories for 2003. Although the lists of new products are long, don't let that intimidate you. Best of all, you needn't buy tons of accessories to get the most out of your bow. Above all, never consider an accessory as a "shortcut" to success. Accessories are designed to improve what's already there.

Another key point to remember is this: Don't go bow-hunting if you are unsure about the capabilities of your equipment. Instead, visit a pro shop and have a bow technician help you become properly equipped.

Shoot-Through or Shoot-Around?

Arrow rests have come a long way since the days of those little glue-on plastic rests. Archers have so many choices that even choosing a style seems almost impossible.

With so many innovative products on the market, hunters needn't worry what style they choose. Most rests fall into one of two categories: shoot-through and shoot-around.

Most of the high-performance rests are shoot-throughs, including the innovative designs by Carolina Archery Products, Golden Key-Futura, New Archery Products and Bodoodle. Two other winners are the Super Slam from Chuck Adams Bowhunting Equipment Co. and the Scout Mountain Magna Launch.

DANIEL E. SCHMIDT

> **ALMANAC INSIGHTS**
>
> Despite the fact nonhunting residents of Abington, Pa., pleaded with their county commissioners to allow bow-hunting within a local park, animal rights activists still turned out to interfere with the hunt.
>
> Abington residents had been complaining that the park's overpopulated deer herd was damaging landscaping, causing car accidents and increasing the risk of Lyme disease. The county granted the residents' request, allowing 44 bow-hunters into the park. However, along with the bow-hunters came anti-hunters carrying devices that sound like burglar alarms, hoping to scare deer out of the area.
>
> In addition, the protesters poured gasoline around stand sites and sabotaged tree stands.
>
> Despite the interference, hunters killed 17 deer.
>
> — *U.S. Sportsmen's Alliance*

If you're a simplistic bow-hunter, be warned that some high-end rests have more features than you'll ever want or need. In that instance, you might want to consider a flipper-style rest by New Archery Products or the Huntmaster from Golden Key-Futura.

What about overdraws? Thought you'd never ask! Overdraws are designed to increase arrow speed to compensate for misjudged yardage. However, overdraws are best for experienced hunters — those who can consistently shoot accurately at distances beyond 25 yards.

Vanes or Feathers?

Each year, dozens of hunters ask me what I prefer on my arrows: plastic vanes or natural feathers. Under perfect conditions, I'll pick feathers every time. Although feather fletching cause more "wind drag" than plastic vanes, feathers are more forgiving off the arrow rest and result in more consistent shots. That's helpful when your shooting form is like mine — not perfect.

That's not to say I never use vanes. In fact, I switch between the two choices throughout the season. I use plastic vanes almost exclusively during wet weather. However, several companies offer powder-based products that provide outstanding weather protection for feathers.

Be wary of short fletchings. Most seasoned bow-hunters use 4- or 5-inch fletchings on their arrows. However, many target shooters use short fletchings — some shorter than 3 inches. Although short fletchings improve arrow speeds, don't be tempted to switch to short fletchings for bow-hunting. Longer vanes help stabilize an arrow in flight, especially when it's propelling a broadhead.

Another common gray area among bow-hunters is the dilemma of whether to use straight offset or helical fletchings. Helical fletchings help an arrow rotate. They also help prevent broadheads from planing. Helica is offered in right- and left-hand configurations. Shooting either style is a personal choice, but right-hand shooters typically benefit more from a left-hand fletch, which allows the arrow to spin away from the bow and the arrow rest.

Releasing the Shot

Over the past 10 years, the string release has probably seen the most innovation of any archery accessory.

In fact, although I took up archery in the 1980s, I waited until 1995 before switching to a release. My budget was limited, and I had trouble learning the nuances of the less-expensive releases.

That all changed when I started shooting a caliper-style release. Today, a quality caliper release can be had for less than $20, and the Cadillacs — which include releases like the TRU Ball Tornado — retail for $50 to $60.

The Tornado features a patent-pending, four-way adjustable trigger that allows hunters to custom-adjust tension, providing for "punch-free" shooting.

If you use a string loop, consider the TRU Ball Loopmaster, a Jim Fletcher Fletchunter, Cobra Pro Caliper or Scott Archery Rhino. The Pro Release Roll Aid is a good choice for hunters who don't use string loops.

Dozens of other releases are available. If possible, visit a pro shop and ask to shoot several styles and determine which one best suits your needs.

Carbon or Aluminum?

Call me old-fashioned, but I'm a tough-sell when it comes to technology. Unfortunately for me, that attitude kept me from improving my archery skills for many years. The arrow debate — carbon or aluminum — is a perfect example.

Despite shooting a bow that was capable of blistering speeds, I didn't switch to the lighter carbon arrows until just recently. Of course, speed isn't everything. Furthermore, carbon/graphite arrows often require upgrading to more expensive rests, quivers and broadheads.

When it comes to arrows, remember that speed isn't everything. In fact, just because an arrow is made of carbon or graphite doesn't mean it will fly faster. Speed is directly related to weight. The lighter an arrow, the faster it will fly. However, a light arrow has drawbacks: The lighter the arrow, the less kinetic energy it provides.

How fast is fast enough? A bow that shoots arrows 230 to 250 feet per second (AMO) is plenty for bow-hunters who pursue whitetails.

Although new aluminum arrows are straighter than carbons and graphites, they can't withstand continued punishment quite like high-tech shafts can handle. However, make no mistake, aluminum is still king of the hill, especially when you're talking about the new high-tech shafts from companies like Easton.

From Beman to Gold Tip to Carbon Impact to Game Tracker, carbon/graphite arrows come in all sizes and price points. With the emergence of large mail-order companies like Cabela's now offering carbon shafts, the price of a dozen carbon arrows is more affordable than ever.

If you're new to the carbon/graphite game, give strong consideration to internal-component arrows.

That's not to say carbon/graphite arrows are superior. Far from it. In fact, Easton's A/C Kinetic II is one of the most exciting arrows to come along in quite some time.

IT'S BEST to leave bow repairs and adjustments to a skilled pro-shop employee.

Introduced at the 2002 Archery Manufacturers and Merchants Organization Show, the A/C Kinetic II is an aluminum-and-carbon hybrid. The shaft features .01-inch aluminum wall thickness, coupled with a stiff layer of carbon fiber for extra mass. The result is a flat-shooting arrow that delivers additional kinetic energy.

Sights and Such

Bow sights and other aiming devices fall into another category with seemingly endless possibilities.

Today's fiber-optic advancements have allowed bow sights to reach the next level. Combined with the advancements in bows, rests and releases, today's sights are so reliable that most seasoned hunters can shoot accurately out to 30 yards without much problem.

My favorite sights are ones that feature few moving parts and include tightening devices that ensure pins and components won't wiggle loose after long hours at the practice range. Montana Black Gold is one company that builds sights to such specifications. Its lineup of premium sights feature lifetime guarantees on everything — including the pins!

Regardless of your budget, you can find a sight to meet your needs. Remember, not all sights are compatible with all bows. That's why it's important to check out the models from all companies, including those from Toxonics, Truglo, Timberline, Scout Mountain, Savage and Trophy Ridge.

Miscellaneous Gear

Let's face it, archery is highly addictive! Although wise hunters leave repairs and "construction projects" to the highly skilled pro shop employees, some hunters derive more enjoyment out of the sport by becoming "do-it-yourselfers."

If you fall into the latter category, one look at a Bass Pro Shops Redhead catalog will give you ample ideas for converting a corner space in the basement into a full-service archery center.

If you like building your own arrows, invest in a quality cut-off saw like those made by Apple Archery Products. A good saw will retail for $100 to $170, but you can easily make that up through the money you'll save by building a few dozen arrows from raw shafts.

Other must-haves would be a bench-mounted bow press, bow scale, 1,000-grain scale and at least one quality-made fletching jig.

Fletching jigs come in all shapes and sizes. One of the most user-friendly units is the Arizona E-Z Fletch. This hand-held tool applies all three fletchings at once. It's so easy to use that even novice archers can fletch a dozen arrows in about a half-hour.

Home-based archery centers should also include quality adhesives and cleaners, such as those offered by Bohning. Be sure to keep these products in locked child-proof cabinets.

ALMANAC INSIGHTS

Bow-hunting's value as a deer-management tool is constantly increasing as lands become more urbanized. Although gun-hunting in highly developed areas is often impractical or dangerous, bow-hunting remains safe and effective.

Not surprisingly, more urban areas are adopting legislation that permits bow-hunting within city limits.

For example, in November 2002, Radford, Va., ratified its town ordinance to allow bow-hunting. The new legislation requires that hunters use tree stands at least 12 feet tall and be hunting tracts of land no smaller than 5 acres.

A similar program has proved effective in Marion, Iowa. For the past five years, Marion has permitted bow-hunting to control its booming deer herd. The hunts have resulted in no accidents, while reducing property damage and vehicle-deer collisions.

— *U.S. Sportsmen's Alliance*

Conclusion

With so many products on the market, selecting archery accessories can seem like an overwhelming task. However, that shouldn't be the case.

First, buy items you only absolutely need. After that, consider upgrading on a year-to-year basis. Then, if you want to dabble with some of the really neat "add-ons," give yourself a budget and improve your bow one step at a time. The process will not only be more manageable, you'll find yourself deriving much more fun out of archery practice and bow-hunting!

WHETHER YOU'RE A NOVICE or a seasoned archer, at times, everyone has flaws in their shooting form. Follow these tips to keep you on top of your game.

11 Tips to Becoming A Better Archer

Everyone knows recurve and longbow shooters must practice extensively to gain the strength, hand-eye coordination and muscle control needed to shoot accurately without sights or let-off. Plus, traditional shooters must continue to practice consistently to maintain their skills.

Shooting a compound bow, on the other hand, can seem dangerously simple. You draw, look through the peep sight, and line up the proper pin on the target. Using the peep and sight pin like the front and rear sights on a rifle, you hold the bow on target and squeeze the trigger on your release. If all goes well, your arrow hits where you intend.

Considering this, it seems logical that an archer shooting a modern compound equipped with sights and a mechanical release could theoretically sight in his bow in one or two brief shooting sessions, set it down, and shoot it a year or two later with the same accuracy and consistency as he did the day he sighted it in.

Of course, this is true in theory alone. Although modern compound shooters — who, according to recent industry estimates, make up more than 95 percent of bowhunters — must practice and worry about form much less than traditional archers, shooting is hardly as simple as lining up sights on a rifle.

Here are 11 tips for sighting in your bow and maintaining your shooting ability.

Tip 1:
When sighting in your bow, take it slow. Shoot a few arrows, make adjustments to your sight as needed, shoot a couple more arrows, then call it a day. Shooting more, especially if you're not used to it, will only tire you out. Your form will deteriorate, and you'll begin compensating for your misses. As a result, any adjustments you make to your sights might actually decrease your accuracy.

Tip 2:
Although you should begin sighting in your bow at short distances, shoot at longer distances than you would during hunting situations after sighting in. Long-range practice forces you to maintain your form, release more smoothly and hold on target. When you move in to more reasonable ranges, you'll shoot much better.

Tip 3:
Follow through. Bow-hunters hear this advice so much it begins to sound cliche. However, it's worth repeating. As you shoot, concentrate on keeping your bow

RYAN GILLIGAN

arm and hand motionless until long after the arrow has cleared the rest. Dropping your arm or torquing your hand as you release destroys accuracy.

Tip 4:
Don't grip the bow. Instead of wrapping your thumb and fingers around the handle, let them relax, holding the bow steady by pulling it into the heel of your hand as you draw. If you grip the bow, you invariably torque it to the side.

Tip 5:
Pick the smallest target possible while target-shooting and hunting. Don't aim at a paper plate — aim at a quarter-sized dot on that plate. Wind, nerves, unseen vegetation, bulky hunting clothes and the fact deer often move as you shoot decrease accuracy dramatically. If you're used to aiming at — and hitting — a tiny target, such factors probably won't affect your accuracy so much as to cause a miss or a poor hit. However, if you settle for hitting a pie-plate during target practice, you might be in trouble during hunting situations.

Tip 6:
Be the arrow. It sounds silly, but visualizing your arrow hitting the target as you shoot helps your accuracy.

HOLD YOUR BOW in the heel of your hand. If you grip it, you will torque the bow to the side.

Tip 7:
Follow a routine. Whether you shoot a high-tech compound or a hand-carved osage orange longbow, accuracy depends on consistency. If you don't draw, aim and release the same way every time you shoot, you won't hit anything. It's relatively easy stay consistent while target-shooting by yourself, but things get a little tricky in high-pressure hunting situations. When the tension is high, it's easy to miss your anchor, point instead of aim, or punch your release.

To avoid these mistakes, go

through a mental checklist every time you shoot. Even if it's as simple as thinking "Draw, anchor, aim, squeeze," it will do wonders for your accuracy in hunting situations.

Tip 8:

Shoot at 3-D targets. Conventional target-shooting is fine for sighting in your bow and mastering archery fundamentals. However, the experience gained through shooting at 3-D targets is invaluable when a buck walks past your stand. You'll not only become more used to shooting a target that actually looks like your quarry, you'll become better at shot placement, especially on angled shots.

WHEN SIGHTING IN your bow, shoot a few arrows, make adjustments, shoot a few more, and call it a day. Shooting too much will wear you out and hurt your accuracy.

Tip 9:

Practice shooting in different positions — crouching, kneeling, etc. As any bow-hunter knows, shooting opportunities often come in places and situations that don't allow for conventional shooting. For example, in Fall 2002, a mature buck passed my stand at just 17 yards. Unfortunately, he used a trail shielded by brush. As the buck paused, I realized I could shoot. However, I needed to back out to the outside edge of my tree stand platform and lean out against my safety harness.

The awkward position wreaked havoc with my sense of balance and I missed the buck cleanly. Had I practiced such shooting, that story might have had a happy ending.

Tip 10:

Tune your bow. While talking about tuning his archery equipment, a friend of mine once said "Who cares if the arrow flutters a little on the way to the target? It's still gonna hit the target and poke a hole in a deer's chest, right?

Wrong. An out-of-tune bow is a missed or wounded deer waiting to happen — it's simply less accurate and less consistent than a properly tuned bow. Further, because arrows fly more erratically on their way to the target, poorly tuned bows produce less kinetic energy on impact.

To keep your setup in optimum shape, refer to tuning instructions on Page 90.

Tip 11:

Don't force it. With even the steadiest hand, it's impossible to hold your bow perfectly still at full draw. Unlike shooting a rifle, it's impractical to hold a bow rock steady while you line up the sight pin on target, hold, and squeeze the trigger on your release. Rather, your sight pin will invariably move around the target at any range. The key to accurate shooting, therefore, is going with the flow and releasing when you're on target.

If you try to force yourself to hold rock steady, you'll probably miss.

ARCHERY INSIGHTS

Setting Up A Clinometer

Ray Howell

In steep terrain, it's hard to know what pin to use. To make angled shots, I use a Suunto clinometer.

The clinometer shows the exact degree of angle up or down and your range-finder will give you the distance to your target. By combining these two tools, you can figure out where your arrow is going to hit at any angle. (See chart below.)

For example, if your target is 40 yards away at a 60-degree angle, you would use your 20-yard pin (draw a line from the two numbers — where they intersect is the pin you use). To develop a chart that works for your archery equipment, take your target, range finder and clinometer to an area where you have very steep terrain. You will need to have grid lines across and down on your chart. One will be for distance and the other for angle. Use increments of 5, starting from 20 yards and 20 degrees, up to 60 or more. See example below:

After gaining confidence in your chart, and knowing that your range finder and clinometer are working well together, tape the clinometer to your range finder. Make sure the chart is no wider than your bow limb, and tape it to the lower limb for easy reference.

		20	25	30	35	A N G L E 40	45	50	55	60
D	100	94	90	85	82	77	71	64	58	50
I	95	89	85	80	78	73	68	61	55	48
S	90	85	81	76	74	69	64	58	52	45
T	85	80	77	72	70	65	61	55	49	43
A	80	75	73	69	66	61	57	51	46	40
N	75	70	68	65	61	57	53	48	43	38
C	70	66	63	61	57	54	49	45	40	35
E	65	61	59	56	53	50	46	42	37	33
D	60	56	54	52	49	46	42	39	34	30
I	55	52	50	48	45	42	39	35	32	28
S	50	47	45	43	41	38	35	32	29	25
T	45	42	41	39	37	34	32	29	26	23
A	40	38	36	35	33	31	28	26	23	20
N	35	33	32	30	29	27	25	22	20	18
C	30	28	27	26	25	23	21	19	17	15
E	25	23	23	22	20	19	18	16	14	13
	20	19	18	17	16	15	14	13	11	10
		20	25	30	35	40	45	50	55	60
					A N	G L	E			

Urban Areas Seek Solutions to Deer Overcrowding

Deer entering urban areas continues to be a problem across the country. Many urban areas are turning to bow-hunting as an effective solution to controlling overabundant deer herds. However, others have turned to non-lethal methods to control skyrocketing deer populations.

DEER ARE OVERPOPULATING urban areas across the country. Some areas are turning to bow-hunters for help, while other municipalities seek non-lethal solutions to thin burgeoning deer herds.

✓ Sudbury, Mass. — Sudbury permits bow-hunting on its conservation land to reduce the size of a deer herd that, according to Debbie Dineen, Sudbury conservation agent, "was destroying other habitat in our conservation land." Dineen said birth-control medication for deer is very expensive and impractical.

Ellie Horwitz, chief of information and education for the Massachusetts Department of Fisheries, Wildlife and Environmental Law Enforcement, added that hunting "is more safe than most things people routinely do."

✓ Midland, Mich. — The Midland City Council voted to reduce acreage requirements for bow-hunting within city limits. The previous requirement was a 100-acre tract of land. The new regulation states hunting will not be allowed within 300 feet of another owner's property.

✓ Radford, Va. — The Radford City Council has permitted bow-hunting on two city-owned properties. Vice Mayor Gale Collins also suggested the council write a letter to the state Board of Game and Inland Fisheries to encourage it to extend the deer season and take other measures to reduce the deer population.

✓ Mt. Pleasant, Mich. — Bow-hunters will hunt deer in Veits Woods for a second year. Sara Schaefer, a wildlife biologist with the Michigan Department of Natural Resources, said the hunts are the best option for managing the population. Mt. Pleasant is plagued by deer/auto accidents, deer consuming and destroying expensive landscaping and overpopulation. Schaefer calls the overpopulation "social stress" and likens it to, "putting 100 people in a room that was designed for 10."

Bow-hunters are also being ousted from areas they were previously allowed to hunt, and other areas are

ARCHERY INSIGHTS

Fall-Away Range-Finders

I like to carry my range finder where it's easily accessible. Then after getting the reading, I let go of the range finder so I can quickly lock my release to the bow-string without worrying about the range finder. One way to accomplish this is to use an old bow-string or a strap long enough so that your range finder will hang down (slightly lower than your belt line), out of the way, on your right side if you are right-handed. By putting your head and your right arm through the loop, your range finder will always fall to your side after using it. Your range finder can be carried in a protective case attached to your belt until needed. The case should be made from a quiet material, such as fleece, so when removing the range finder at a critical moment, you won't spook deer.

Ray Howell

seeking alternative methods to deal with their deer problems.

✓ Beverly Shores, Ind. — The Beverly Shores Town Council banned an urban bow-hunt that had previously been permitted. The town's clerk-treasurer cast the tie-breaking vote in the absence of Councilman Rick Rikoski — a hunt advocate. Councilwoman Ellen Firme submitted the resolution to suspend the hunt, saying arrows might injure children. Councilman Bill Kollada voted against suspending the hunt and said the vote was "pre-orchestrated" and "unethical."

✓ Asheville, N.C. — The Western North Carolina Nature Center will use birth control on its deer herd. It will use PZP (porcine zona pellucida), a drug that has not received approval from the Food and Drug Administration, and will administer it annually to the deer.

✓ Pittsboro, N.C. — Fearrington Village, a retirement community, had considered instituting a bow-hunt to control deer overpopulation, but the community's developer would not allow it. In a message to community residents, he said, "I am not convinced that bow-hunting would, in itself, be an effective tool in reducing the deer that frequent Fearrington, and until I am, we will not allow hunting on any of our undeveloped property." Instead of a hunt, Fitch suggested residents attend a workshop called "Landscaping with Deer," form a committee to study and implement ways to lessen the impacts of deer, reconsider landscape choices and consider a "Deer Off" program for ornamentals.

✓ Princeton Township, N.J. — In addition to a deer cull, a committee evaluating Princeton's deer population has suggested birth control and sterilization programs. The birth-control program could cost up to $50,000 and the sterilization program has a start-up cost of around $10,000. Councilman Leonard Godfrey raised concern about liability problems that could arise from families that eat deer treated with the birth-control drug. The committee also recommended that the Humane Society of the United States be invited to observe net-and-bolt procedures if they are implemented. As of yet, no actions have been taken on these recommendations.

— National Bowhunter Education Foundation, U.S. Sportsmen's Alliance

Drop-Away Arrow Rests

Technology is constantly advancing in the world of bow-hunting. One of the most popular recent advances is the drop-away arrow rest.

As the name implies, the drop-away rest falls out of the way as your arrow is released. Most models function on a similar principle: the rest is attached to your bow cable via a cable or string. As the bow is drawn, the rest is pulled into the upright position. As the bow is released, tension on the string connecting the rest to the cable is relaxed, and the rest drops down and out of the way.

Drop-away rests provide several benefits to the shooter. First, they reduce torque on your shaft, which increases accuracy. Also, because they move out of the way before the arrow's fletching reaches the rest, you can use shafts with more helical, which improves arrow flight. Drop-away rests also reduce friction, which extends launcher life and makes for a quieter release.

Many companies offer drop-away arrow rests, including Carolina Archery Products' Drop-Tine QS, Golden Key-Futura's Power Drop, New Archery Products' QuickTune, High Country's Vertical Drop Pro, Trophy Ridge's Drop Zone, Montana Black Gold's Trap Door LR, Bodoodle's Game Dropper, Quality Archery Designs' Ultra-Rest, APA Innovations' Ultimate Rest and many others.

Montana Black Gold Trap Door LR

Quality Archery Designs Ultra-Rest

Trophy Ridge Drop Zone

JOE SHEAD

Don't Lose Your Deer!
Keep Broadheads Shaving-Sharp

As I settled into my tree stand one cool November morning, I pulled an arrow out of my quiver and nocked it on my bow-string. As an afterthought, I reached toward the broadhead and pulled my fingernail against its blade. It was sharp, but it was certainly showing signs that it had been pushed in and out of a quiver several times in the previous weeks.

"No matter," I thought arrogantly. "My bow is going to fling this arrow at 250 feet per second. I could practically shoot a deer with a field point and I'd kill it."

Of course, in my youth and inexperience, I was dead wrong, and I was about to find out.

A few minutes after first light, a mature doe appeared in the gully behind me and began feeding toward my stand. As she stepped behind a tree just 13 yards away, I stood and drew my bow. When the doe emerged on the opposite side of the tree and lowered her head to feed on acorns, I held my pin on her vitals and released.

As the arrow hit, the doe hopped, tucked her tail between her legs and bolted for a nearby thicket. A few seconds later, the woods were again silent.

A half-hour later, I descended from my stand and walked to my arrow. However, what I saw didn't match my expectations. Although I was sure the arrow had penetrated both lungs and possibly clipped the heart, there was relatively little blood on the shaft or fletching. I found just as little sign as I began walking along the doe's path — one drop of blood here, another there, but nothing like you'd expect from a double-lung hit.

Fortunately, the doe left a trail of scuffed-up leaves far more easy to follow than her sparse blood trail, and I soon found her lying dead about 100 yards from my stand.

Amazingly, the arrow entered the doe behind her shoulder, about halfway up her body, and exited through the opposite "armpit," yet left virtually no blood trail. Although the incident might have been a fluke, it probably had much to do with my dull broadhead.

As I learned that day, "pretty sharp" isn't sharp enough when it comes to broadheads. In fact, as many seasoned bow-hunters have told me, if you're not scared of your broadheads, they shouldn't be in your quiver.

Razor-sharp broadheads slice organs, arteries and blood vessels cleanly, causing rapid blood loss and preventing clotting. Dull broadheads, however, rip and tear

RYAN GILLIGAN

such tissues — or worse, push them out of the way. Wounds caused by dull broadheads are more likely to clot, resulting in more unrecovered deer — even on seemingly perfect hits.

To avoid this, sharpen your broadheads regularly. Manufacturers offer several sharpening systems designed to sharpen virtually every broadhead design. The easiest designs to sharpen are one-piece fixed-blade broadheads like those made by Zwikey and G5. In fact, these heads can be used repeatedly on game, as long as their blades are touched up between uses.

G5 offers specialized sharpening systems for its Montec and B-52 heads. The sharpeners are shaped to hold the broadhead blade at the perfect angle, ensuring quick and precise sharpening.

Whatever sharpener you use, begin by using fairly heavy pressure. Gradually decrease the pressure of your strokes until you are just gently pushing the blade against the stone.

For even better results, finish by stroking the blades against a leather strop. If you don't have a commercially manufactured strop, use an old leather belt or flat-edged knife sheath. This will remove any burr edge from the blades.

Finally, don't just use sharpeners for maintenance — use them for sharpening broadheads right out of the box. Like fishing hooks, broadheads usually don't come optimally sharp from the factory. Even if they did, oxidation while they sit on store shelves often dulls the blades before hunters ever take them out of the package.

DULL BROADHEADS cut or tear tissues, or push vital organs out of the way. Keep broadheads shaving sharp so you don't lose your deer.

ALMANAC INSIGHTS

➤ **DO YOU THINK OF** arrows as primitive weapons? Think again. The U.S. Army is using a modified arrow as the primary weapon on Abrams tanks. The anti-tank projectile consists of a dense metal rod, measuring 18 inches long and 1 inch in diameter. The "arrow" is fired through the Abrams' smoothbore cannon, and is stabilized in flight by metal fins similar to fletchings.

Unlike most modern military weapons, the anti-tank arrow uses no explosives. Rather, it penetrates all known tank armor using only its momentum — not surprising, considering the projectile flies at a rumored 6,000 fps!
— *Peter P. Roemer*
Trueflite vice president

Diffraction: Why to Hate It

Before I started bow-hunting, my brother hunted with a bow. My brother is a teacher, so he often went hunting in the evenings after school. He told me of all the deer he had seen and shot at. Once he emptied his entire quiver at a 6-point buck that refused to leave the scent he had set out. In five years of bow-hunting, he never harvested a deer. My brother no longer hunts with a bow.

About six years ago, I was bow-hunting along the Mississippi River. I am always the last one out of the woods, so I was surprised to find a truck still parked near mine. The fellow standing by the truck was waiting for his buddy. We visited as I casually packed away my gear. You know curiosity. I was stalling, thinking his buddy had shot a deer. I wanted to hear all about it.

When his buddy finally arrived, he had no deer! "I'll never go bow-hunting again!" he exclaimed as he threw his tree stand in the back of the truck.

"I've been bow-hunting for three years and I haven't got a deer yet. I even bought a 3-D target. Every evening I've been shooting that fake deer from my deck. I never miss."

The more he talked the angrier he got.

"Tonight a huge doe stood broadside in front of me. She was only 18 yards away. I shot all five of my arrows at her, and missed every time. She walked off as if nothing had happened."

By now the anger was turning to disgust.

"Do you know what I've been doing? For the last hour I have been trying to find my arrows. I Quit!"

He slammed the tailgate closed. My brother could have said the same thing.

Switching Dominance

If you are curious why these bow-hunters could never shoot accurately when hunting, try this simple experiment. With both eyes open, focus on a spot about 10 feet away. Point at the spot with a finger. Using the other hand, block your vision, (dominant eye) with the tip of one of your fingers. Start with your fingertip about a foot from your eye. Slowly bring your fingertip toward your eye, keeping your focus on the spot. When your fingertip is about six inches from your eye, you will notice you are no longer pointing at the spot. Instead you will be pointing to the left or right of the spot.

What happened? Your eyes

KEN JOHNSON

switched dominance. You started sighting with your dominant eye and ended up sighting with your non-dominant eye. Under these circumstances, at 18 yards you will shoot two to three feet to the right

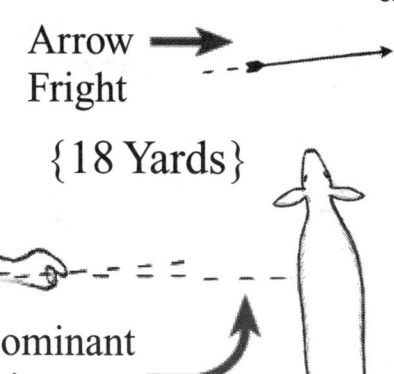

Arrow ➞
Fright
{18 Yards}

Figure 1

Non-Dominant Sight Line

or left, and all the practice in the world will not help you hit your target.

You might say, "I don't shoot with my finger in front of my eye." I would hope not. But you do shoot with a peep sight in front of your eye. Under low-light conditions, your peep sight and your finger produce the same results. Note the drawing.

Another Near Miss

Tom is an excellent archer with his share of tournament wins. One evening at the end of our hunt, Tom was standing in front of his truck.

"Is it a buck or a doe?" I asked.

"It's a doe, but I think I gut-shot her," Tom responded, shaking his head in disbelief.

"I had the pin just behind her front shoulders, and I gut-shot her!" On our hands and knees we followed tiny blood specks for over a mile. At 1 a.m., we finally found Tom's deer. The arrow had passed through just in front of the deer's rear flanks.

Why did an excellent archer make such a poor shot? Tom had the pin just behind the deer's front shoulder. It should have been an easy double-lung shot. The problem was, Tom didn't know he was aiming with the wrong eye and shot two feet to the left.

Light Diffraction

Look at the end of your nose. You will see a fuzzy border along the edge of it. This fuzzy border is caused by light diffraction. Light passing near the edge of your nose is diffracted, or bent away, making the edge of your nose appear fuzzy. Hold any object just in front of your nose and look at its edge. You will again see this fuzziness. Look through your peep sight, you will also see a fuzziness along the inside edge. This is because all edges diffract light.

Light diffraction controls the size of your peep sight's peephole. In Figure 2, the small arrows show the

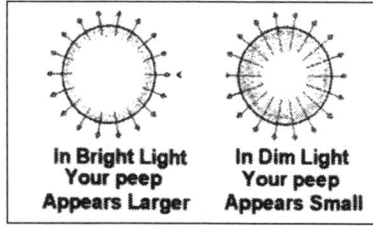

In Bright Light Your peep Appears Larger

In Dim Light Your peep Appears Small

Figure 2

ARCHERY INSIGHTS

Be Stealthy

With your feet: When stalking use a pair of Sneaky Petes — a cloth shoe cover designed to keep your steps quiet when it's dry.

Ray Howell

For your legs: Use knee-high wool socks, pulling them over the top of your pant legs, to keep the noise down when walking through thick brush.

Outer clothing: Use a material such as fleece or wool. This will eliminate 99 percent of the noise encountered from brushing up against brush and tree limbs. It also allows you to draw your bow without being detected.

Take it Slow

While stalking your prey, do not be in a hurry. Wait for the deer to make the mistakes and then capitalize on them. A lot of times if you get too anxious, you might blow your shot opportunity. Always remember that one set of eyes is a lot easier to stalk up on than several sets.

General Tactics

Use a powder-device to constantly check wind direction. Keep the wind in your favor and use scent-eliminating clothing.

While sitting in a tree stand and moving to and from your tree stand, use knee-high rubber boots with a scent-eliminating spray.

Cover your bow limbs with camouflage cloth tape to prevent reflections.

Use sound-dampening equipment on your bow to keep deer from jumping the string.

Use scentless face paint to take the glare off your face.

Use the landscape to your benefit and never silhouette yourself.

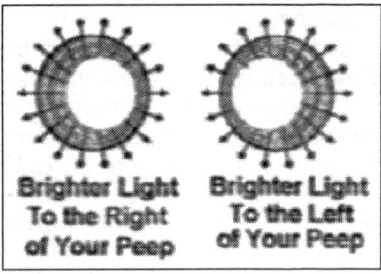

Brighter Light To the Right of Your Peep | Brighter Light To the Left of Your Peep

Figure 3

direction light is diffracted. Like spokes in a wheel, light is bent perpendicular to the edge of the peephole and, out and away from your eye. Your eye's retina will not sense light that is bent at such an angle, so the edge appears fuzzy.

Figure 2 also shows how diffraction decreases as light becomes brighter and increases as light becomes dimmer. This is why target shooters use small peepholes and hunters use large peepholes. At twilight, dusk or in heavy cover, hunters need the large peepholes to provide more space for the increased diffraction.

A Convincing Example

Diffraction is a powerful deceiver. One summer, we had a solid week of wonderful weather, blue skies and windless days. Every afternoon a young man was at the local archery range. The last day of this wonderful weather, the young man was feeling his oats. He was shooting at a playing card from distances of 30 to 60 yards. His arrows never missed. As he proudly demonstrated his skills, a heavy bank of clouds slowly moved in out of the west. When the clouds shut off the bright sunlight, the young man's next arrow struck 14 inches low. Was he surprised! He fooled with his front pin sight, and tried a few more arrows, but finally quit in confusion.

You may not have seen such an obvious example of someone being fooled by diffraction, but if you think back, you may remember situations when you and your friends have been deceived in a similar way.

If you shoot outdoors, where light is constantly changing, the following will help explain some of your misses. Remember, the brighter the light, the less the effects of diffraction, and the dimmer the light, the greater the effects of diffraction.

Figure 3 shows how inconsistencies in light intensity affect the diffraction in your peephole. When the light on the right side of your peephole is brighter then the light on the left side of your peephole, the diffraction will cause the center of your peephole to appear off center to the right. The opposite happens when light is brighter to the left. As the light changes, the diffraction changes, and the center of your peephole changes. This is what happened to the young man. When the clouds shut off the bright sunlight, the diffraction in his peephole changed, the center of his peephole changed, and he unknowingly aimed 14 inches low. Diffraction controls the location of the center of your peephole.

Perform the following experiment. Early in the morning on a sunny day, set up a target 20 yards away so you are shooting to the north. Aiming at the center of the target, shoot a group of five arrows. Mark the group. Next, move your target so you shoot the same distance to the south. Again, aim at the center of the target and shoot five arrows. Examine your two

Allan Martin Inducted Into Archery HOF

Allan Martin of Fairfield, Ohio, was inducted into the Archery Hall of Fame in January 2003.

He has been involved in archery since the 1950s as a competitor, administrator and judge.

He won the Sextuple American event at the U.S. Nationals in his first year of archery. He was also on the National Archery Association men's championship team.

Martin was NAA president and board member, a delegate to the U.S. Olympics Committee, and helped form and direct the NAA's National Officials and Rules Committee. He wrote the first officiating goals and guidelines book and was NAA's shooting director.

Starting in the 1980s, Martin administered many local and international programs and organizations. He served as president of the Cincinnati Archers, board member of the Midwest and Northern Region, chairman of the Brown County Archery Association, and a delegate to both the Pan Am Committee and the International Archery Federation.

He gained international fame as an archery judge at the World Field Championships, Pan Am Games, Championship of the Americas, World Target Archery Championships, NAA Nationals and National Sports Festivals.

As the AHF's 53rd inductee, Martin joins such famous inductees as Fred Bear, Saxton Pope, Art Young and Earl Hoyt.

— *Archery Trade Association*

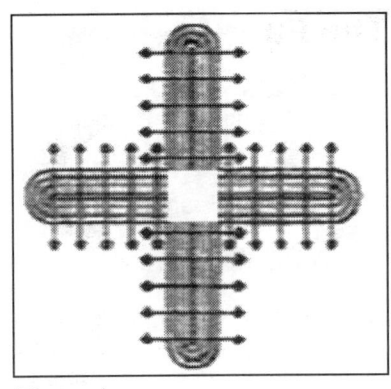

Figure 4

groups. You will see that your groups vary. One will be further to the right than the other. When you shot facing North, the sunlight was from the right. When you shot facing South, the sunlight was from the left. This change in light direction caused the light in one side of your peephole to become more intense than the light in the other side. The diffraction changed, the center of your peephole changed and you unknowingly misaligned your sights and shot at two different points and produced two different groups.

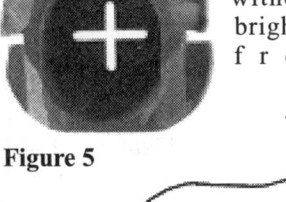

Dealing With Diffraction

Light diffraction cannot be eliminated. But it can be controlled. There are two characteristics of diffraction that makes it controllable.

First, diffraction only occurs when light passes an edge. Second, light diffracts perpendicular to the edge that causes the diffraction.

Figure 4 shows how diffraction can be controlled. By replacing the round peephole with two intersecting slots, a peephole is created that has no edge. The intersecting slots allow light to diffract within the slots, but not within the square hole. The light entering the slots diffracts perpendicular to the edges of the slots and parallel to the outside of the square hole. The result is a square hole free of light diffraction. An archer looking through the peep will not see the slots, because the light passing through the slots is diffracted. The archer sees a square hole that is always consistent in size and shape.

Figure 5 shows what an archer sees when sighting through a Night Hawk peep. The archer sees a perfectly clear picture of his target (Figure 6) framed by a square formed by diffraction. The sight picture (Figure 7) appears extra bright and perfectly clear.

When I first witnessed the extra brightness that came from viewing a target through a Night Hawk peep, I was skeptical, but not anymore. The only way I can explain the extra brightness is that it is the result of the square peephole limiting the area your eye can focus on, and at the same time,

Figure 5

Figure 6

Figure 7

Carbon Arrow Shafts: The Future is Now

Carbon arrows are simply the next evolution of bow-hunting shafts. In virtually any category, carbon is a better shaft material than aluminum.

Durability is a definite carbon advantage. If you stumble on the way to your stand and fall on or drop your bow with carbon arrows, they are still straight. With aluminum arrows, who knows?

Quietness is another carbon advantage. You'll hear none of the metallic ringing that you get with aluminum.

Penetration, which is always a main goal of bow-hunters, is often better with carbon shafts. With today's selection of carbon shafts, virtually any weight shaft is available, so the argument that slower and heavier shafts penetrate better can be ignored.

In reality, in most cases, carbon arrows are smaller in diameter than most aluminum arrows, which reduces friction and allows more penetration. More importantly, carbon shafts maintain their straightness, even after striking something hard. This allows the shaft to cleanly pass through the hole the broadhead created. Aluminum tends to deflect when it hits something, robbing it of energy needed for penetration.

If you shoot carbon arrows, you know just what I'm talking about. If you haven't tried carbon, there has never been a better time.

— *Johnny Grace*
Parker Compound Bows

---

allowing all the light entering the peephole to pass undisturbed. It is this combination that helps you see more clearly. You can witness a similar result if you look through a pinhole in a well-lit room.

Conclusion

Too often I see archers blaming their inaccuracies on their form or their equipment, when neither are to fault. They waste much of their practice time and show no improvement. This brings on confusion and reduces their confidence. With no improvement, they become frustrated and quit.

It need not be this way. Try some of the things suggested here. By doing so, you will get a better understanding of how your peep sight works and how diffraction affects your success. With this new understanding, you will find yourself improving as a bow-hunter and an archer.

For more information contact Night Hawk Archery at www.nighthawkarchery.com or (952) 854-3530.

How to Select Fletchings for Your Hunting Arrows

For hunting arrows tipped with broadheads, three 5-inch feathers or four 4-inch feathers work best. Individual differences in equipment and shooting style sometimes require the use of larger feathers. It is also possible that good flight can be achieved with smaller feathers. Test shooting is the best way to decide which setup is right for you.

It's important to remember that broadheads need more guidance than field points. Without proper guidance, a broadhead will cause the arrow to yawn or fishtail during flight. Yawning arrows cause inconsistent flight patterns, and lose velocity and penetration.

Use the following question-and-answer segment to determine which setups are right for your arrows:

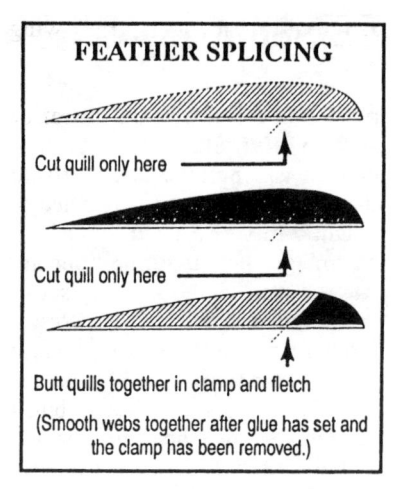

➤ **Should I use right- or left-wing feathers?**

You can shoot either wing successfully. An arrow does not rotate noticeably until it is well clear of the bow. Left-wing feathers should be used to rotate the arrow counter-clockwise, while right-wing feathers rotate the arrow clockwise.

➤ **How can I determine the alignment of the feather on my arrows?**

Two methods can be used to determine right- or left-wing alignment. First, look at the nock end of the arrow (aligned as though the arrow is ready to be shot), and rotate it so one fletching is on top of the shaft. If the "catch lip" is to the left of the web, it is a right-wing feather. If the "catch lip" is to the right of the web, it is a left-wing feather.

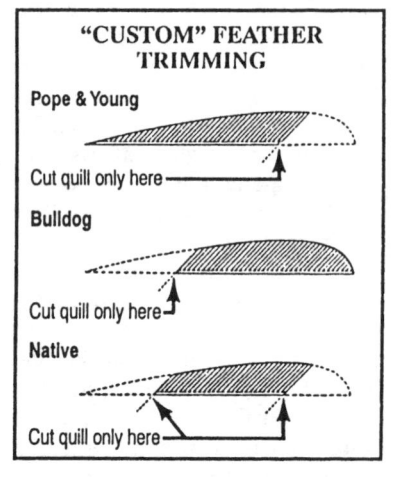

The second method involves holding the forward end of the die-cut (pointed end) or full-length feather (larger end) toward yourself. Look down from the top, and rotate the feather so its web is horizontal and its natural curve droops the end pointed away from you downward ("shedding rain" as opposed to "catching rain"). If the web is to the right of the quill base, it is a right-wing feather. If the web is to the left of the quill base, it is a left-wing feather.

▶ **Should I use straight, offset or helical fletchings?**

Archers often ask about flight differences of arrows with angled or helical fletching

For compound bows, it is recommended that shooters use offset or helical fletchings on all arrows. Offset and helical fletchings cause arrows to rotate in flight just like the rifling in a gun barrel causes a bullet to rotate. This is important for arrows because the rotation acts like a gyroscope to stabilize the arrow during flight.

Helical fletchings offer more stability than a simple offset, and therefore should be the first choice for all broadhead-tipped arrows.

▶ **How much fletching offset should I use?**

If the forward end of a 5-inch feather is offset $1/16$-inch from its rear, this equals about three-quarters of one degree. This works well for most offset or helical-fletched arrows.

▶ **How should I prepare my arrow shafts for the fletching process?**

Begin by wiping the fletching area of the arrows with alcohol, then lightly scuffing the area with 600-grit sandpaper or fine steel wool. It's wise to perform a final alcohol wipe before starting the fletching process.

For more information on fletchings, contact Trueflight, Box 1000, Manitowish Waters, WI 54545.

Silence that Bow!

I've had the privilege of shooting a wide variety of bows, from wooden recurves and early compounds to today's most advanced one-cams. And although today's newest bows are generally faster, quieter and more efficient than any ever produced, virtually all bows could stand to be quieter. Fortunately, there's plenty you can do to take the twang out of even the loudest bows.

If your bow rattles the windows every time you shoot, first concentrate on the bow itself. Tighten any loose screws on the rest, quiver and other accessories. If the bow is still loud, shooting a heavier arrow shaft might help, as the increased mass will absorb more of the bow's energy. Incidentally, this will also probably increase your setup's kinetic energy and penetration.

Next, outfit your bow with a set of string and cable silencers from the wide array available today. Larger, heavier silencers generally dampen more noise and vibration than small, rubber-band-style models. However, these heavier silencers will slightly reduce arrow speeds.

Manufacturers also offer innovative limb attachments for reducing noise, such as Sims Vibration Laboratories' Stealth Limb Savers. Stabilizers also help minimize noise and vibration.

— *Ryan Gilligan*

Selecting Accurate, Hard-Hitting Broadheads

Quality broadheads aren't cheap, and it's easy to spend a lot of money trying to determine which ones are right for you. With that in mind, follow this simple, four-step game plan to reduce your costs and select the perfect broadhead for your setup:

1. Conduct your own field test.

Most broadheads are sold in three- and four-packs, so get two or three of your hunting partners to split the cost of several packs of broadheads.

2. Research what types of broadheads are out there. You will want to try mechanicals and fixed-position heads, so do some homework and select three or four different brands of each category that you want to try.

Don't let cost scare you from trying what you want. For example, if three shooters spend $40 apiece on a field test, they could shoot at least six brands of broadheads. Furthermore, they will know exactly what heads they want to shoot, rather than spending $40 on two packs of one brand that "looks good."

3. Set up a test course. Present huge soft targets — foam blocks work best — and start by shooting the broadheads from short distances (10 to 15 yards).

First, however, organize the shoot. Give each shooter one broadhead from each pack. Shoot one arrow at a time, plot its performance on a sheet of paper, and retrieve the arrow before shooting again. You can ruin a lot of arrows, and perhaps a few broadheads, if you allow shooters to shoot several broadheads at the same 6-inch circle on the target.

4. Select the broadhead that shoots best for you, and purchase six or more that will be used strictly for hunting. Also, purchase replacement blades for heads you use. You will save a lot of money.

Finally, use the original field-test broadheads as your practice heads. And, unless your broadheads fly exactly like your field points, always practice with your broadheads.

— *Daniel E. Schmidt*

Paper-Tuning Instructions

Proper tuning is a vital, but often overlooked, part of bow-hunting success. In short, poorly tuned bows are inaccurate, unpredictable and produce less arrow penetration and energy on impact.

There's no excuse for shooting an out-of-tune bow, because paper tuning is simple. To begin tuning, set your nocking point $1/16$ inch above the top of an arrow squared to the bow-string. Also make sure you're using the right size arrow for your bow. Shooting a shaft that's too stiff or weak might make proper tuning impossible.

Next, set up a poster-sized sheet of paper in a frame set a few feet in front of a safe backstop. Then, stand about four feet away from the frame and shoot two or three arrows into different parts of the paper. The way the paper tears will indicate whether the arrow is flying correctly.

Optimal arrow flight is indicated by a tear that shows the fletching hitting $1/4$ to $3/4$ inch higher than the

Photos Reveal Trueflight Fletching Integrity

TRUEFLIGHT captured these shots of an arrow making contact with a branch using a camera with a shutter speed of 12 microseconds. Shot 1 shows slight fletching contact with a branch, Shot 2 shows moderate contact, and Shot 3 shows severe contact.

An experiment conducted by Trueflight shows the amazing resistance of its fletching.

Using a camera with a shutter speed of 12 microseconds (12 one-millionths of a second) Trueflight took photos of arrow fletching making slight, moderate and severe contact with a tree branch positioned 1.3 yards downrange. Arrow speed was 256 feet per second.

The feathers fold down on contact, then pop back and smooth down. In fact, in Shot 3, with severe contact, the feathers straighten out after traveling only 16 inches beyond the branch. Total elapsed time from contact to smooth fletching: 0.0047 second!

What's more, the shot was repeated 30 times without touching the fletching.

What does this mean for archers? Although it's uncertain how contact will affect arrow flight, at least the fletchings will stand up to repeated contact.

— *Trueflight Inc.*

---

point, between 11 and 1 o'clock. However, chances are your bow will produce one of the following tear patterns, which indicate improper arrow flight.

To remedy these problems follow the instructions accompanying the tear pattern that matches yours. The left and right tear instructions are for right-handed shooters. Left-handed archers must use reverse solutions. High and low tear solutions are identical for right- and left-handed archers.

Left Tear

This indicates a weak-spined arrow.

Solutions:

✓ Decrease the draw weight by backing out the limb bolts a quarter turn at a time. Adjust limbs equally to prevent changing the tiller and nock point. To avoid injury and damage, be careful not to back out the limb bolts too far.

✓ Decrease the point weight. A lighter point will increase shaft stiffness. However, too light a point might result in unstable arrow flight.

✓ A slight tear can sometimes be fixed by moving the arrow rest away from the riser.

✓ If none of these measures reduce the length of the tear, change to a stiffer shaft.

Right Tear
This indicates the arrow is too stiff.
Solutions:

✓ Increase the draw weight by tightening the limb bolts a quarter turn at a time. Adjust limb bolts equally to avoid changing the tiller and nock point.

✓ Increase the point weight. A heavier point will decrease shaft stiffness. However, it will probably decrease arrow speed.

✓ A slight tear can sometimes be fixed by moving the arrow rest away from the riser.

✓ If these solutions don't reduce the length of the tear, change to a weaker shaft.

High Tear
Solutions:

✓ Lower nocking point in small increments.

✓ If you're using a launcher or shoot-through rest, raise the support arm. Increasing spring tension also might help.

✓ Check for fletching clearance and adjust rest accordingly.

Low Tear
Solutions:

✓ Raise nocking point in small increments.

✓ If you're using a launcher or shoot-through rest, lower the support arm. Increasing spring tension might also help.

Proper Tuning For Today's Broadheads

Broadheads should be checked for flight after shafts have been paper tuned. It's not uncommon for the impact point of a broadhead to be different than a field point.

1. Set up a broadhead target 20 to 30 yards away. Using the same arrow (with field point) that you used for paper tuning, shoot at the target. This will give you a reference point. If the shot is off, make the necessary adjustments to your sights.

2. Remove the field point and install a broadhead onto the shaft. Use the same aiming point, and shoot again. If the broadhead hits close to where the field point did, shoot the same arrow several times to be sure you are within a respectable group size.

3. The shot group is the key. If you are shooting good groups but the impact is off from your aiming point, simply make sight adjustments.

✓ Check for fletching clearance and adjust rest accordingly.

Are Expandables Right For You?

Expandable broadheads have made huge strides in the archery world during the past 10 years, and hunters have taken notice. More archers are using expandable broadheads than ever before, but should you? Thanks to ever-improving designs and materials, that question is constantly becoming easier to answer.

Today's Hot New Bows

- The V-Lock zero-tolerance limb system makes **Mathews'** LX highly accurate and dependable. The bow's HP (High Performance) single cam and idler wheel feature precision sealed ball bearings for smooth drawing and shooting. It is available in 65 percent or 80 percent let-off.

- The AR-34 bow from **Archery Research** has chambers in the riser that direct vibration away from your hand. The bow features a torque-free grip, a Cam-Lock cable guard system, pivoting limb pockets with vibration-dampening inserts and a machined Ram Cam with a wide-track design and rubber cable stopper.

- The NV vibration dampening system and Phase III grip make the **Precision Shooting Equipment** Nitro smooth and quiet. The new Nitro is lighter and quieter than last year's model. The bow features Trimline pivoting limb pockets, a fully adjustable Cam-Lock cable guard mount and a Kolorfusion finish. It is available with PSE's Centerfire One-Cam or Maxi-Plus Twin-Cams.

- **Golden Eagle's** Obsession is quiet, fast and maneuverable. The bow features a machined reflex riser, a Shock Stop string suppressor, Carbon Air Quad limbs and Golden Eagle's modular Gold Dot Perimeter OneCam. The Obsession also features a two-piece checkered hardwood grip and Mossy Oak's new Break Up camouflage pattern.

Leonard Lee Rue III

Try the Winter Challenge!

When it is 10 degrees below zero and most people are snuggling up with a good book or watching TV, some people defy the need for warmth and brave the cold in search of the elusive white-tailed deer. No, this isn't November anymore, it's December — the last month of bow-season.

You might think that anybody who dares to venture into the bitter cold must be a little crazy, and you might be right! You have to try it before you can judge us die-hard hunters. If you dress properly, make sure you stay dry and don't sweat, it isn't so bad.

I go out for the thrill. Bucks don't realize we are still after them at this point. The once elusive whitetails are a little dim-witted now. They know when they are being hunted in rifle season because there are a lot of hunters moving around in the woods, but when the snow flies and the temperature drops, people tend to clear out of the woods and head back to their warm homes.

I have found ways to stay warm that I normally wouldn't think of in the winter. For example, I dry all of my clothes. Even though they feel dry to the touch, they may still be wet if you don't dry them properly.

The first places I usually get cold are my feet or my hands. It would be easy to keep my hands warm with hand-warmers if I didn't have to wear a trigger for my bow or if I put another pair of gloves on my hands.

My feet, on the other hand, get so cold that when I get up from my stand, it seems they don't work. And the problem is not something to be solved easily. If I wear extra socks, my boots get too tight and my feet get cold. If I wear foot-warmers, they warm my feet for a short while, make my feet sweat, and then my feet get cold.

During late-season bow-hunting, the deer's habits change rapidly from during rut. They are looking for a nice wintering spot. If you can find where they like to feed, then you have a good shot at bagging one. Also, late-season hunting provides you a better chance to get to place you normally couldn't because everything has snow on it and the water is frozen. If you want to be quiet, use snowshoes, but if you want to get somewhere fast, use a snowmobile and hope the deer ignore the noise.

Late-season bow-hunters have the odds stacked against them, but hunting at this time of the year is exciting. I'll keep taking my chances to defy the odds.

CODY BRANDON

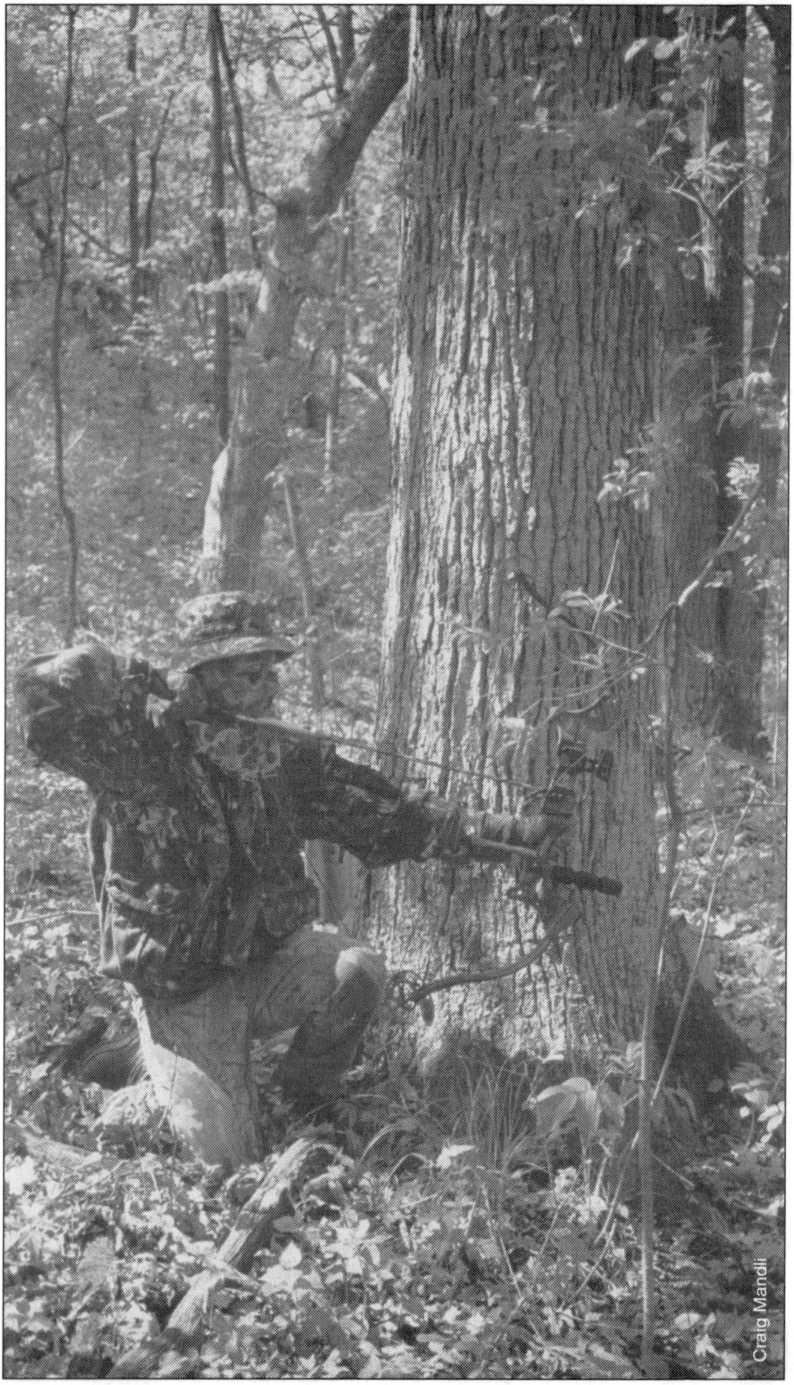
Craig Mandli

The Buck at 4 Yards

It wasn't my first bow-hunt, but it was one of my first.

I'd grown up in a hunting family, and I remember counting the years until I'd be old enough to hunt when I was only in elementary school.

And while hunting was practically a way of life in my family every fall, one thing we didn't do was bow-hunt.

After a few years of gun-hunting, it dawned on me there were a lot more opportunities to bag a deer while bow-hunting, and it would be a lot more exciting watching unpressured deer, instead of watching them tear wildly across open fields until they were buried in thick cover or dead.

So, like a lot of bow-hunters, I took up the sport on my own.

On my first memorable bow-hunt, I returned to an area where friends and I had hunted during an antlerless-only gun-hunt days before. It was early November, and we'd watched rut-crazed bucks chasing does on our hunt. Things looked promising.

The place we hunted was a river-bottom silver maple forest. It was a peninsula, if you want to get technical, but it was essentially an island. That alone made it fun to hunt.

My friend had watched a herd of deer approach his stand from the west on our gun hunt before he picked out and shot a buck fawn. With a quick walk, I found where the "island" narrowed 100 yards from where he'd taken his stand, and decided it was a great ambush point.

I found an old, rotten stump next to a deer trail, and after clearing the ground of leaves, kneeled down behind it.

I don't remember how long I kneeled there, or frankly, many details of the hunt, but I do know that I spotted a deer coming at me right down that deer trail.

It was about 40 yards away when I first saw it. I ducked down behind the stump and drew. I didn't know how long it would take the deer to reach the stump, but I didn't want it to see me draw.

I didn't know what it was, but that didn't matter. I could legally kill any deer, and any deer would do for my first bow-kill.

The deer was taking its sweet time approaching me. At least I think it was. My head was hidden behind the stump, and I wasn't watching the deer; only the trail I hoped it would pop out on. And in hindsight, my memory is probably more influenced by my burning arms than any rational judgment.

After a few seconds, my arms felt weak, and they began shaking. I braced my left elbow against my knee, trying to steady myself, but still I shook. I could hold it no longer. Just as I told myself it was time to let down, the deer emerged on the trail, 4 yards in front of me.

The deer was walking and was

JOE SHEAD

ALMANAC INSIGHTS

➤ **ALTHOUGH MOST** gun-deer hunters were brought into the sport by friends or family members, bow-hunters follow a different trend. According to a recent survey by the Archery Merchants and Manufacturers Association, 39 percent of active bow-hunters took up the sport on their own.

totally oblivious to my presence.

The arrow's flight startled me. Had I not seen the arrow fly off my bow-string, I'd deny ever shooting. But I saw white hair fly like a puff of smoke, and I watched my arrow hit the ground 15 yards away.

The deer was equally startled, and trotted 15 yards before stopping to look back at the commotion. It was then that I saw a single, inch-long spike. It was no buck fawn, but apparently a yearling with a meager lone antler. As the buck watched me, I longed for my rifle. It would have been an easy shot with a gun, but I carried the bow, and my strength was gone. And I doubt if I even carried another arrow.

The deer trotted off, and I struggled to my feet, confused by the details swirling around me. I wondered if it was all a dream.

There was no blood on my arrow, so I followed the buck's tracks as best I could. I'd never lost a deer before, and I felt sick. But I knew I was looking for a perfectly healthy deer, and there would be no catching up to it. Plus I had no blood trail to follow. Deep down, I knew the deer would be fine. His belly might just get a little cold from now on.

I returned to the trail to examine the deer hair, and my eyes swiveled back and forth to the stump and to the trail, so close together.

ARCHERY INSIGHTS

Eight Tips for Accuracy

Ray Howell

1. Use a shorter draw with a slightly bent arm and three anchor points: Put the release under your chin, kisser button on your canine tooth and string on the tip of your nose.

2. The weight of your arrow should be predominantly forward of the arrow's center, so the broadhead is doing the pulling.

3. Learn how to properly paper-tune your bow.

4. Visually tune your shots to check for abnormalities (planing, whipping, porpoising, etc.) by using bright-colored fletching and shooting into a black-faced target at 30 to 40 yards.

5. Apply the right amount of helical to your fletching to achieve more control during flight. Even the largest of fixed-blade broadheads can be tuned to perfection with the right amount of helical.

6. Practice with the same equipment as you would use in the field.

7. Wear your hunting clothing while practicing to check for loose fabric that the string might catch. You may have to sew your sleeve and chest area tight for string clearance.

8. Practice long-range shots to improve your accuracy and confidence at close range.

For more tips, stories or advice from Ray Howell or information on his Kicking Bear One-on-One mentoring program, log onto www.rayhowell.com.

I tucked a clump of hair in the pocket of my bow-hunting jacket, and every now and then I still find a stray hair from the buck that got away at 4 yards.

ARCHERY INSIGHTS

Tips for Cold Weather

One of my most productive times for taking large whitetails is in December and January because deer are easier to pattern. They are often herded up and are stressed due to the cold and snow. Abundant feed is hard to find during these months. Also, I rarely encounter other hunters.

Ray Howell

A few things that have made me successful in bitter cold are wearing the proper clothing, shooting a quiet bow and shooting accurately in cold weather.

The best way to stay warm and dry is to layer clothing. The first layer should wick moisture away from the skin. The next layer is a light-weight wool sweater, followed by a layer of fleece material. You may need more layers, depending on the temperature. The outer layer should be a quiet fleece that blocks the wind and is also water resistant to keep wind, rain, sleet or snow from penetrating your insulation layers. The clothing should allow total freedom of movement.

This type of clothing is extremely quiet, enabling you to draw without being detected. To ensure the clothing is quiet, have someone listen as you move your arms as if drawing your bow. No matter how much money you have invested in your clothing, if it makes noise, it's not worth wearing!

Keeping yourself dry while walking to your stand is critical for staying warm the rest of the day. Give yourself plenty of time so you can walk slowly in deep snow and bitter cold in order to keep yourself from sweating. One way to do this is to carry some of your clothes to your stand and then put them on when you get there. It's also a good idea to bring a change of hats. Face masks can be used as long as they don't obstruct your vision and accuracy with your bow.

If you are a right-handed shooter, sew the left sleeves of your undergarments and outer clothing to tighten them and give you clearance with your bowstring. You may also have to sew in or tighten the chest area of your outer layer of clothing to keep your string from making contact.

Well-insulated boots, wool socks over polypropylene socks and warm gloves are essential. Keeping your feet and hands warm will help keep your whole body warm. If they get cold, your hunt is over! Wear your outer pants over your boots to keep the snow out and to keep the metal eyelets from making noise against your tree stand. Carry a piece of heavy cloth big enough to stand on in your tree stand or on the ground. It will help keep your boots from squeaking after clearing the frost or snow off the area that you'll be standing on. Ninety-five percent of the animals I have harvested in bitter cold conditions have been taken from the ground. Once I've patterned an animal, I'll use whatever snow bank or brush pile is available for concealment.

In extreme cold, wear a thin polypropylene glove underneath a heavier glove. (Using a scissors, cut the palm out of the outer glove on the hand you hold your bow with. This will help keep you from torquing your bow and give you normal contact with the grip). The thinner glove will keep your palm warm. My release hand (with the release aid strapped over a thin glove) stays inside my jacket pocket next to my stomach. Then there's no bulky glove when it's time to shoot.

Cold weather can bring out noises in your bow that you normally wouldn't hear. To check for quietness, leave your bow outside for several hours and then have someone listen while you draw. Make whatever alterations are necessary. Using moleskin where the arrow contacts the rest will keep it dead silent while coming to full draw.

Using the proper vibration and silencing system on the bow, with a heavier arrow, will make deer less likely to jump the string. This is critical in cold weather because sounds seem to magnify. A deer can "outjump" the fastest bow, therefore, a quiet bow is better.

Practice outside in the same conditions you'll be hunting in while wearing your cold-weather clothing.

RIFLE CARTRIDGE TECHNOLOGY is constantly improving, helping hunters increase their shooting range and improve their accuracy.

5

INSIGHTS FOR RIFLE AND SHOTGUN HUNTERS
Choosing the Best Bullets

Choosing the top five deer bullets is no easy task. However, after 35 years of real-world hunting experience, I've found a few bullets that stand above the crowd. Here are my five favorites.

Nosler Partition

The Nosler Partition bullet has two lead cores separated by a solid partition of jacket material. The front end of the bullet expands rapidly while the rear section is protected by the partition. The bullet does not expand past this partition, which ensures the rear portion remains intact and continues driving through the target — even after the front core is gone.

On impact, the Partition almost always expands until it loses the front core and about 40 percent of its weight. The jacket then folds back against the rear section, creating a smaller frontal area.

Nosler Partition

Barnes X-Bullet

The Barnes X-Bullet is a unique solid copper bullet with no lead core to separate it from the jacket. It features a deep hollow point that splits into four distinct petals, which expand until reaching the bottom of the hollow point. This leaves a long, solid rear section to continue driving through the target.

Deep, reliable penetration is the trademark of this bullet, but it still expands at long range or when hitting mild targets like a whitetail's rib cage. The downside is that not every rifle shoots X-Bullets well. On the other hand,

Barnes X-Bullet

BRYCE M. TOWSLEY

guns that shoot X-Bullets well shoot them like target rounds.

Winchester Fail Safe Supreme

The front half of the Winchester Fail Safe Supreme bullet is made of solid copper alloy with a deep hollow point, similar to the X-Bullet's. The Fail Safe's rear section has a lead core enclosed with a steel sheath and covered in a jacket formed from the same metal used for the front. The two are separated by a thick belt of solid copper alloy.

The moly-coated Fail Safe expands quickly until it reaches the solid belt at the end of the hollow point, and then it stops expanding. Denser lead causes the rear section behind the bullet to weigh more than the front. This provides weight to push the bullet through the target.

Winchester Fail Safe Supreme

highly engineered super bullet like some of the others listed here. However, it's not a simple bullet. It uses a jacket with inner grooves at the tip to initiate expansion and tapered thickness to arrest expansion. The jacket is locked to the core with a raised ridge of jacket material around the inside of the jacket near the base.

Swift Scirocco

The plastic-tipped Swift Scirocco has a sharp profile with a small meplat, which results in a high ballistic coefficient. The bullet features a thick, tapered copper jacket bonded to a pure lead core. The thin front section works with the wedging action of the plastic tip to initiate expansion.

The Scirocco is ideal for long-range shooting, but it's tough enough for close shots.

Hornady InterLock

The Hornady InterLock is not a

Swift Scirocco

Conclusion

Although today's array of bullets is daunting, the good news is most of them perform well on whitetails. However, by choosing bullets I've listed here, you'll be best prepared for virtually any shot.

Hornady InterLock

Break In Your New Deer Rifle Properly

It's a good idea to take a few hours to properly break in a new rifle. The barrel will be much easier to clean and it might help hold accuracy longer between cleanings. The idea is to burnish away tooling marks and not impregnate the steel with carbon initially. Barnes has used the following break-in process successfully:

1. Shoot once using a jacketed lead-core bullet. The hard jacket material will do a better job of burnishing the barrel during the break-in process than other bullets.

Remove the bolt and clean the barrel thoroughly, as detailed below. When cleaning a rifle, remember, it's best to angle the muzzle downward and use a bore guide. This ensures solvents and grime won't drip through the action, gumming the trigger and ruining the bedding. Use a one-piece cleaning rod.

A. Use a proper jag and tight-fitting patch or nylon brush wrapped with a patch soaked with CR-10 to remove the powder fouling. Use two to four patches and push each patch completely through the bore with one long stroke.

B. Install the proper size bronze brush. Soak the brush with CR-10 before brushing. The brush should be stroked through the bore 10 to 20 times (it must be pushed completely through the bore before reversing direction). Add CR-10 to the brush halfway through the process. Clean the bronze brush when you're finished.

C. Use the proper size jag or nylon brush, with CR-10-soaked patches, running them down the barrel until they come out clean. This step removes all copper fouling. The first two patches after

Revive a 'Shot-Out' Deer Rifle

Neglected gun barrels can frequently be brought back to life with a special cleaning procedure called "deep cleaning." This procedure can return a "shot-out" rifle to a tack-driving deer gun.

If you have a rifle that isn't shooting consistently and is extremely difficult to clean, this might be worth trying.

✓ With the gun in a cradle or vise, install a bore guide. Attach a jag to a cleaning rod. Place a patch on the jag and saturate it with solvent. Push the patch slowly through the bore.

✓ Put a clean patch on the jag. Using your fingers, work bore compound into the patch until it's completely saturated. Be sure to use a bore compound that won't harm your barrel.

✓ Run the saturated patch into the bore. Mentally divide the barrel into four equal lengths. Using short strokes, work the rod into each area, using at least 10 strokes in each area. As the patch becomes looser, replace it with another one saturated with bore compound. Continue scrubbing until the patch moves through the bore with uniform smoothness.

✓ Remove bore compound residue from the barrel with patches moistened with carbon solvent. Run patches through the bore until no bore compound residue remains. Clean the compound from your cleaning rod, jag and bore guide.

✓ Resume standard cleaning.
— *Ian McMurchy*

brushing should be pushed completely through the barrel in one long stroke. The remaining patches should be short-stroked through the barrel a few inches at a time.

D. Run one dry patch inside the chamber.

E. Run two dry patches inside the bore.

F. Examine the muzzle and throat areas for signs of copper fouling. If copper is still visible, repeat steps B through E.

G. Wipe any excess solvent from the muzzle and the action.

2. Lube the bolt lugs with grease and clean out lug recesses. Apply a small amount of grease to the bolt handle and cocking piece camming surfaces on the bolt. Do this after each cleaning.

3. Repeat the cleaning process (steps A through G) for 10 shots, cleaning after every shot.

4. Shoot five sets of two-shot groups, cleaning after every group.

5. Shoot two five-shot groups, cleaning after every group.

6. Apply a light coat of oil to the bore if the gun is to be stored for a long period.

The importance of having a clean bore cannot be overemphasized. Copper fouling is a primary contributor to poor shooting accuracy. Following the above cleaning and break-in procedures is vital for proper shooting.

— *Courtesy of Barnes Bullets*

Tracking the History of Semi-Automatic Rifles

The first semi-automatic rifle was patented in 1878 by John Browning. Semi-autos were commercially available through the Sears catalog, among other places, at the turn of the last century. The U.S. military adopted its first semi-auto rifle, the M-1 Garand, in the days preceding World War II.

Semi-automatics incorporate modern designs that use the force of the expanding gas from a fired cartridge to load the next cartridge. The 1994 "Assault Weapons" ban limited certain features on semi-automatics that made them appear similar to fully automatic or machine guns, and semi-autos manufactured today comply with all these restrictions.

It is important to remember that no semi-automatic rifle, pistol or shotgun — or any firearm — can be sold without the buyer passing a background check conducted of police records by the FBI. No other product sold in America is as tightly regulated, and gun shops, wholesalers and firearm manufacturers all must be licensed by the federal government and meet state and local requirements to operate their business.

Firearms capable of firing a single shot accurately at distances up to 150 yards have been in civilian hands in America since before there was a United States. Some 80 million Americans have firearms safely stored in their homes, and each year millions enjoy the recreational use of firearms.

The National Shooting Sports Foundation (NSSF) has for more than 40 years been the trade association for the makers and sellers of firearms, ammunition and associated products, and a promoter of the safe and responsible enjoyment of such products. Learn more about NSSF and firearm safety at www.nssf.org.

— *National Shooting Sports Foundation*

Barnes' Rules for Reloading Rifle Ammo

1. Modern ammunition uses smokeless powder as an energy source. Smokeless powder is much more powerful than black powder and Pyrodex, and therefore, should never be substituted or mixed with these substances when reloading.
2. Follow loading recommendations exactly. Don't substitute components for those listed. Start loading with the minimum powder charge for the load shown.
3. Never exceed the manufacturer's reloading data. Excess pressures caused by overloaded rounds could severely damage a firearm, causing injury or death to the shooter.
4. Understand what you are doing and why it must be done a specific way.
5. Stay alert when reloading. Don't reload when distracted, disturbed or tired.
6. Set up a loading procedure and follow it. Don't vary your sequence of operations.
7. Set up your reloading bench where powder and primers won't be exposed to heat, sparks or flame.
8. Do not smoke while reloading.
9. Always wear safety glasses while reloading.
10. Keep everything out of reach of small children.
11. Keep your reloading bench clean and uncluttered. Label components and reloads for easy identification.
12. Do not eat while handling lead.
13. Never try to dislodge a loaded cartridge that has become stuck in the chamber by hitting it with a cleaning rod. Have a component gunsmith remove the round.

Smokeless Powder

All smokeless powders have to burn very fast, but handgun powders must burn faster than rifle powders. You will readily note the differences in physical size and shape of various powders, but you cannot see differences in chemical composition that help control the rate of burning. Burn rate is also affected by pressure. "Hot primers," seating the bullet too deep, over-crimping the case, tight gun chambers, oversized bullets, heavy shot loads and anything that increases friction or confinement of the powder will increase the pressure. Obviously, reloading requires attention to detail, patience and meticulousness to ensure the safety and quality of loads.

1. Never mix powders of different kinds.

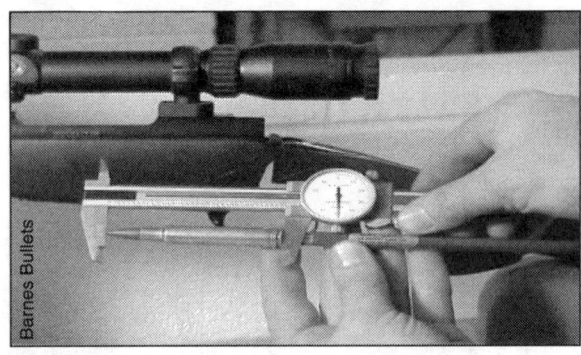

2. Use the powder only as recommended in manufacturer reloading manuals.

3. Store powder in a cool, dry place.

4. If you throw or measure powder charges by volume, weigh the charges every time you begin loading, occasionally during loading and when you finish.

5. Pour out only enough powder for the immediate work.

6. Never substitute smokeless powder for black powder or Pyrodex.

7. Don't carry powder in your clothing. Wash your hands thoroughly after handling it.

8. Store powders only in original packages. Don't repackage.

9. Keep powder containers tightly closed when not in use.

10. Specific powders are designed for specific uses. Don't use them for other purposes.

11. Smokeless powder is extremely flammable. To dispose of deteriorated powder, follow recommendations in the "Properties and Storage of Smokeless Powder" — SAAMI Reprint #376-2500, which is available from the National Reloading Manufacturers Association.

12. Empty your powder measure back into the original powder container when through with a reloading session. Do not mix powders.

13. Clean up spilled powder with a brush and dust pan. Do not use a vacuum cleaner because a fire or explosion might result.

Primers

Priming materials differ in brisance — initial explosive force — and in the amount of hot gas produced. Therefore, don't mix primers of different makes.

1. Don't decap live primers. Fire them in the appropriate gun, then decap.

2. Don't ream out or enlarge the flash hole in primer pockets. This can increase chamber pressure.

3. Over-ignition creates high gun pressures. The best results are obtained by using the mildest primer with good ignition.

4. Don't use primers you can't identify. Ask your local police or fire department about disposal of such primers.

5. Keep primers in the original packaging until used. Return unused primers to their original package. Don't dump them together or store in bulk.

6. If you feel resistance when seating or feeding primers, stop and investigate. Do not force primers.

7. Store primers in a cool, dry place. High temperatures, such as

those found in an attic during summer, cause them to deteriorate.

8. Don't handle primers with oily or greasy hands. Oil contamination can affect ignition.

9. Primer dusting may get inside the tubes of loading tools due to vibration. Therefore, clean machines after each use.

10. Refer to the SAAMI reprint "Sporting Ammunition Primers: Properties, Handling & Storage for Handloading."

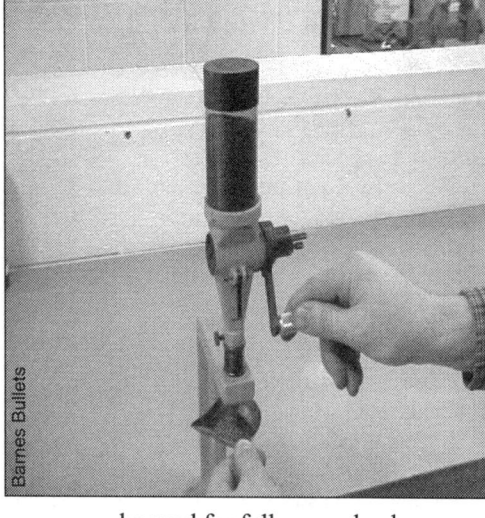

Handling Rifle and Pistol Cartridges

1. Examine cases before loading. Discard any that are in poor condition.

2. Put labels on boxes of loaded cartridges. Identify caliber, primer, powder and charge, bullet and weight and date of reloading.

3. In handgun cartridges, the seating depth of the bullet is extremely important. Handgun powders must burn very quickly because of the short barrel. They are sensitive to small changes in crimp, bullet hardness, bullet diameter, primer brisance and bullet seating depth.

4. Check the overall length of the cartridge to be sure the bullet is seated properly.

5. If you cast your own bullets, remember their hardness, diameter and lubrication will affect chamber pressure.

6. Plastic cases designed for practice loads (where the bullet is propelled by primer gas only) can't be used for full-power loads.

7. Consult the manufacturer regarding disposal of unserviceable ammunition. Ask your local police or fire department to dispose of small quantities.

Double Charges

1. It is easy to double-charge if you are momentarily distracted. Use a depth gauge to check powder height in the casing. A piece of doweling rod can be used as a depth gauge.

2. Observe the powder level of cases with missing or double powder charges.

3. Take care to operate progressive loaders as the manufacturer recommends. Don't back up the turret or jiggle the handle. Don't use a shell to catch the residue when cleaning out the powder train.

— Courtesy of Barnes Bullets

How to Mount a Riflescope

A state-of-the-art scope is useless if it is mounted incorrectly. Although your local gun shop should be up to the task, doing the work yourself can save money and add another rewarding dimension to your hunts.

Follow these steps to meld your rifle and scope into a tack-driving combination.

Tools required
- ✓ Hex wrench set (English)
- ✓ Gunsmith screwdrivers
- ✓ Scope-mounting adhesive
- ✓ Gun oil
- ✓ Long cotton swabs
- ✓ Soft cotton cloth
- ✓ Acetone, ether or other cleaning/degreasing agent
- ✓ Riflescope bore-sighting device and arbors
- ✓ Scope alignment rods
- ✓ Shims
- ✓ Rubber hammer
- ✓ Rifle vise
- ✓ Short steel ruler
- ✓ Lapping kit
- ✓ Reticle leveler

Instructions

1. Place the gun's safety in the "on" position. Unload firearm and remove bolt, cylinder, clip, etc. Make sure the chamber is empty.

2. Remove old bases or rings. If the gun is new, you might have to remove the factory screws from the receiver. These screws protect the scope's mounting holes until needed.

3. Degrease the base screws and the receiver's mounting holes.

4. Temporarily install the bases. Shimming might be required under part of the base if the top of the receiver is not parallel to the axis of the bore. Mismatches might require a different set of bases.

WHEN THE SCOPE is mounted on the gun, make sure there is at least 1/8 inch of clearance between the bell of the scope and the gun.

5. Install the scope-alignment rods into the rings and place them on the firearm. If there is a misalignment, some shimming might be required. Very small adjustments can be made later by tapping the base with a rubber hammer.

6. Remove the rings when the rods indicate the system is aligned. Apply a light coating of gun oil to the underside of the base and the top of the receiver.

Also install the base and screws, using adhesive. Be sure the adhesive does not drip into the action. Use cotton swabs to clean spillage.

7. Re-install the rings with the alignment rods. Again, if there is a small alignment problem, tapping with the rubber hammer might correct it. If there's gross misalignment, shimming might be required.

8. Once you are satisfied the rings and the base are aligned, install the riflescope in the rings. Degrease the inner surface of the rings and the area of contact on the scope.

Inspect the fit of the rings to the

scope. Some inexpensive rings are not perfectly round, making for a poor fit between the ring and the scope's body tube.

If you're using Weaver-style rings, install them loosely, then attach them to the base. For Redfield-style rings, attach the twist-lock front ring by using a 1-inch metal or wooden dowel.

When the scope is mounted, ensure there is at least $1/8$ inch of clearance between the bell of the scope and the gun. Also, make sure the action doesn't touch the scope during cycling.

9. Set up the bore-sighting system on the firearm. Adjust the ring screws so the scope can rotate, but not wobble. Adjust the distance from the scope to your eye to prevent injury during recoil. It should be about 3 inches.

10. Turn the scope to high power and adjust the windage and elevation so the image of the bore-sighting grid and the scope reticle don't move with each other as the scope is rotated.

11. Gently rotate the scope in the rings so the horizontal portion of the reticle is level when the gun is held in the shooting position. To aid this adjustment, use a bubble level or reticle leveler. Next, tighten all rings and base screws. Use adhesive on the screws, and let set overnight.

12. Adjust the windage and elevation to place the center of the reticle on the center of the bore-sighting grid. Shimming might be required to bring it in alignment with the bore. If so, consider using a system with windage control.

13. With everything secure, the scope is ready for the range. The shooter should pick a common distance — 25, 50 or 100 yards — and adjust accordingly. Remember, ammunition, outside temperature, temperature of the barrel and cleanliness of the barrel all affect a gun's accuracy.

14. Make sure the scope's rings and bases are tight.

— FOR MORE INFORMATION ON SCOPE MOUNTING, CONTACT BUSHNELL SPORT OPTICS, 9200 CODY ST., DEPT. DDH, SHAWNEE MISSION, KS 66214.

Use a Partner to Sight-In Your Rifle with Two Shots

The best way to sight in your deer rifle is to shoot from a bench and steady rest at a paper target 50 to 100 yards away.

If your scope is equipped with an adjustable objective, be sure it is adjusted to the range at which you are sighting.

The traditional method of sighting a rifle from a solid rest is to aim at the bull's-eye and carefully fire one or more shots. Note the vertical and horizontal distances between the resulting bullet holes and the desired point of impact. Adjust the scope the required number of clicks to move from the initial point of impact to the desired point of impact. Fire additional shots and make adjustments as required to achieve the desired result.

The "two-shot" sighting method is much easier, but it requires another person's help.

With the rifle on sandbags, take careful aim at the bull's-eye and fire one shot. Arrange the rifle back on the bags and aim at the bull's-eye again. Without moving the rifle, have a friend adjust the scope reticle while you watch through the scope. Direct the person to move the reticle until it's centered on the first bullet hole. Now the rifle should shoot where the scope is looking.

Fire a second shot to confirm the rifle is sighted. You might need to perform some fine tuning, but this method is quick, easy and accurate.

— Courtesy of Pentax Corporation

Average Centerfire Rifle Cartridge Ballistics

Cartridge	Weight	Velocity in feet per second			Energy in foot pounds			Trajectory in inches			Box Price
		Muzzle	100 yds	200 yds	Muzzle	100 yds	200 yds	100 yds	200 yds	300 yds	
.270 Win.	130 gr.	3,060	2,776	2,510	2,702	2,225	1,818	+2.5	+1.4	-5.3	$17
.270 Win.	150 gr.	2,850	2,585	2,336	2,705	2,226	1,817	+2.5	+1.2	-6.5	$17
.30-06 Spfd.	150 gr.	2,910	2,617	2,342	2,820	2,281	1,827	+2.5	+0.8	-7.2	$17
.30-06 Spfd.	180 gr.	2,700	2,469	2,250	2,913	2,436	2,023	-2.5	0.0	-9.3	$17
.300 Win/Mag	150 gr.	3,290	2,951	2,636	3,605	2,900	2,314	+2.5	+1.9	-3.8	$22
.300 Win/Mag	180 gr.	2,960	2,745	2,540	3,501	3,011	2,578	+2.5	+1.2	-5.5	$22
.300 Wby/Mag	150 gr.	3,600	3,307	3,033	4,316	3,642	3,064	+2.5	+3.2	0.0	$32
.300 Wby/Mag	180 gr.	3,330	3,110	2,910	4,430	3,875	3,375	+1.0	0.0	-5.2	$32

Source: *2001 Gun Digest*, Krause Publications

Find Gun-Hunting Gear on the Web

Looking for more information on gun-hunting equipment? Check out these Web sites:

Ammunition
Federal:
www.federalcartridge.com

Hornady:
www.hornady.com

Remington:
www.remington.com

Winchester:
www.winchester.com

Riflescopes
Bushnell Sport Optics:
www.bushnell.com

Leupold:
www.leupold.com

Nikon:
www.nikonusa.com

Simmons:
www.blount.com

Swarovski/Kahles:
www.swarovskioptik.com

Firearms
Browning:
www.browning.com

Ithaca:
www.ithacagun.com

Marlin:
www.marlinfirearms.com

O.F. Mossberg & Son:
www.mossberg.com

Remington:
www.remington.com

Savage Arms:
www.savagearms.com

Sturm, Ruger & Co.
www.ruger-firearms.com

Tar-Hunt Slug Guns:
www.tar-hunt.com

Thompson/Center Arms:
www.tcarms.com

Weatherby:
www.weatherby.com

U.S. Repeating Arms:
www.winchester-guns.com

Cleaning Products
Birchwood Casey:
www.birchwoodcasey.com

Hoppe's:
www.hoppes.com

Outers:
www.outers-guncare.com

Safes and Gun Locks
Americase:
www.americase.com

Heritage Safe:
www.heritagesafecompany.com

Winchester Safes:
www.fireking.com

Reloading Equipment
Corbin:
www.corbins.com

Hornady:
www.hornady.com

Lee Precision:
www.leeprecision.com

Lyman:
www.lymanproducts.com

Mayville:
www.mayvl.com

MTM Case-Guard:
www.mtmcase-guard.com

Stony Point Products:
www.stonypoint.com

Hearing Protection
Walker's Game Ear:
www.walkersgameear.com

Publications
Krause Publications:
www.krause.com

Today's Hot New Deer Rifles

■ **Remington's** Model 7400 Weathermaster rifles feature an all-weather gas-operated action that maintains uniform bolt velocities to improve reliability and durability. The black synthetic autoloader has a nickel-plated receiver, barrel and magazine to protect it from inclement weather. The rifle has a slim-line design and weight distribution similar to a shotgun's for balance and pointability. The Model 7400 Weathermaster features a 22-inch barrel and is drilled and tapped for scope mounts.

■ **U.S. Repeating Arms** offers the Model 70 Super Shadow, featuring a high-tech stock assembly, made out of fiberglass microfibers. The synthetic stock features an energy-absorbing recoil pad, oval-dot textured grip and forearm, a mock cheekpiece and flat comb, ergonomic grip and a slimmer forearm. All of these features make the rifle lighter and more user-friendly. Controlled Round Push Feed lets the bolt face control the cartridge from magazine to chamber.

■ The **Marlin** Model 336 SpikeHorn is designed for small-statured shooters. The gun weighs just $6^1/_2$ pounds and has an overall length of 34 inches and a $16^1/_2$-inch Micro-Groove barrel. The .30-30 has a blued finish, a black walnut pistol-grip stock with fluted comb and cut checkering and an offset hammer spur for use with a scope. The rifle has a semi-buckhorn folding rear sight and a ramp front sight with a brass bead and a Wide-Scan hood.

■ The **Ruger** M77 Mark II left-handed bolt-action rifle has a one-piece bolt and a nonrotating Mauser-type controlled feed extractor. The rifle is chambered in .300 Win. Mag. and has a black laminate stock and forearm and a stainless steel 24-inch barrel. The rifle also features a three-position manual safety, scope rings that attach directly to the receiver's machined mounting surface and a floorplate latch mounted flush with the front of the trigger guard, which secures the floorplate against accidental cartridge dumpage.

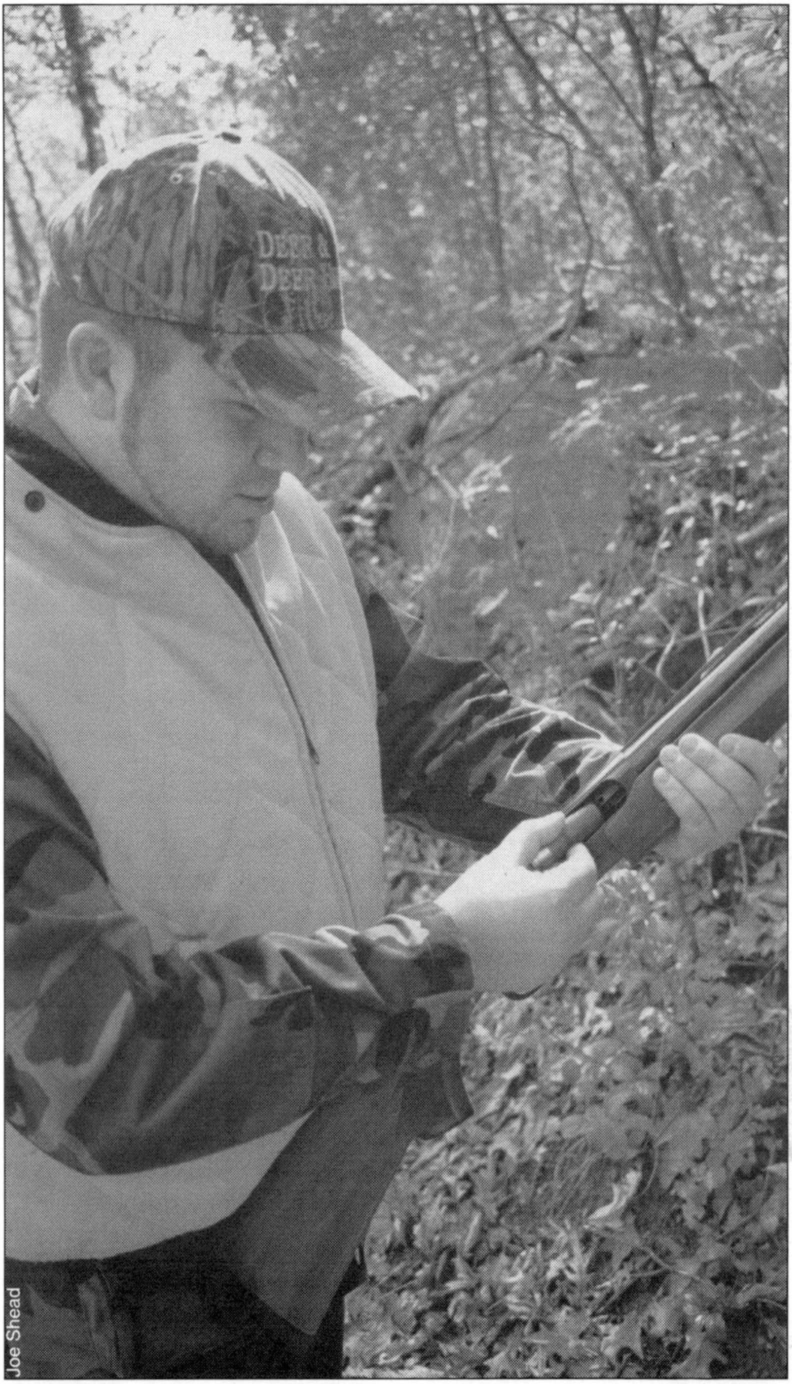

Joe Shead

Remington Unveils Beefy New Slug

Remington has paved new ground with the introduction of its new Express BuckHammer slug.

The attached-sabot slug weighs 1¼ ounces, making it the heaviest Remington slug ever offered. What's more, it maintains almost 100 percent of its weight on impact.

The slug produces a tremendous amount of energy at the muzzle — 2,935 foot-pounds — offering ample knockdown power for even the toughest whitetails.

I saw the BuckHammer in action at Remington's 2003 New Products Seminar at Florida's Bienville Plantation, and was impressed with its accuracy at the range. However, I was even more stunned when I saw what it could do on one of the plantation's 325-pound wild hogs. A BuckHammer penetrated the big boar's shoulder, mushrooming completely.

THE REMINGTON EXPRESS BUCKHAMMER slug weighs 1¼ ounces and is the heaviest slug Remington has ever offered. The saboted slug generates 2,935 foot-pounds of energy at the muzzle.

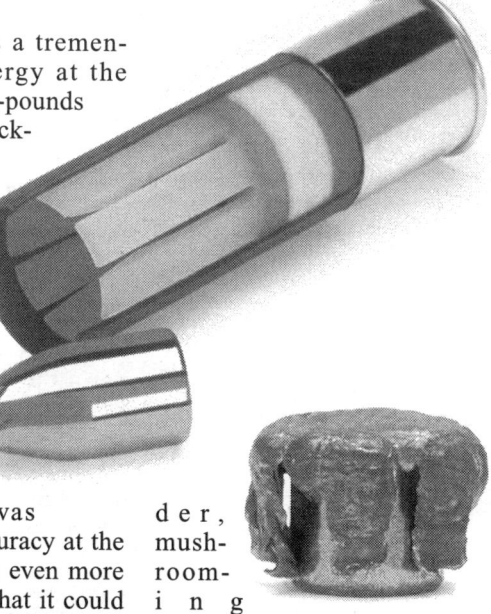

RYAN GILLIGAN

The Dos and Don'ts of Firearms Cleaning

Most hunters appreciate the importance of proper gun cleaning. However, even the most experienced hunters sometimes make gun-cleaning mistakes that reduce their firearm's accuracy, performance and life. Here are a few pointers for keeping your favorite deer gun in its prime.

▶ **Always clean from the breech to the muzzle.**

When you fire a gun, powder residue and dirt foul the barrel, but stay out of the receiver. By running a brush or patch from the muzzle, you push dirt and residue into the chamber. This frequently causes problems with lever-action and autoloading rifles and shotguns.

▶ **Center the rod in the firearm's barrel while cleaning, and do not let it rub against the bore.**

A firearm's bore is a record of the gun's cleaning history. When a cleaning rod rubs a firearm's bore, it creates marks and scratches, hampering accuracy.

▶ **Always use a clean patch.**

Reusing cleaning patches is like cleaning a floor with a dirty mop. During normal use, abrasive dirt collects in rifle and shotgun barrels. By reusing patches, you redeposit dirt and push it into the gun's chamber and neck. The next round you fire through the gun picks up this dirt as it leaves the chamber, thus eroding the throat.

▶ **Never run a brush down the barrel first.**

A brush picks up dirt, moisture and powder residue and redeposits it in the receiver and chamber. Also, never dip a brush in solvent, as this enhances this effect.

▶ **Use only a few drops of solvent or lubricant.**

Although many people think the more solvent the better, this damages firearms. Use only as much solvent as the patch can absorb. If you use too much, the solvent or oil will drip into the trigger mechanism, causing a gummy trigger, or into the stock, destroying the wood.

▶ **Put the patch on the cleaning rod correctly to ensure it fits within the barrel as tightly as possible.**

Doing this lets the patch mold itself to the bore and scrub deep within the rifling.

▶ **Run successive patches down the barrel until they come out clean.**

After doing this, cleaning is finished. If you plan to store the gun for an extended period, run a loose, oiled patch down the barrel and let the oil stay in the bore.

▶ **If you plan to shoot the gun immediately after cleaning, run a dry, tight-fitting patch down the bore.**

This removes any excess oil or solvent, eliminating the need for a fouling shot.

— *Courtesy of Otis Technology, Inc.*

CLEAN YOUR FIREARM thoroughly after each hunt. Doing so will ensure optimum performance and extend the weapon's life.

Joe Shead

Today's Hot New Shotguns

■ **Remington** introduces the Model 1100 synthetic field shotgun — the only autoloading 16 gauge currently produced. The gun features a weather-resistant black matte stock and forearm, and a non-embellished black matte receiver. The low-recoiling shotgun features a 28-inch vent rib barrel, also with a black matte, nonreflective finish. The shotgun is chambered for $2^{3}/_{4}$-inch shells only, and accepts interchangeable Rem Chokes. This is the first time Remington has offered a 16 gauge autoloader in 20 years.

■ **Mossberg** expands its 500 pump series to include the .410 Bantam Slugster. It features a 24-inch cylinder bore barrel, black synthetic stock and forearm, adjustable fiber-optic sights and swivel studs for sling attachment. The Bantam Slugster also has a shortened length-of-pull and is ideally suited to youths and smaller-framed hunters. A special magazine plug renders the gun a single-shot shotgun until removed.

■ The **Marlin** Model 410 .410 lever-action shotgun is based on a 70-year-old design — the Model 1895. The gun features a folding open rear sight and a high-visibility fiber-optic front sight. The 22-inch barrel has a cylinder bore and accepts $2^{1}/_{2}$-inch shells. The shotgun has a pistol-grip walnut stock with cut checkering, a Mar-Shield finish, a blued steel forend cap and a rubber butt pad.

■ The Gold Rifled Deer shotgun from **Browning** has thicker rifled barrel walls designed for use with Foster or sabot slugs. The 12-gauge semi-auto features a Cantilever scope mount and Mossy Oak Break-Up camouflage. The stock and forearm are coated with Browning's Dura-Touch armor coating, which has a velvety smooth feel, and gives you a secure grip while protecting the shotgun's finish. The Gold Rifled Deer shotgun is chambered for 3-inch shells.

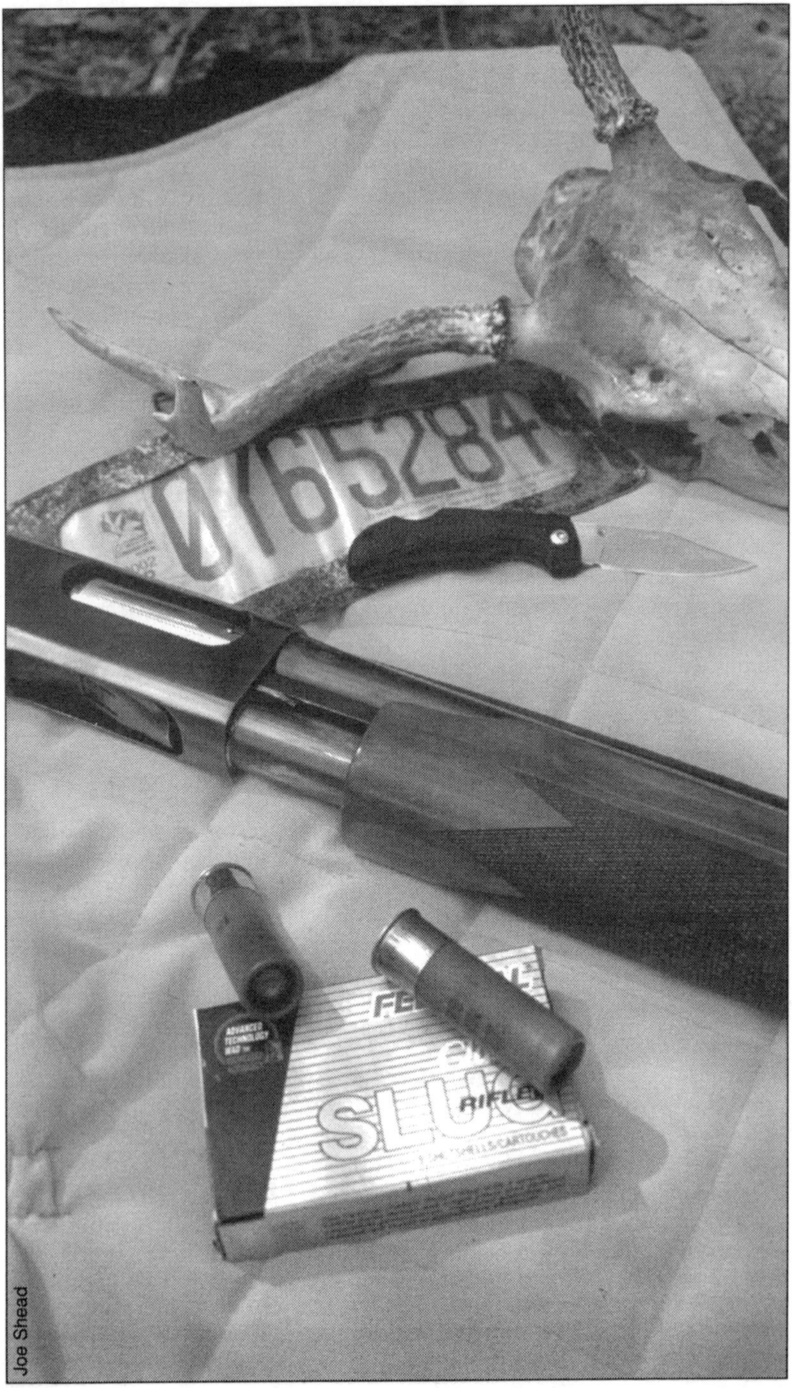

Joe Shead

Hunting Accessories:
Endless Possibilities

Today's hunters may assume that interest in accessories is a recent development. Nothing could be further from the truth. American frontiersmen would no more have been without their "possibles" bag than their trusty Hawken rifle or knife. The contents of that leather pouch varied from one mountain man to the next, but they all had the accessories they deemed essential to successful hunting and their general well-being.

Today's hunter has infinitely more choices. Hunters have to decide what items fall into "must-have," "nice but not necessary" and "non-essential" categories.

After arriving at camp or my stand only to discover some important accessory had been left behind too many times, it finally dawned of me that the answer to such foul-ups was a checklist. The list I developed started with gun, ammo and clothing, but its real focus is accessories. Now the list (actually there are two — one for hunts from home and the second for hunts in which I travel and stay overnight) stays on the wall in my closet throughout the year. Making additions as new products become available is simple enough, and it offers me a sure, simple way of making sure nothing is left behind.

I recommend you try a similar approach, whether in written form or on your computer. It will save you some time and potentially a bunch of trouble. Keep in mind that an integral part of your gear ought to be a survival kit — fire starter, high-energy food, space blanket and the like.

With that suggestion out of the way, let's look at some new items that might find a place on your list.

Finding Your Way

Almost anyone who hunts and has even a hint of willingness to get "back of beyond" in them has been lost. Even Daniel Boone, when asked if he had ever been lost, said, "No, but I was temporarily misplaced for three days one time." With today's GPS systems, there's no reason for any hunter not to know precisely where he is. The systems keep getting better, and cheaper, and most have a whole bunch of accessories. Two standard-bearers in the field have been Magellan and Garmin, and both have new hand-held units for 2003. From Magellan there is a new Meridian Color GPS, with a vivid image readily visible even in bright sunlight. Garmin's new GPS 72 is waterproof, floats and has other useful features as well.

Another useful tool is a two-way radio. It can be particularly useful in a hunt camp situation or when a

JIM CASADA

successful hunter has a deer down and needs help tracking or getting the animal out. Midland has two new units, the G-222 and G-227 GMRS. They offer up to 7 miles of range and 22 operation channels.

Should you need to find your way into or out of remote areas after dark, some type of artificial light is essential. Every hunter needs a light and extra batteries, in his daypack. The Optronics Nightblaster, a rechargeable headlamp, is perfect for following a blood trail or easing out of the woods when you have stayed in a stand until it is pitch dark. It comes with a rechargeable six-volt battery and has a magnifier for varying the beam from spot to flood as desired.

Two other lights need mention. MPI Outdoors' Pathfinder, a pocket penlight that operates on a pair of AAAA batteries, doesn't glare and is ideal for flicking on and off as you ease to a stand before daylight. Browning's Odyssey 2100, with four LEDs, uses three AA batteries and can provide up to 300 hours of use. With these lights, or others for that matter, Reflective Trail Tacks from Hunter's Specialties are a simple way to find you way to and from a stand in the dark. They come 50 to a pack and are visible for up to 200 yards. Then, for an interesting approach to finding your stand, there is the Lem-O-Ward Stand Locator. This is a 24-hour clock, with an attached Velcro strap, that you set as you would an alarm clock. When the "alarm" goes off, it isn't a sound, but a high-intensity light that guides you to your stand. The light is visible for 400 yards or more.

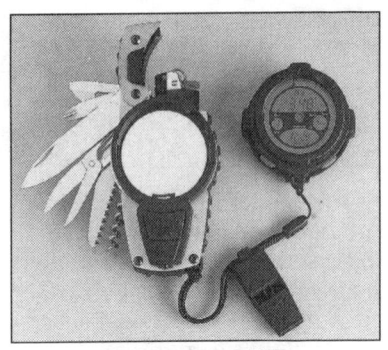

Schrade i-QUIP

My favorite new item in this general area is the Schrade i-QUIP. This is sort of a location multi-tool. It contains a computer module that is outfitted with an altimeter, barometer, digital compass and a clock (with alarm and stopwatch functions). Yet that is only the start. The pod that holds the computer module contains a bunch of stainless steel tools, including a saw, cutting blade, scissors, flathead and Phillips screwdriver, bottle opener, can opener and even a corkscrew. Add a belt clip, a whistle, built-in flashlight, signal mirror and even a compartment to hold a standard cigarette lighter, and you have a single item that serves an incredible array of needs.

Carrying Your Stuff

Most hunters favor some type of day pack to carry their gear, although some opt for a fanny pack or hang items from their belt. MPI Outdoors offers a dozen or so selections. The MPI Outdoors Trail Master is an ideal hunting pack that places weight where it should be — on your hips. It features three storage compartments; silent zippers and a removable Annex clip for attaching accessories such as the MPI Outdoors Hydration System and rain flaps. The MPI Outdoors Outlander is a versatile waist pack.

From Browning is the Water Hole Fanny Pack. Its single shoulder strap design leaves your shooting arm free. The pack also has a 1-liter water system. It also has pockets for shells or calls and a foam roll-away seat attached to the bottom of the pack.

Bear Cutlery 8-Inch Feathermate

Once you have carried your gear to a stand, you want it aloft and handy, but out of the way. The Tree Belt from Hunter's Specialties is the answer. It straps around the tree and holds a day pack, water bottle, calls or other items.

Gun Cleaning and Care

Cleaning a gun after a hunt in inclement weather, on a multi-day hunt or after a shot is fired is a must. One of the handiest cleaning gadgets around is Atsko's little Rapid-Rod. This collapsible rod comes with a carrier that can be attached to your belt, and it is a simple way to run a patch down the barrel a few times. Kleen-Bore offers Kleen-Brite gun polish. It is suitable for most surfaces and cleans and brightens without making surfaces oily or slick.

Outers has several new products for 2003, including an Ultra Deluxe Pow'r Scrubber and the Universal Field Kit. The latter comes with a zippered pouch that fits nicely in a day pack or gun case.

Remington Bullet Knife

Odor Control

A whitetail's first line of defense is its nose, and over the last two decades, use of masking scents, attractants and the like has gotten a great deal of attention. Hiding scents begins at the skin, and Atsko's Sport-Wash has a well-deserved reputation when it comes to odorless clothing. Yet one step into a kitchen where bacon is frying or a quick stop for a cup of coffee ruins that. With that in mind, Atsko has N-O-DOR liquid spray for destroying odor as you set out for your stand. In a remote hunt camp or in the field, you might find Browning's Dry Wash handy. Without water or a towel, this soap goes on wet and dries in seconds. It flakes off, taking dirt or blood with it.

Knives

A good, sharp and sturdy knife is

Remington Bird's Eye Gut Hook Knife

an exceptionally versatile tool. For deer hunters, its primary use is gutting and skinning deer, but around camp and in the woods it has many other uses. A whetstone, small sharpening stick, a fixed-blade sheath knife and a two- or three-blade pocket knife should be an integral part of every deer hunter's must-have accessories.

Buck Knives recently celebrated its 100th anniversary. It has many new offerings for collectors, but on the practical side, the Alpha Hunter line (particularly those with gut hooks), along with the Buck Zipper, deserve special mention. Buck's caping knife is also a fine field-dressing tool, and it features a small gut hook.

From Bear Cutlery, the 787 8-inch Feathermate, designed by legendary knife guru Blackie Collins, features a gently curving 3^1/$_2$-inch blade and a non-slip Zytel handle. Remington, though most frequently associated with firearms and ammunition, has long been a presence in the knife world as well. In addition to a new Bullet knife in its collectors' series, it has four new Bird's Eye maple laminated-handle fixed-blade knives. The drop-point model with a gut hook behind its 4^1/$_2$-inch blade is tailor-made for field-dressing work, and the skinner model's 3-inch cutting edge makes removing a whitetail's hide a breeze.

Everyone who uses a climber or, for that matter, hunts in any situation where they are aloft and wearing a safety belt, needs ready access to a knife they can operate with one hand and which doubles as a pocket knife. One such offering comes from Gerber Legendary Blades, with their new Air Ranger pocket knives. They come in striking colors of red or blue and feature aluminum handles, a clip, and thumb studs for one-hand opening. Also new from Gerber are the AR 3.00 the E-Z-Out Utility knife. The latter has a serrated sheepsfoot blade (the last ^{1}/$_4$ inch is fine edge) and both offer one-hand opening. The one-hand opening feature is also available on the Schrade Simon, which weighs

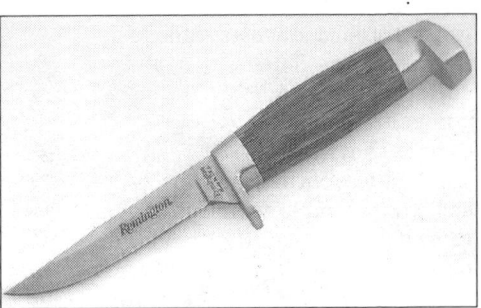

Remington Bird's Eye Skinner Knife

only one ounce and readily attaches to a key ring or belt loop. Case has been making fine pocket knives for well over a century, and for 2003 their Amber Bone Small Stockman, with clip, pen and sheepsfoot blades, is visually appealing and a good utility knife. For those who prefer a larger folder, the SpyderHawk C 7 7 S B K features an arcing curve for a pulling cut and a serrated blade. Even though the blade is more than 3 inches long, it can be opened with one hand to its full 8¼-inch length.

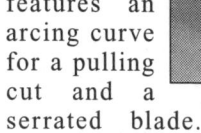

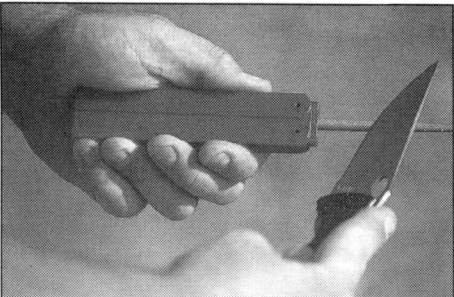

Eze-Lap Diamond Sharpener

Sharpening Tools

To keep knives performing at their best, Buck's Diamond Pocket sharpening stone is quite convenient from a size standpoint. For those who have or use knives or gut hooks with wholly or partially serrated blades, the Model 571 Diamond Sharpener from Eze-Lap, with its fast sharpening diamond-grit surface and compact design, is the answer.

Miscellaneous Gear

In cold weather many prefer a good hand warmer to gloves, which can be cumbersome at the moment of truth. Shotgun hunters might find an item from Browning designed for duck hunters quite useful: a neoprene hand warmer with an attached shell pouch.

Most deer hunting is done "on high," but there's still considerable interest in and appeal to hunting on the ground. Such tactics usually mean setting up much like turkey hunters or watching quietly for long periods while standing. Should a shot offer itself, some type of gun rest really helps. PMI's Cover System Quik Stik, which combines the features of a blind and a gun rest in a unit weighing only two and a half pounds, hides the hunter and steadies his shot.

Finally, the R3 Recoil Pad from Remington gets my seal of approval. It utilizes LimbSaver technology familiar to bow-hunters to reduce felt recoil from a rifle or shotgun up to 40 percent. It fits most modern Remington rifles and shotguns.

Conclusion

The products mentioned above do not cover everything new and noteworthy in deer hunting accessories. Every year scores, maybe even hundreds, of accessories are introduced to the market. The biggest problem is picking and choosing from them to suit your hunting style. That quest may not offer the same measure of pleasure as pursuing a big whitetail, but there's undeniable fun in visiting sport shows, spending time in sporting goods stores or browsing retail catalogs to add a cherished item (or several) to your accessories checklist. I'm betting that you'll find one or more of the above items something you simply must have this fall.

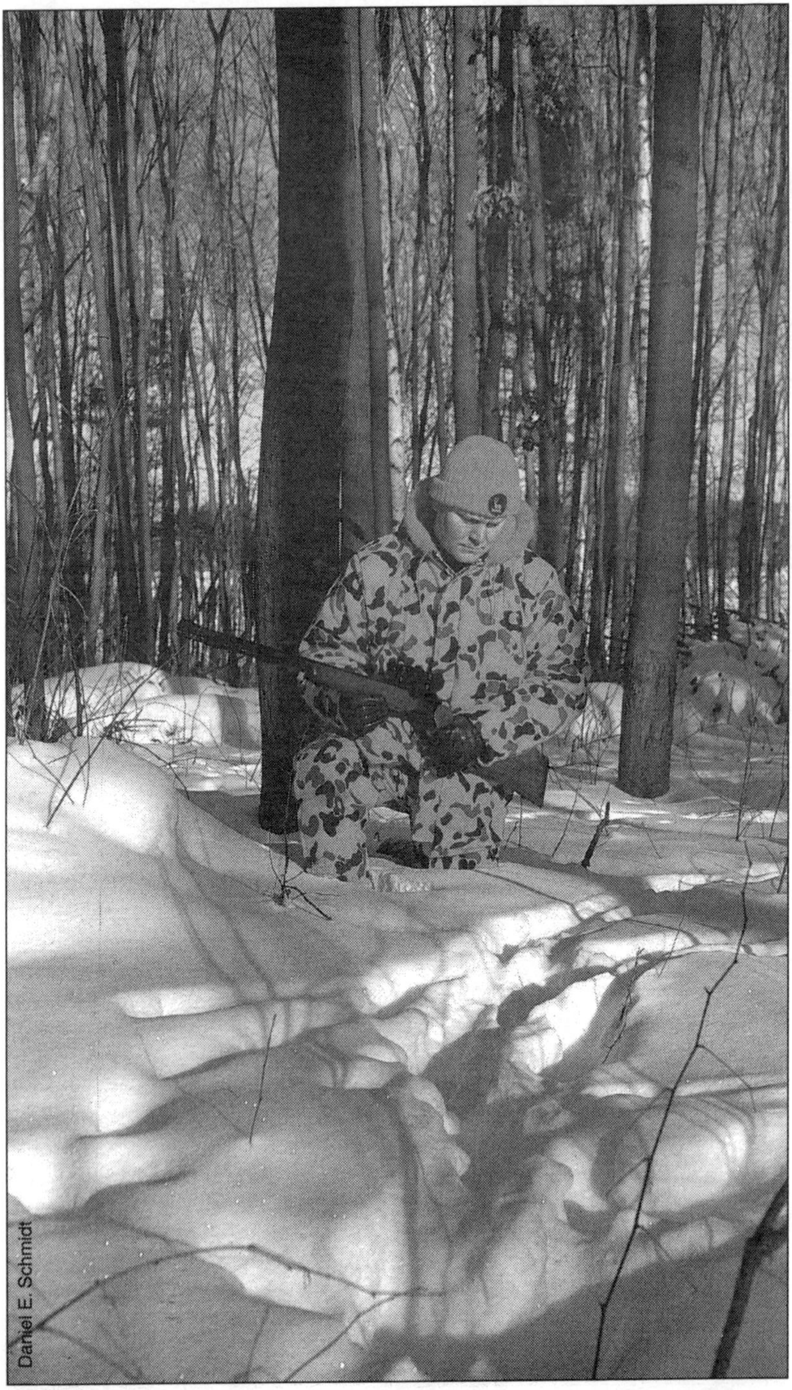

Daniel E. Schmidt

Into The Fog

I didn't hold high hopes as I eased my truck door closed and slid my muzzleloading rifle from its case. The slate-gray sky was spitting a light but persistent rain, and the air drooped with a heavy fog. I poured a charge of powder down the barrel, tapped the muzzle and seated the bullet. However, considering the soggy conditions, I doubted a percussion cap would be enough to dislodge it.

No matter. I doubted I would see a deer. Sure, I held several antlerless tags and a buck tag, but memories of a dismal gun season and a frustrating bow season were too strong to shake as I cradled the rifle and began my silent trek through the hemlocks.

As I meandered through the heavy, moist air, fluttering leaves caught my peripheral vision, causing me to turn my head sharply, subconsciously hoping the soft, wet ground might have let me unwittingly walk within range of a bedded whitetail.

Nope.

That would be uncharacteristically lucky for me, I thought, mentally donning blinders and quickening my pace to my stand on the little oak-covered knob.

Revisiting Old Disappointments

The knob. It had always *seemed* like a great place to kill deer. The small island of oaks was bordered to the east by a low, often flooded stand of mature hemlocks, and to the west by the thick regrowth of an aging cleat-cut. Aside from being an acorn oasis along classic edge cover, the spot had another plus: A large cattail marsh within the old clear-cut sandwiched a 20-yard-wide swath of aspen and maple regrowth against the oak stand, creating a tight funnel for deer traveling along the clear-cut to the acorn-laden knoll.

Despite all this, the spot had never really produced. Although my hunting partners and I had seen a handful of does and fawns there and had killed a couple of them, the results had been nothing like we'd hoped when we erected an elaborate permanent stand there a few years earlier. Still, I kept walking toward the stand. It seemed fitting to end a disappointing deer season — one that I thought held so much promise — in an equally disappointing stand. Why get unrealistically ambitious on the last day of the season?

As I reached the stand, however, a fresh rub caught my eye along the edge of the clear-cut. I shrugged it off, though, reasoning it had probably been there since October and was only apparent now that the cold December rain had soaked and darkened the sapling's remaining bark. I climbed the ladder, settled in

RYAN GILLIGAN

> ## Disposing of Smokeless Powder
>
> Although smokeless powders basically don't deteriorate when stored properly, safe practices require a recognition of the signs of deterioration and its possible effects.
>
> Powder deterioration can be checked by opening the cap on the container and smelling the contents. Deteriorating powder has an irritating acidic odor. Don't confuse this with common solvent odors such as alcohol, ether and acetone.
>
> Make sure powder is not exposed to extreme heat, because this causes deterioration. Such exposure produces an acidity that accelerates further reaction and has been known to cause spontaneous combustion. Never salvage powder from old cartridges, and do not attempt to blend salvaged powder with new powder. Don't accumulate old powder stocks.
>
> The best way to dispose of deteriorated smokeless powder is to burn it out in the open at an isolated location in small, shallow piles not more than 1 inch deep. The quantity burned in any one pile should never exceed 1 pound. Use an ignition train of slow-burning combustible material so the person can retreat to a safe distance before powder is ignited.
>
> For a free copy of the *2001 Basic Reloaders Manual*, write Hodgdon Powder Co., Box 2932, Dept. DDH, Shawnee Mission, KS 66201, or call (913) 362-9455.

the stand and began my vigil.

As the minutes slowly passed, the fog changed from a low mist that hovered a few feet off the ground to an all-encompassing haze, rising above the treetops, and back again. The rain changed, too — from large, sporadic drops to a mist that coated my orange jacket with millions of barely discernable droplets.

The only thing that seemed constant was the lack of animal activity. Although the stand was never a good bet for deer, it was a consistent hub for other creatures. Squirrels always scampered up my stand tree when I hunted the knob, and turkeys often scratched through the oak leaves at the clear-cut's edge, gobbling acorns. Nuthatches usually flitted among the nearby hemlocks and red-tailed hawks often screamed from above the hayfield on the opposite side of the clear-cut. Once, while I was set up on a gobbler a stone's throw from the stand, a skunk scampered by, mere feet from my boots. But no such visitors were at the knob that afternoon.

It felt like I was underwater.

A Season of Missed Opportunities

Savoring my bad mood, I thought about the doe I had almost killed 30 minutes into opening day of archery season. As if on cue, she had appeared on the trail I had anticipated deer would use, and passed my stand at 25 yards. At full draw, I followed her through my peep sight, waiting for her to clear some blackberry brambles, but the moment never came. As my arm trembled with fatigue, the doe continued stepping behind shooting obstacles until she was out of range.

I recalled the wide-racked 10-pointer I had seen while hunting from a ground blind to the north. That buck, accompanied by two similar bachelors and five yearlings, had walked by at about 75 yards, seemingly accustomed to following a well-worn trail that wound along the edge of a stand of red maples. Three days later, I was perched in a stand along that trail, confident I would see the bucks again. But, like the previous days, luck refused to smile on me.

I thought about the two Pope and Young-class bucks that came within 25 yards of my calling on a calm November afternoon. The larger of the two came in slow and cautious, while the other charged toward my calling, tumbling through the swamp muck and thrashing a sapling that stood in his way. Despite their different personalities, the bucks shared a trait: neither presented a shot.

Finally, I thought about the yearling buck that walked by a different stand a few days later, giving me a 12-yard shot. Everything looked perfect as I squeezed the trigger on my release, but I was quickly jarred back into reality as my arrow hacked into a sapling a few feet from the buck's chest.

Looking back, it had been a season of disappointment — one of missed opportunity piled on missed opportunity. As I stared into the drizzle and fog, I wasn't hunting because I thought I might get anything — or even because I was enjoying myself. I was hunting out of obligation and boredom. It was muzzleloader season. I had a muzzleloader. I had a tag. It stood to reason I should at least try to fill it. I had nothing better to do.

Things Change

However, as I watched droplets collect, merge and roll down my rifle's barrel, something made me look up. Shadows were moving through the old clear-cut. A twig snapped.

Suddenly, the pessimistic attitude I had carried since opening day of archery season melted away. Patches of darker fog transformed

ALMANAC INSIGHTS

➤ **"A MAN MAY NOT CARE** for golf and still be human, but the man who does not like to see, hunt, photograph, or otherwise outwit birds or animals is not normal. He is supercivilized, and I for one do not know how to deal with him. Babes do not tremble when they are shown a golf ball, but I should not like to own the boy whose hair does not lift his hat when he sees his first deer."
— Aldo Leopold

into vague shapes, and shapes soon became legs shuffling through the wet leaves near the cattail marsh.

One deer, then three, then eight, emerged from the fog and clustered at the edge of the clear-cut. My heart was pounding in a way it hadn't since those first disheartening days of bow season. I was a hunter again.

Although it had been calm all afternoon, a breeze suddenly blew from behind me, and the lead doe nervously sniffed the air. But it was too late for caution. I had already shouldered my rifle and had lined up the iron sights on the doe's vitals. I could hear the trigger grinding slightly as my index finger crept backwards, when a dark figure appeared behind the does and a massive nontypical rack snapped into view. The big buck stiff-legged through the fog, intently watching the does.

With the lead doe now stamping and bobbing her head, I swung my rifle from her chest and tried to find the buck in a gap between the saplings. But it wasn't going to happen. The suspicious doe wheeled around and headed back into the fog, and the other deer followed. Obscured by a tangled alder, the buck lingered a moment,

Muzzleloading Supplies

Barnes Bullets
Box 215
318 S. 860 E., Dept. DDH
American Fork, UT 84003

Connecticut Valley Arms
Box 7225, Dept. DDH
Norcross, GA 30091

Goex Black Powder
Belin Plant, Dept. DDH
1002 Springbrook Ave.
Moosic, PA 18507

Gonic Arms Inc.
134 Flagg Road, Dept. DDH
Gonic, NH 03839

Hodgdon Powder Co.
6231 Robinson, Dept. DDH
Shawnee Mission, KS 66202

Hornady
Box 1848, Dept. DDH
Grand Island, NE 68802

Knight Rifles
234 Airport Road, Dept. DDH
Centerville, IA 52544

Markesbery Muzzle Loaders Inc.
7785 Foundation Drive, Suite 6
Florence, KY 41042

Muzzleloading Technologies
25 E. Hwy. 40, Suite 330-12
Roosevelt, UT 84066

Prairie River Arms
1220 N. 6th St., Dept. DDH
Princeton, IL 61356

Remington Arms Co. Inc.
870 Remington Drive, Dept. DDH
Madison, NC 27025-0700

Thompson/Center Arms
Box 5002, Farmington Road
Rochester, NH 03867

Traditions
1375 Boston Post Road, Dept. DDH
Old Saybrook, CT 06475-0776

White Shooting Systems
25 E. Hwy. 40 (330-12), Dept. DDH
Roosevelt, UT 84066

---

then bounded toward the does, apparently unaware he had ever been in danger. I guess he was right.

Season End, New Beginnings

As the fog swallowed up the fleeing deer, I exhaled deeply and lowered the rifle. Although about an hour of shooting light remained, I knew my season was over.

Surprisingly, not shooting the buck didn't bother me — at least not too much. Rather, I felt renewed. I remembered how I savored feeling the mixture of anticipation, excitement, happiness and all-out terror that always comes with shooting a deer. It's the same feeling I imagine most hunters got as awkward teenagers slowly dialing a girl's phone number — you know you want to push that last digit, but you're paralyzed.

I remembered how much I liked the fact every time I step in the woods, almost anything — even killing a record-class buck — might happen.

I recalled how I loved the refreshing, cause-and-effect logic the deer woods followed — the same logic so much of the "real world" doesn't. The deer I had seen had been hunted hard for almost five months. It made sense they were skittish. Everything they had done made sense. They had been walking into the breeze, following the brushy strip of woods from thicket to thicket. The lead doe winded me, and she reacted understandably.

It wasn't what I wanted, but I couldn't help but take comfort in seeing the world follows logic and reason — if only for a few instants at a time. As the doe ran, taking the

ALMANAC INSIGHTS

✓ **MEPPS** bucktail fishing lures were originally called "bucktails" because at one time, only bucks were legal targets, so the tails used for lure making were all from bucks. The terminology stuck, and even though tails from both white-tailed bucks and does are now used when making bucktails, the name remains unchanged.

✓ **THE TOP FIVE COUNTIES** for white-tailed deer entries into the Pope & Young and Boone & Crockett record books from 1991-2000 were 1. Buffalo County, Wis. (309); 2. Pike County, Ill. (188); 3. Dane County, Wis. (160); 4. McHenry County, Ill. (123) and 5. Waukesha County, Wis. (119).

MOSSY OAK BRAND CAMO

MOSSY OAK BLIND-HUNTING TIPS: PLAYING IT SAFE

If you're planning to rattle or grunt from a ground blind, make safety a priority when selecting a location.

Sitting on the ground while making sounds that resemble bucks fighting is an excellent way to increase your chances of seeing big deer, but you must make sure other hunters won't mistake your movement as a target.

Choose a calling location with a solid cut bank, large tree or other impenetrable obstacle behind you.

Also, be on the lookout for other hunters moving toward you. If you see another hunter approaching, don't shout or wave. Address them in a calm voice and let them know what and where you are.

A little defensive thinking goes a long way toward preventing accidents.

---

buck of my lifetime with her, it wasn't because of some complex social chess game or unexplainable act — it was cause-and-effect logic

True, my hunting season had been unproductive. Promising places, situations and strategies failed time and time again. It was a bummer, but all of those failures adhered to logic. The wind was wrong. I misjudged the distance to my target. Warm weather shut down deer activity. I contaminated the deer trail with human scent. Whatever the reason, failure, though disheartening, added up. And with that realization, I knew the same cause-and-effect logic would eventually work the other way — at least in the woods.

Instead of throwing down my rifle in disgust and turning my thoughts to ice-fishing, football and the distant turkey season, my mind was already popping out strategies for hunting the big buck the following autumn. I took a second glance at the impressive, rain-soaked rub I had found on my walk in, and suddenly noticed a host of other big-buck sign dotting the knob.

Content for perhaps the first time that fall, I slung the rifle over my shoulder and walked back to my truck. Before hopping in the driver's seat for the trip home, I pulled back the rifle's hammer and squeezed the trigger as my sights met a rotten stump, officially ending my hunting season. I swabbed the barrel and slid the rifle in its case.

That night, I slept as soundly as I had in months.

Tips for Keeping Your Muzzleloader Clean

After you've fired your muzzleloader, the real work begins — cleaning. That's because Pyrodex and black powder leave a much thicker, more corrosive residue than smokeless powder. As a result, cleaning is not only more difficult, it's vital for preventing rust.

The simplest and most common way to clean a muzzleloader is to fill a bathtub or large bucket with hot, soapy water. Stand the barrel in the water nipple-end-down and run a patch back and forth down the bore. The scrubbing action will suck water up the bore through the nipple, rinsing out residue.

When the water coming out of the bore is clean, remove the barrel from the soap solution and rinse it with clean hot water.

CLEANING YOUR MUZZLELOADER is essential to prevent rust. The simplest way to clean a smokepole is to soak it in a tub of hot, soapy water.

This removes any loose residue and heats the steel, speeding drying.

Next, run dry patches down the bore until they come out clean. Then, dry all parts and apply a coat of oil-displacing lubricant.

During the following days, inspect the barrel and bore for any signs of rusting.

Prepare for Long Shots With Your Muzzleloader

Long-range accuracy with scoped muzzleloaders entails two things — knowledge and ability. You must know the bullet drop or trajectory, distance to the target and the effect of any wind that might be present. You must also refine some of the former, and obtain the shooting skills to ensure that your shot will strike the vitals of a deer. Here are some key tools that hunters should use for long shots.

1. Drop chart — Memorize or write a drop chart on the side of your rifle.
2. Laser range finder — These items are crucial for determining distances.
3. Shooting rest — Underwood shooting sticks, Harris bipods, Snipe Pods or any handy rest can be helpful.
4. Back-up — If possible, have your buddy ready to help put down a wounded animal.
5. Practice — Take shots at a variety of distances and learn what effect wind has on your bullet.
6. Be prepared to pass on shots — Only take ideal shots within your ability. Wishing to undo a shot is no way to end a hunt.

Today's Hot New Muzzleloaders

■ The **Knight** Disc Elite muzzleloader features a Full Plastic Jacket (FPJ) ignition system and a KnightLite fully contoured barrel, which makes it lighter and easier to carry and aim. The barrel has a cantilevered lug, making it virtually free-floating, which improves accuracy. The Disc Elite is available in .45 or .50 caliber and in a variety of stock designs.

■ **Thompson/Center Arms'** G2 Contender 209x45 Magnum is a closed-breech, break-action muzzleloader with an exposed hammer. The .45 caliber muzzleloader takes charges of up to 150 grains, and can be converted to a centerfire rifle by switching barrels. The removable breech plug makes cleaning easy.

■ **Savage Arms** builds on its line of Model 10ML-II muzzleloaders. The latest offering accommodates smokeless powder, black powder and Pyrodex. The muzzleloader features a heavyweight 24-inch button-rifled tapered barrel with crowned muzzle, a stock with dual-pillar bedding, 209 primer ignition, a removable breech plug and vent liner and a three-position top-tang safety.

■ The **Connecticut Valley Arms** Optima Pro Magnum 209 is a break-action in-line muzzleloader. The 209 ignition system is protected from the elements and requires no capping tool. The muzzleloader has a solid composite stock with a dual cheekpiece and a radical pistol grip. The Optima Pro has a reversible hammer spur for unobstructed cocking with a scope, DuraBright metallic fiber-optic sights and a solid-metal loading rod.

■ The **Traditions** Evolution LD muzzleloader uses a 209 shotgun primer and has a 150-grain powder capacity. The synthetic rifle features a stainless steel Ultra Glide bolt, Tru-Glo fiber-optic sights and a 26-inch fluted barrel with a Projectile Alignment System that centers the bullet.

Tips for Sighting-In Your Muzzleloading Rifle

MUZZLELOADERS ARE efficient deer killers when sighted in properly. Follow these tips for best results.

1. Be sure your muzzleloader has good iron sights, or, if it's topped with a scope, be sure the mounts are secure. A shooter cannot properly sight-in a rifle with lousy open or peep sights, or a scope that's going to wiggle out of place.

2. Make sure the firearm is sound. Tighten all screws, including the sight screws.

3. Be sure of your load. Inaccurate loads will not print consistently. All things must be equal — especially the charge — to ensure tight shot groups.

4. Use a benchrest, and use it right. Make sure that both the forend of the rifle and the toe of the stock are well padded and secure on the benchtop. A rifle should be set up so that it all but aims itself when properly resting on the benchtop. The shooter should be comfortable with both feet flat on the ground and spread apart a bit for stability. If recoil is a problem, the left hand for a right-handed shooter can be used to grip the forestock. If recoil is not a problem, it's best to rest the left hand flat on the bench. The right hand should control the aim and the trigger.

5. Use a target you can see — one with a well-defined aiming point.

6. Start by just getting a shot on paper. Do not frustrate yourself with 100-yard shots. Save those for later. Start by dialing the gun in at 10 to 15 yards. Adjust sights to hit dead center at close range, then move out to 100 yards.

7. Know your trajectory before shooting. There's no point in sighting-in a big-game rifle with its top load at only 50 yards. Skilled shooters should be able to sight-in a round ball at 75 to 100 yards. Therefore, top loads should increase your range to 150, 175 and, in some cases, 200 yards.

— *The Complete Blackpowder Handbook,* Krause Publications

Pyrodex Pellets Produce Consistent Results

While examining Pyrodex Pellets, one word comes to mind: consistency. Each pellet weighs about 37 grains and consists of 50 grains of powder.

A random sample of five Pyrodex Pellets weighed 36.8, 36.7, 36.7, 36.9 and 36.9 grains, with an average of 36.8 grains. The same test performed on five two-pellet sets yielded 73.2, 73.6, 73.4, 73.8 and 73.3 grains, for an average of 73.46 grains.

That's close enough to 71.5 grains weight, considering muzzleloader propellant efficiency, or lack thereof, to call it a 100-volume charge. And this size charge with proper bullets is considered a whitetail load for most muzzleloaders, while some frontloaders are allowed even more powder.

Weighing five three-pellet sets, these figures were produced: 110.2, 110.0, 110.6, 110.8 and 110.6 grains, averaging 110.44. That's about 140 grains of volume, which would be a magnum charge. In most deer hunting situations, two pellets are plenty.

Although loose Pyrodex provides excellent ignition, the Pyrodex Pellet, to ensure super ignition, has a base impregnated with black powder. In tests, ignition was 100 percent.

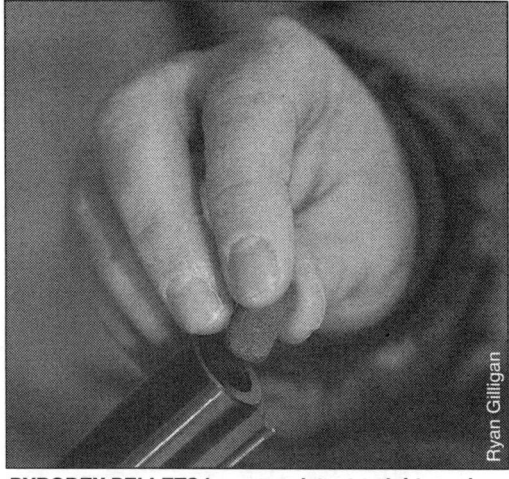

PYRODEX PELLETS have consistent weights and produced consistent velocities in shooting tests.

Incidentally, laboratory tests of the pellet without the blackpowder base still revealed excellent ignition.

To test ignition, a shooter properly loaded two pellets with the black-powder bases down. The three shots averaged 1,426 feet per second, with a high of 1,432 fps and low of 1,422 fps. Another test resulted in an average of 1,433 fps, with a 1,454 fps high and 1,411 fps low.

A third test had the shooter load the pellets incorrectly, with the blackpowder bases up. The three shots averaged 1,411 fps, with a high of 1,449 fps and a low of 1,375 fps.

As the numbers show, the Pyrodex Pellet, when loaded properly, provides consistent and impressive results.

— The Complete Blackpowder Handbook, Krause Publications

Muzzleloader Projectiles

Round Balls

The Round Ball

The earliest and most traditional projectile; an all-lead sphere. Used with a lubed patch; either pre-cut or trimmed during loading (with a patch knife). A .50-caliber round ball weighs approximately 175 grains. Using 100 grains of FFG Black Powder, muzzle velocity is about 2,000 feet per second. At 100 yards, terminal energy will be only half of what a conical delivers.

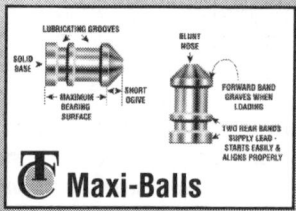

Maxi-Balls

Lead Conicals

An all-lead, conical-shaped projectile, with grooves to hold a lubricant. Although weights might vary, the most popular weight used (.50 cal.) for deer is approximately 350 grains. Using 100 grains of FFG black powder, muzzle velocity is about 1,400 fps. At 100 yards, terminal energy will be about twice that of a round ball.

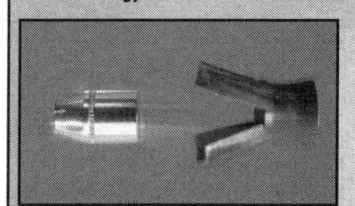

Mag Express Sabots

Sabots

A jacketed bullet (usually .44 or .45 cal.) housed in a plastic or polymer sleeve. The weight of a .50-caliber bullet is usually between 240 and 250 grains. Using 100 grains of FFG black powder, muzzle velocity is approximately 1,600 fps. At 100 yards, terminal downrange energy is between 1,100 and 1,250 ft lbs; on par with a 350-grain all-lead conical. At longer ranges, 150 yards or greater, down-range energy starts to surpass that of a conical because of the higher retained velocity.

.50 Cal. Ballistics - Lead Conicals with Black Powder or Pyrodex

Bullet	Black Powder or Pyrodex®	Range in Yards	Impact from line of Sight	Velocity f.p.s	Energy ft./lbs.
350 Grain Maxi-Hunter® or 370 Grain Maxi-Ball®	100 Grains	50	+1.9	1383	1572
	100 Grains	100	0.0	1176	1137
	100 Grains	150	-8.1	1041	891
	100 Grains	200	-21.8	951	743
350 Grain Maxi-Hunter® or 370 Grain Maxi-Ball®	150 Grains	50	+1.5	1574	2036
	150 Grains	100	0.0	1326	1445
	150 Grains	150	-4.6	1142	1072
	150 Grains	200	-15.2	1016	848

.50 Cal. Ballistics - Mag Express Sabots with Black Powder or Pyrodex

Bullet	Black Powder or Pyrodex®	Range in Yards	Impact from line of Sight	Velocity f.p.s	Energy ft./lbs.
240 Grain XTP™	100 Grains	50	+1.1	1696	1532
	100 Grains	100	0.0	1539	1261
	100 Grains	150	-4.8	1399	1043
	100 Grains	200	-14.1	1276	867
240 Grain XTP™	150 Grains	50	+.7	2006	2143
	150 Grains	100	0.0	1830	1783
	150 Grains	150	-3.2	1660	1468
	150 Grains	200	-9.6	1507	1210
275 Grain XTP™	100 Grains	50	+1.4	1571	1506
	100 Grains	100	0.0	1420	1232
	100 Grains	150	-5.7	1289	1014
	100 Grains	200	-16.6	1177	846
275 Grain XTP™	150 Grains	50	+.8	1887	2175
	150 Grains	100	0.0	1705	1775
	150 Grains	150	-3.8	1540	1447
	150 Grains	200	-11.4	1393	1185
300 Grain XTP™	100 Grains	50	+1.4	1573	1649
	100 Grains	100	0.0	1452	1404
	100 Grains	150	-5.6	1343	1200
	100 Grains	200	-15.9	1244	1030
300 Grain XTP™	150 Grains	50	+.8	1862	2310
	150 Grains	100	0.0	1718	1965
	150 Grains	150	-3.8	1583	1669
	150 Grains	200	-11.1	1461	1421

THE INFORMATION PROVIDED HERE is based on testing done by Thompson/Center Arms with 26-inch barrels and components specified in the chart. Caution: 150-grain magnum loads of FFG black powder or the Pyrodex equivalent should be used only in guns approved by the manufacturer for use with magnum charges.

BEN JOHNSON shot this mule deer near his home in southeastern Minnesota — hundreds of miles from typical mule deer range.

6

The Weird World of the Whitetail

Hunter Kills Mule Deer... In Minnesota!

If you spend enough time in the woods, you're bound to see strange things. But probably not as strange as what Ben Johnson of Byron, Minn., saw last fall.

Johnson was bow-hunting for whitetails near his hometown — about 8 miles from Rochester in southeastern Minnesota in early November.

Johnson had placed a doe decoy near his tree stand. It was the first time he had ever used a decoy. And he was about to find out just how effective fakes can be.

After a rattling sequence, Johnson spotted a buck coming toward him.

"As he got closer, I thought, 'Man, he's got some funny-looking ears,'" Johnson said.

He thought the buck was a mule deer, but it would be absurd to see that species in southeastern Minnesota. But as the buck circled the decoy, Johnson was pretty sure of what he was seeing. Suddenly a white-tailed buck appeared, and when he compared the newcomer to the first buck, there was no doubt the first buck was a muley.

Johnson practices quality deer management, and because neither buck was large, he passed them up. But as the deer wandered out of sight, Johnson had regrets. Who would believe his amazing story?

Just as quickly as the mule deer disappeared, it returned, coming within 15 yards of Johnson's tree stand. Johnson capitalized on his second chance at a once-in-a-lifetime deer and arrowed the muley. The deer ran only about 30 yards before expiring.

After the deer was down, Johnson called his father for help.

"I told him, 'You're never going to believe what I shot,'" Johnson said.

Indeed he didn't. Neither did Johnson's friend. The skeptics hurried to the successful hunter's stand to verify the deer for themselves.

Johnson's analysis was correct. He had killed a 7-point mule deer that weighed about 150 pounds. Johnson hung the deer in the garage, and by the next day, news had spread about his unusual kill, and people flocked to his home to see the wayward muley.

JOE SHEAD

DEER HUNTERS' ALMANAC®
BROWSE LINES
NEWS AND NOTES FROM WHITETAIL COUNTRY

Toy Tire Deforms Oklahoma Buck

Most hunters know white-tailed bucks sometimes grow deformed racks after suffering an injury. Usually, the injury is caused by a collision with a vehicle or a fight with another buck. However, those aren't the only things that cause such malformations.

Take, for example, the buck Nathan Christie of Coakron, Okla., shot during his state's 2000 muzzleloader season. Christie saw the unusual 6-pointer walk past his stand, accompanied by three does. After watching the buck rub his antlers on a bush and work a small scrape, Christie lined up his sights on the buck's vitals and pulled the trigger. Christie saw the buck go down, and soon walked over to claim his prize.

To his surprise, Christie immediately noticed the buck had a deformed right beam. But what was more amazing was what presumably caused the malformation: A small rubber tire — like those on toy trucks — was firmly attached to the buck's left hind foot, between the hoof and dewclaws. According to Christie, it appeared the tire had been on the buck's foot for a long time, as the hoof was deformed and it appeared that it was slowly being cut off by the tire's grip.

Interestingly, the buck showed no signs of the bizarre injury before Christie shot it.

— *Ryan Gilligan*

NATHAN CHRISTIE of Coakron, Okla., shot this 6-point buck during the 2000 muzzleloader season. The buck had stepped on a toy truck tire, which was deforming its hoof. The injury likely caused the buck's deformed right antler.

Michigan Bow-Hunter Shoots 'Basket Rack'

The term "basket rack" has a whole new meaning for one Michigan bow-hunter.

Larry Noorman of Grand Rapids was bow-hunting with his son Oct. 27, 2002. Noorman was watching some deer in front of his stand when he heard a noise behind him. When he turned to look, he saw the bottom half of a deer.

Noorman turned his attention back to the deer in front of him. When he looked behind him again seconds later, he did a double take. The deer, which was now 30 yards away, had a basketball in its antlers!

Noorman decided to try to shoot the 8-pointer, knowing it was a once-in-a-lifetime opportunity. However, the stand creaked and the buck made eye contact with him. Noorman thought he was busted. However, the deer put its head down and kept coming.

When the buck was 20 yards away, Noorman shot, and the deer ran off.

Noorman called his wife before taking up the blood trail, and she and their other son joined Noorman and his son to see the bizarre buck.

They trailed it past a neighbor who was hunting and had seen the deer go down and easily recovered the deer.

Several other hunters had seen the buck with the basketball in its antlers, and presumably, the ball had become lodged weeks ago.

When Noorman examined his trophy, he found no velvet and assumed the blue and yellow ball became wedged in the antlers in late September or early October.

— *Joe Shead*

A BASKETBALL lodged in the antlers of this Michigan buck. Larry Noorman killed it while bow-hunting Oct. 27, 2002. He estimated the buck had carried the ball for several weeks.

Hunter's First Big Buck Sports Deformed Rack

Scott Newman of Waupun, Wis., usually gun-hunts the big woods of northern Wisconsin, near Michigan's Upper Peninsula. Although the area occasionally produces some big bucks, deer densities are low and action is often slow. Not surprisingly, Newman has faced an uphill battle for bagging mature bucks.

He hoped his luck would change during Wisconsin's 2002 firearms season, as he headed to central Wisconsin's Waupaca County to hunt the property of a family friend, Harvey Schaub.

Although he hadn't planned to hunt the afternoon he reached the property, Newman arrived with plenty of time to head to his stand for an evening hunt. His last-minute change of plans was about to pay-off.

About a half-hour before the end of shooting hours, Newman spotted a deer moving across the oak-covered ridge near his tower stand. At first, Newman thought it was a smaller buck, but then the deer turned it's head, revealing a wide nontypical rack.

Excited by the chance at killing his first mature buck, Newman raised his shotgun and rested it against the rail of his stand. Despite his high hopes, Newman knew killing the deer wouldn't be a simple proposition. The buck was angling away from him, walking steadily at about 150 yards.

Newman steadied his rifled shotgun barrel on the shooting rail, centered the buck in his sights and squeezed the trigger.

SCOTT NEWMAN killed this strange 11-pointer while hunting in central Wisconsin during the 2002 firearms season. The deer was Newman's first mature buck.

At the shot, the buck flinched and began trotting along the ridge, finally crashing against a tree.

After the shock of what had just happened began to wear off, Newman descended from his stand and rushed over to the buck. Although he knew the buck's rack was unusual before he shot it, he had no idea how strange it really was.

The rack featured a normal 4-point left beam and a bizarre 7-point right beam that snaked almost perpendicular to the buck's head. The reason for the weird antler was immediately apparent: the buck was missing the bottom 9 inches of his left hind leg.

According to Newman, the buck was walking normally before he had shot it, despite the handicap.

— Ryan Gilligan

Odd Racks Come In All Shapes and Sizes

The word "nontypical" conjures up thoughts about rocking chair-racked bucks with points numbering in the double digits. But not all nontypical bucks have massive racks.

Scott Scarbrough of Akron, Ohio, took up bow-hunting in the mid-1990s. He shot his first deer (with gun or bow) in 1999. That year he killed a doe with his compound bow.

In 2000, Scarbrough was looking to tag a buck with his bow. On Oct. 28, he was hunting from a tree stand overlooking a well-used corridor trail. He passed up a few does, waiting for his chance at a buck.

Later in the evening, Scarbrough heard a deer coming toward him from the top of a hill. When he saw the deer, he had to look twice. The deer was a buck, which was surprising enough, but something was unusual about the buck's right antler. Instead of growing up, it grew nearly straight down alongside the buck's head. In fact, the antler was actually pushing the eyebrow over the buck's right eye.

Believe it or not, Scarbrough nearly passed on the unusual buck. However, he was more concerned with the buck's health than taking an unusual trophy. Thinking the buck may have trouble surviving with its vision obscured by the eyebrow, Scarbrough shot the odd-racked buck.

When Scarbrough recovered the deer, he finally got an up-close

SCOTT SCARBROUGH had never killed a buck, but that changed in October 2000 when he shot this buck. The buck's right antler hung down alongside its head and pushed the deer's eyebrow over its eye.

look at the unusual rack. The right antler hung down about $6^{1}/_{2}$ inches and was teardrop-shaped at the bottom. Scarbrough speculated the antler may have resulted from a fight with another buck or a collision with a car while still in velvet. Scarbrough said there were no injuries to the opposite side of the buck's body. The left side of the buck's rack also appeared normal.

When his emotions from the hunt set in, Scarbrough realized how lucky he was to shoot such an unusual deer. He said if he ever gets another chance at a buck with a similar rack, he won't think twice before shooting.
— *Joe Shead*

Technology Detects Lyme Disease Faster

It is estimated that 20,000 cases of Lyme disease are reported every year. However, the Centers for Disease Control estimates this number may be closer to 200,000, due to inefficient testing and the lack of available medical technology.

Many Americans could have Lyme disease and not know it. For example, a California women was bitten by a tick and contracted Lyme disease. The women suffered memory loss and painful arthritis until she was finally diagnosed with Lyme disease more than a year after contracting it. Now she has to administer antibiotics every day through an IV surgically implanted in her chest.

However, recent technology isolates Lyme disease and detects infection quicker. Laboratories such as, IGeneX in Palo Alto, Calif., have the technology to reference Lyme disease earlier, which may cut down on long- and short-term symptoms.

Symptoms of Lyme disease may include arthritis, memory loss, fatigue and neurological damage. If Lyme disease is not detected or caught in an early stage, these symptoms may worsen or become permanent.

The Lyme Disease Association offers support and information on Lyme disease and may also locate a local lab that has advanced diagnostic equipment.

— *Leigh Ann Ruddy*

Peanut Butter Fails To Deter Airport Deer

The crew at the Lake in the Hills Airport in Illinois tried a drastic measure to deter deer from the runway, where pilots spot several deer a week, and where a plane/deer collision cost $32,000 in damage.

A 30-inch-high electric fence was erected to stop deer from crossing the runway to reach a watering hole. To increase effectiveness, airport officials spread peanut butter on the hot wires. They hoped the smell would draw deer in, and the shock they received would teach them to stay out of the area.

The plan didn't work! People have seen deer crawling under or jumping over the fence.

The airport is seeking a new solution to its deer problem, possibly a tall, chain-link fence.

— *Joe Shead*

2004 Whitetail Calendar

Includes 2004 Rut Prediction Guide

Your new 2004 Calendar brings the world of the whitetail to vivid life with a new full-color photo for every month of the year.

In addition, you'll also get:

- An on-the-money forecast that predicts the peak of the rut and related chase phases-North and South-so you can hunt bucks in your area when they are the most active.
- Daily moon peak phases that will help you pick key times to be in the field
- A complete deer anatomy and shot placement guide to pinpoint vital areas and help you determine the most lethal shots.

From the Publisher of
DEER & DEER HUNTING MAGAZINE

Order Today
While Supplies Last

Credit Card Customers Call Toll-Free
800-258-0929 Offer DHCA4
M-F 7am-8pm Sat 8am-2pm

Order Online at www.krausebooks.com

Yes! Please send _____ copies of the 2004 Whitetail Calendar

- ❑ 1 copy $9.95
- ❑ 3 copies $26.95
- ❑ 6 copies $49.95

Shipping & Handling:
1-3 copies $2.00; 4 or more copies $4.00
Subtotal: $_____
Sales Tax: CA, IA, IL, KS, NJ, PA, SD, TN, WI residents please add sales tax. $_____
Total: $_____

Mail to: **Deer & Deer Hunting**
Offer DHCA4, 700 East State Street
Iola WI 54990-0001
Write for non-US rates

❑ Check or MO Enclosed
(payable to *Deer & Deer Hunting*)

Charge my ❑ Mastercard ❑ Visa
❑ AMEX ❑ Novus/Disc

Card # _____
Exp. Date _____
Signature _____
Name _____
Address _____
City _____
State/Zip _____
Phone _____
Email _____

RECORD DEER HERDS provide ample hunting opportunities. By filling tags, hunters put meat on the table and help reduce social problems, such as crop damage and car-deer collisions.

7

National Whitetail Trends

There's No Better Time To Fill Your Tag!

The adaptable nature of white-tailed deer is truly remarkable. Whitetails are spreading their range ever westward, extending into Wyoming, Montana, Colorado, Idaho and even Washington.

Deer inhabit the big forests of Maine, bayous of Louisiana and even the suburbs of Chicago.

Despite their ability to adapt to a wide range of habitats, perhaps the most impressive feature of whitetails is their ability to increase their herd.

At the end of the 19th century, only about 500,000 deer inhabited all of North America. That number has grown exponentially. To put things in perspective, in modern times, the 1987 Texas harvest, 1999 and 2001 Michigan harvests, 2000 and 2002 Pennsylvania harvests and the 2000 Wisconsin harvest would have caused deer to go extinct 100 years earlier! However, despite these high deer harvests, deer in these states and others are flourishing to the point where in many areas they have become problems to society.

Deer cause millions of dollars in damage to agricultural crops and

All-Time Single-Season Whitetail Harvests

Rank	State	Year	Total Harvest
1.	Wisconsin	2000	618,274
2.	Michigan	1999	544,895
3.	Michigan	2001	541,701
4.	Pennsylvania	2002	517,529
5.	Texas	1987	504,953
6.	Pennsylvania	2000	504,600
7.	Wisconsin	1999	494,116
8.	Pennsylvania	2001	486,014
9.	Michigan	1995	478,960
10.	Alabama	2001	478,700
11.	Texas	1989	477,491
12.	Michigan	2002	476,215
13.	Texas	1988	474,968
14.	Texas	1991	474,047
15.	Texas	1992	468,893
16.	Wisconsin	1995	467,100
17.	Michigan	2001	463,706
18.	Wisconsin	1996	460,524
19.	Texas	1993	452,509
20.	Michigan	1989	452,490
21.	Texas	1995	450,593
22.	Michigan	1998	450,000
23.	Wisconsin	2001	446,957
24.	Georgia	2001	446,000
25.	Texas	1986	445,119
26.	Texas	1999	438,627
27.	Texas	2002	436,949
28.	Michigan	1991	434,340
29.	Michigan	1990	432,690
30.	Pennsylvania	1995	430,583
31.	Texas	1990	429,532
32.	Georgia	1998	427,000

Statistics compiled by:
Deer hunters' 2003 Almanac, Krause Publications.

Single-Season Record Whitetail Harvests by State

State	Year	Harvest
Alabama	2001	478,700
Arizona	1984	7,181
Arkansas	1999	194,687
Connecticut	1995	13,740
Delaware	2001	12,200
Florida	2001	140,000
Georgia	2000	446,000
Illinois	2002	150,348
Indiana	1996	123,086
Iowa	2002	137,443
Kansas	2000	108,000
Kentucky	2000	157,321
Louisiana	2000	276,000
Maine	1959	41,735
Maryland	2002	94,114
Massachusetts	2002	12,264
Michigan	1999	544,895
Minnesota	1992	243,068
Mississippi	1995	334,962
Missouri	2002	279,445
Nebraska	2001	59,518
New Hampshire	1967	14,186
New Jersey	2000	77,444
New York	2002	308,216
North Carolina	1992	217,743
North Dakota	2002	88,325
Ohio	2002	204,114
Oklahoma	2000	101,935
Oregon	2001	1,457
Pennsylvania	2002	517,529
Rhode Island	2000	2,307
South Carolina	2002	319,920
South Dakota	2002	62,591
Tennessee	2002	168,809
Texas	1987	504,953
Vermont	1980	25,932
Virginia	1995	218,476
Washington	1991	18,000
West Virginia	2002	255,356
Wisconsin	2000	618,274
Wyoming	1992	14,749

Editor's note: Several Western states, including Idaho, Colorado and Montana, do not distinguish between white-tailed deer and other deer species in their annual harvest statistics. The whitetail harvests in those states are marginal and, therefore, are not represented in this chart.

Statistics compiled by: *Deer Hunters' 2004 Almanac*, Krause Publications.

in car-deer collisions, to name a few.

Gargantuan deer populations can be a blessing or a curse to deer hunters. For the person who is looking to put meat on the table, skyrocketing deer herds make accomplishing that goal easier. However, overpopulated herds may result in increased competition among deer for limited food and minerals, reducing the health and vigor of deer herds, which could reduce both the size of deer and the antlers they carry.

Hunters, therefore, have the perfect opportunity to benefit the deer herd, society and themselves, simply by killing deer.

A reduced deer herd means healthier deer because of less competition. It also means a healthier environment. Trees, shrubs and plants benefit from reduced browsing. In fact, some species that have been browsed completely out of existence in some areas may be able to regenerate when deer populations are less dense. Animal species, such as moose, also benefit from smaller deer herds. When deer densities grow too high, moose populations suffer, due to increased presence of brainworm, which is fatal to moose but has no effect on deer.

Society benefits from reduced deer populations because fewer car insurance claims means car insurance prices stay lower. Farmers have more crops to bring to market and people can rest a little easier at night, knowing when they walk into their gardens in the morning that they will appear as they had the night before — with no surprises from raiding deer. Plus, lives will undoubtedly be saved — both human and deer — if herd size in kept in check, and deer are kept off the highways.

Hunters have the most to gain by filling their tags. Not only is venison a great delicacy, but the time spent deer hunting with friends and family is a sacred gift. Longer hunting seasons and expanded opportunities help hunters get afield more often and spend quality time communing with nature and with deer camp chums.

And if your freezer space is limited, consider donating a deer to a venison-donation program such as Farmers and Hunters Feeding the Hungry. These charities collect hunter-killed deer, pay for butchering, and distribute deer to food pantries, providing the needy with meat — a commodity they may not otherwise be able to afford.

With record-high kills in practically every state within the last few years, it's apparent there's no time like the present to fill deer tags. Plus, by helping keep deer herds at socially tolerable levels, hunters strengthen the case for using hunting as a herd-control device in urban areas, and in general. And that means we're only helping ourselves.

Editor's note — *This chapter is designed to educate hunters on various aspects of deer hunting in the United States. Regulations are provided in general terms.*

Annual White-tailed Deer Harvests in the U.S.

5-Year Averages: 1998 through 2002
(Last year's rankings in parenthesis)

Rank	State	Harvest
1.	Michigan (2)	495,303
2.	Wisconsin (1)	467,808
3.	Pennsylvania (3)	452,925
4.	Alabama (4)	424,420
5.	Georgia (6)	420,800
6.	Texas (5)	417,462
7.	Mississippi (7)	311,676
8.	New York (9)	276,696
9.	South Carolina (10)	274,890
10.	Louisiana (8)	247,800
11.	Missouri (11)	245,261
12.	West Virginia (12)	217,878
13.	Minnesota (14)	197,469
14.	Virginia (13)	196,937
15.	Arkansas (15)	172,551
16.	Tennessee (18)	154,763
17.	Ohio (21)	149,692
18.	North Carolina (16)	146,086
19.	Illinois (17)	143,138
20.	Iowa (19)	124,320
21.	Kentucky (20)	114,997
22.	Florida (23)	105,950
23.	Indiana (22)	101,279
24.	Kansas (24)	94,043
25.	Oklahoma (25)	89,785
26.	Maryland (26)	86,485
27.	New Jersey (28)	68,911
28.	North Dakota (29)	65,750
29.	Montana (27)	58,515
30.	South Dakota (30)	49,053
31.	Nebraska (31)	48,016
32.	Washington (38)	37,500
33.	Maine (33)	32,394
34.	Idaho (34)	20,892
35.	Vermont (35)	17,690
36.	Connecticut (36)	11,760
37.	Delaware (37)	10,802
38.	Massachusetts (39)	10,420
39.	New Hampshire (38)	10,316
40.	Wyoming (NR)	8,770
41.	Arizona (40)	4,005
42.	Rhode Island (41)	1,993
43.	Oregon (42)	978

Editor's note: Several Western states do not distinguish between whitetails and other deer species in their harvest statistics. Those states are not represented in this chart.

Statistics compiled by: *Deer Hunters' 2004 Almanac*, Krause Publications.

ALABAMA
Camellia State
Harvest Ranking: #4

For more information, contact:
Dept. of Wildlife and Freshwater Fisheries
64 N. Union St.
Montgomery, AL 36130
(334) 242-3469   www.dcnr.state.al.us

HISTORY OF ALABAMA'S WHITETAIL HARVEST

Year	Firearms	Bow	Total
1964-65	NA	NA	59,230
1965-66	NA	NA	37,819
1966-67	NA	NA	47,842
1967-68	NA	NA	68,406
1968-69	NA	NA	63,674
1969-70	NA	NA	74,239
1970-71	NA	NA	63,502
1971-72	NA	NA	80,184
1972-73	NA	NA	82,555
1973-74	NA	NA	121,953
1974-75	NA	NA	120,727
1975-76	NA	NA	125,625
1976-77	NA	NA	144,155
1977-78	NA	NA	147,113
1978-79	NA	NA	152,733
1979-80	NA	NA	140,685
1980-81	NA	NA	130,532
1981-82	NA	NA	202,449
1982-83	NA	NA	141,281
1983-84	NA	NA	192,231
1984-85	NA	NA	237,378
1985-86	NA	NA	280,436
1986-87	288,487	17,653	306,140
1987-88	309,517	15,683	325,200
1988-89	257,734	18,854	276,588
1990-91	263,100	31,300	294,400
1991-92	269,500	25,500	295,000
1992-93	261,500	31,600	293,100
1993-94	305,300	45,200	350,500
1994-95	353,000	45,100	398,100
1995-96	334,200	32,600	366,800
1996-97	310,000	40,000	350,000
1997-98	367,900	55,500	423,400
1998-99	349,000	41,300	390,300
1999-2000	372,000	47,000	419,000
2000-2001	435,100	43,600	478,700
2001-2002	376,200	34,500	410,700

Alabama's High Deer Density
According to recent studies by the Alabama Department of Wildlife and Freshwater Fisheries, about half of the state's counties have more than 30 deer per square mile.

ALABAMA WHITETAIL RECORDS

- **Record harvest:** 478,700 (2000-01)
- **Record low harvest:** 31,123 (1963-64)
- **Bow-hunting record:** 55,500 (1997-98)
- **Gun-hunting record:** 435,100 (2001)

- **Season to remember:** 2000-2001. Alabama hunters kill 478,700 deer, setting a new state record and surpassing the 400,000 mark for the third time.

Alabama Governor Urges Venison Donation

Hunters in Alabama will again have an opportunity to provide for the needy this year.

"Hunters Helping the Hungry" is a joint project between the Office of the Governor, the National Rifle Association, The Phillip Morris Company, The Alabama Department of Conservation and Natural Resources and the Alabama Conservation and Natural Resources Foundation.

Hunters desiring to donate deer to "Hunters Helping the Hungry" may do so at one of the many participating venison processors. Posters will be placed in many sporting goods stores and venison processors to inform hunters of the opportunity to donate a deer. The processing is free for the hunter. However, if he chooses, the hunter can make a donation that will provide more venison to be processed.

The names and locations of participating venison processors may be obtained by calling the local Wildlife and Freshwater Fisheries District Office or the Montgomery office at (334) 242-3467.

— *Alabama Wildlife & Freshwater Fisheries*

ALABAMA SNAPSHOT

Deer Population: 1.6 million, 4th in U.S.
Average Harvest: 424,420, 4th in U.S.
Forested Land: 21.97 million acres
Harvest Calculation Method: Surveys
Does State Predict Annual Harvest? No
How Close is Annual Prediction? NA
Gun-Hunters: 225,000
Bow-Hunters: 60,000
Muzzleloading Hunters: 18,180
Hunter Education: Required for persons born on or after Aug. 1, 1977. Bow-hunter education is not required.
Orange Required for Gun-Hunting? Yes

ARIZONA
Grand Canyon State
Harvest Ranking: #41

For more information, contact:
Game & Fish Department
2221 W. Greenway Road
Phoenix, AZ 85023
(602) 942-3000   www.gf.state.az.us

HISTORY OF ARIZONA'S WHITETAIL HARVEST

Year	Firearms	Bow	Total
1958	5,096	NA	5,096
1959	5,421	NA	5,421
1960	4,982	NA	4,982
1961	4,734	NA	4,734
1962	4,194	NA	4,194
1963	4,343	NA	4,343
1964	4,339	NA	4,339
1965	3,612	NA	3,612
1966	2,993	NA	2,993
1967	2,662	NA	2,662
1968	2,927	NA	2,927
1969	2,202	NA	2,202
1970	2,232	NA	2,232
1971	1,535	NA	1,535
1972	1,673	NA	1,673
1973	2,097	NA	2,097
1974	3,248	NA	3,248
1975	2,870	NA	2,870
1976	2,662	NA	2,662
1977	2,319	NA	2,319
1978	2,287	NA	2,287
1979	3,264	NA	3,264
1980	3,523	NA	3,523
1981	3,504	NA	3,504
1982	4,002	60	4,062
1983	4,221	71	4,292
1984	7,116	65	7,181
1985	6,902	138	7,040
1986	5,934	94	6,028
1987	4,895	115	5,010
1988	4,600	108	4,708
1989	4,387	189	4,576
1990	4,449	100	4,549
1991	5,375	129	5,504
1992	5,737	95	5,832
1993	5,556	152	5,772
1994	5,363	1,315	6,678
1995	4,899	239	5,138
1996	4,126	178	4,304
1997	4,229	175	4,404
1998	4,160	204	4,364
1999	3,339	255	3,594
2000	4,250	214	4,500
2001	3,440	225	3,654
2002	3,639	274	3,913

ARIZONA WHITETAIL RECORDS

- **Record whitetail harvest:** 7,181 (1984)
- **Record low deer harvest:** 1,535 (1971)
- **Bow-hunting record:** 1,315 (1994)
- **Gun-hunting record:** 7,116 (1984)

- **Season to remember:** 1984. Arizona hunters kill 7,181 deer — a 60 percent increase from 1983.

Record Low For Deer Permits Recommended

The Arizona Game and Fish Department is recommending the commission set the deer permit tag level for the general deer seasons at 37,025, which is a 4,620-permit reduction from last year. Last year was also a record low for permits.

Arizona experienced a statewide drought that was the most severe drought in more than 100 years in many areas of the state. Deer tag reductions are statewide and are a result of very poor fawn survival in most units

Recommended permit levels represent the lowest level of deer hunting opportunity since records were started in 1946. In 1946, 33,886 deer permits were sold. The majority of the harvest was in northern Arizona. Deer hunting seasons in the 1940s and '50s were limited to four days in most of the southern part of the state.

Unlike in 1946, the southern part of the state now provides the majority of the deer harvest, largely because of white-tailed deer populations, but also because multiple hunt dates offer many more days of hunting opportunities. Regulating harvest through the hunt-permit system allows more liberal hunting seasons rather than severely limiting or closing areas due to drought impacts.

— Arizona Game & Fish

ARIZONA SNAPSHOT

Deer Population: 182,000 (all species)
Average Harvest: 4,005, 41st in U.S.
Forested Land: 19.6 million acres
Does State Predict Annual Harvest? No
How Close is Annual Prediction? NA
Gun-Hunters: 46,430
Bow-Hunters: 22,775
Muzzleloading Hunters: 1,120
Hunter Education: Required for ages 10 to 14. Bow-hunter education is not required.
Orange Required for Gun-Hunting? No

ARKANSAS
Land of Opportunity

Harvest Ranking: #15

For more information, contact:
Game & Fish Commission
#2 Natural Resources Drive
Little Rock, AR 72205
(800) 364-4263   www.agfc.state.ar.us

HISTORY OF ARKANSAS' WHITETAIL HARVEST

Year	Firearm	Bow	Total
1941-42	433	NA	433
1944-45	1,606	NA	1,606
1947-48	2,016	NA	2,016
1950-51	4,122	NA	4,122
1953-54	6,245	NA	6,245
1956-57	8,249	NA	8,249
1960-61	15,000	NA	15,000
1963-64	25,148	NA	25,148
1966-67	20,028	NA	20,028
1968-69	20,063	NA	20,063
1969-70	24,018	1,678	25,696
1970-71	24,784	1,233	26,017

31-YEAR HISTORY

Year	Firearm	Bow	Total
1971-72	23,375	1,345	24,720
1972-73	31,415	672	32,087
1973-74	32,292	1,502	33,794
1974-75	32,168	1,595	33,763
1975-76	32,210	1,112	33,322
1976-77	27,249	540	27,789
1977-78	27,862	1,247	29,109
1978-79	41,018	2,434	43,452
1979-80	32,841	3,233	36,074
1980-81	41,693	3,509	45,202
1981-82	41,567	3,024	44,591
1982-83	35,051	7,822	42,873
1983-84	42,709	17,539	60,248
1984-85	53,679	12,360	66,039
1985-86	48,027	12,049	60,076
1986-87	67,941	11,939	79,880
1987-88	89,422	16,970	106,392
1988-89	94,193	16,014	110,207
1989-90	97,031	16,048	113,079
1990-91	70,498	20,412	90,910
1991-92	NA	NA	110,896
1992-93	NA	NA	110,401
1993-94	106,119	15,944	122,063
1994-95	104,061	16,433	120,494
1995-96	144,932	18,992	163,924
1996-97	133,704	18,756	152,460
1997-98	164,132	15,093	179,225
1998-99	NA	NA	156,431
1999-2000	179,601	15,086	194,687
2000-2001	167,328	14,804	182,132
2001-2002	140,791	9,488	150,279

ARKANSAS WHITETAIL RECORDS

- **Record harvest:** 194,687 (1999-2000)
- **Record low harvest:** 203 (1938-39)
- **Bow-hunting record:** 21,190 (1997-98)
- **Gun-hunting record:** 167,328 (2000-2001)

- **Season to remember:** 1997-98. Decades of trap-and-transplant programs and tightened hunting regulations pay off, as Arkansas hunters kill 179,225 deer.

Arkansas Whitetails Get Clean Bill of Health

Arkansas' deer herd got a clean bill of health after nearly 250 deer were tested for chronic wasting disease by the Arkansas Game and Fish Commission this past season.

Although the disease doesn't seem to affect humans or cows, an appearance in Arkansas would cost the state millions of dollars that would be focused on CWD research, surveillance and management. The Center for Disease Control has conducted a study of CWD and human risk and has stated: "The risk of infection with the CWD agent among hunters is extremely small, if it exists at all."

The AGFC last year passed a law making it illegal to import, ship, transport or carry into the state by any means any live member of the cervid family, including but not limited to white-tailed deer and elk.

AGFC officials said although CWD is not known to be present anywhere in Arkansas, persons who find deer or elk dead from no apparent cause should immediately call the nearest AGFC office or personnel to report it.

— *Arkansas Game and Fish Commission*

ARKANSAS SNAPSHOT

Deer Population: 1 million, 7th in U.S.

Average Harvest: 172,551, 15th in U.S.

Forested Land: 17.86 million acres

Harvest Calculation Method: Mandatory registration

Does State Predict Annual Harvest? Yes

How Close is Annual Prediction? 10%

Gun-Hunters: 161,298

Bow-Hunters: 70,700

Muzzleloading Hunters: 78,956

Hunter Education: Required for persons born on or after Dec. 31, 1968. Bow-hunter education not required.

Orange Required for Gun-Hunting? Yes

COLORADO
Colorful Colorado

Harvest Ranking: Not ranked

For more information, contact:
Colorado Division of Wildlife
6060 Broadway
Denver, CO 80216
(303) 297-1192 www.dnr.state.co.us/

Colorado Approves Special Military Licenses

The Colorado Wildlife Commission approved action to allow members of the U.S. Armed Forces who were unable to comply with big game application deadlines due to the conflict in Iraq to receive a preference point and the opportunity to purchase leftover licenses prior to the public sale.

The decision to approve the proposal was made at the Colorado Wildlife Commission Workshop in Trinidad. It had been brought to the Commission's attention that many armed services members would be unable to apply in time for the big game license draw due to their obligation overseas with Operation Iraqi Freedom. The commission decided that armed services members' commitment to serve should not deter from their hunting privileges in Colorado. The Commission decided to allow any service member to apply for and receive a preference point for each big game species. In addition, they will be allowed to purchase a leftover license prior to the public sale in mid-August. Military personnel will have to show evidence they were on active duty outside of the continental United States at or near the time of the 2003 big-game deadline. The concession will remain in effect until the date of the 2004 big game draw.

There will be two applications available for those who qualify. One application will be to receive a preference point. There will be a $3 fee for applying for a point. The second application will allow those who qualify to purchase leftover licenses prior to the public sale.
— *Colorado Division of Wildlife*

Editor's note: *Colorado does not distinguish between white-tailed deer and mule deer in its harvest statistics. Biologists there estimate that about 1,000 whitetails are taken each year. Most of these deer come from the river bottoms of the eastern plains of Colorado.*

Hunters Can Get CWD Results From Hot Line, Web Site

Hunters who have had their deer or elk tested for chronic wasting disease (CWD) and do not receive a call from the Colorado Division of Wildlife telling them the test was positive should assume CWD was not detected in their animal, Division of Wildlife Director Russell George reminded hunters.

However, hunters who want to check the results for themselves can now call a special CWD hot line and get the results automatically. The CWD hot line number is (800) 434-0274. Hunters will need the head submission number from the test form to activate an automated response system similar to those used by airlines to provide arrival and departure information.

Wildlife Commission Approves Raise in License Numbers

Deer hunters also had a good season in 2002, with the statewide harvest increasing to more than 35,000 deer, an increase of 2,000 over 2001.

An increasing number of herd units are at or above their long-term population objective, resulting in more antlerless licenses available for hunters in selected areas of the state.
— *Colorado Division of Wildlife*

COLORADO SNAPSHOT

Deer Population: 516,458 (all species)
Average Harvest: Not available
Forested Land: NA
Gun-Hunters: 90,551
Bow-Hunters: 20,650
Muzzleloading Hunters: 6,300
Hunter Education: Required for persons born after Jan. 1, 1949. Bow-hunter education is not required.
Orange Required for Gun-Hunting? Yes

CONNECTICUT
Constitution State
Harvest Ranking: #36

For more information, contact:
Dept. of Environmental Protection
391 Route 32
N. Franklin, CT 06254
(860) 424-3105   www.dep.state.ct.us

HISTORY OF CONNECTICUT'S DEER HARVEST

Year	Firearms	Bow	Total
1976	530	100	630
1977	780	125	905
1978	805	125	930
1979	870	140	1,010
1980	2,189	376	2,565
1981	2,463	393	2,856
1982	2,233	391	2,624
1983	3,152	639	3,791
1984	3,742	596	4,338
1985	3,817	722	4,539
1986	4,575	819	5,394
1987	5,618	854	6,472
1988	6,843	799	7,642
1989	7,837	926	8,763
1990	NA	NA	9,896
1991	NA	NA	11,311
1992	NA	NA	12,486
1993	NA	NA	10,360
1994	NA	NA	10,438
1995	11,039	2,701	13,740
1996	9,323	2,691	12,014
1997	9,537	2,300	11,837
1998	7,958	2,186	10,144
1999	8,791	2,561	11,352
2000	10,586	2,687	13,273
2001	9,424	2,262	12,050
2002	9,093	2,889	11,982

Connecticut Deer Harvest Stays the Course

The abundant acorn crop in fall 2002 also partially contributed to reduced hunter success rates. Success rates in the past have been influenced by the amount of acorns available for deer to consume during the fall.

During years of acorn abundance, deer do not need to travel far to feed. Reduced movements by deer make them less visible and less vulnerable to hunting.

— *Connecticut Dept. of Environmental Protection*

CONNECTICUT WHITETAIL RECORDS

- **Record harvest:** 13,740 (1995)
- **Record low harvest:** 550 (1975)
- **Bow-hunting record:** 2,701 (1995)
- **Gun-hunting record:** 11,039 (1995)

- **Season to remember:** 1975. After centuries of unrestricted hunting, habitat loss and encroachment by civilization, Connecticut deer numbers grow high enough to support the state's first modern firearms season.

Connecticut Offers Junior Deer Hunting Training Day

A Junior Deer Hunting Training Day has been established on the Saturday before the regular three-week shotgun deer-hunting season. In 2003, the Junior Deer Hunting Training Day is scheduled for Nov. 15.

On private land, the licensed junior hunter must have a valid private land shotgun/rifle deer permit and written consent from the landowner. The adult mentor must have a deer permit and written consent from the landowner. Harvested deer must be brought to a deer check station.

On state land, the licensed junior hunter must have an appropriate state land shotgun deer permit for the area. The adult mentor must have a valid deer permit. Harvested deer must be brought to a deer check station.

The Junior Hunting Day was initiated to provide junior hunters with an opportunity to learn safe and effective hunting practices from experienced adult mentors.

— *Connecticut Department of Environmental Protection*

CONNECTICUT SNAPSHOT

Deer Population: 75,000, 32nd in U.S.
Average Harvest: 11,760, 36th in U.S.
Forested Land: 1.8 million acres
Harvest Calculation Method: Mandatory registration
Does State Predict Annual Harvest? No
How Close is Annual Prediction? NA
Gun-Hunters: 32,261
Bow-Hunters: 11,039
Muzzleloading Hunters: 2,651
Hunter Education: Required for first-time hunters. Bow-hunter education not required.
Orange Required for Gun-Hunting? Yes

DELAWARE
First State

Harvest Ranking: #37

For more information, contact:
Department of Natural Resources
89 Kings Hwy., Box 1401
Dover, DE 19903
(302) 739-5295   www.dnrec.state.de.us

HISTORY OF DELAWARE'S WHITETAIL HARVEST

Year	Firearms	Bow	Total
1976-77	1,475	19	1,494
1977-78	1,630	22	1,652
1978-79	1,679	20	1,699
1979-80	1,783	20	1,803
1980-81	1,737	17	1,754
1981-82	2,080	31	2,111
1982-83	2,046	48	2,094
1983-84	2,210	21	2,231
1984-85	2,473	41	2,514
1985-86	2,383	58	2,439
1986-87	2,772	78	2,850
1987-88	3,420	121	3,541
1988-89	3,844	154	3,998
1990-91	4,814	252	5,066
1991-92	4,970	362	5,332
1992-93	6,721	524	7,245
1993-94	6,917	548	7,465
1994-95	7,151	673	7,824
1995-96	8,050	728	8,778
1996-97	9,034	786	9,820
1997-98	9,073	930	10,003
1998-99	9,386	926	10,312
1999-00	9,921	835	10,756
2000-01	9,907	834	10,741
2001-2002	10,945	1,037	12,200
2002-2003	9,149	851	10,000

Delaware Hunting License Sales

Year	Resident	Nonresident	Total
1972	23,713	1,357	25,070
1978	25,411	2,443	27,854
1981	23,811	2,600	26,411
1984	23,644	3,516	27,160
1987	23,378	4,320	27,698
1990	21,157	3,848	25,005
1991	21,674	2,995	24,669
1992	21,863	2,362	24,225
1993	21,664	2,184	23,848
1994	21,769	2,042	23,811
1995	19,518	1,945	21,463
1996	19,914	1,693	21,607
1997	20,257	1,731	21,988

DELAWARE WHITETAIL RECORDS

- **Record harvest:** 12,200 (2001-02)
- **Record low harvest:** 1,494 (1976)
- **Bow-hunting record:** 1,037 (2001-02)
- **Gun-hunting record:** 10,945 (2001-02)

- **Season to remember:** 1997-98. Delaware bow-hunters kill a record 930 deer. Although diminutive compared to other states' archery harvests, this figure is amazing considering Delaware bow-hunters killed only 22 deer just 20 years earlier.

Delaware Runs Deer Stand Lottery System

Delaware runs a lottery system for hunting whitetails on state-owned lands. This lottery is conducted annually and guarantees successful applicants a permit to hunt deer on a specific date and location. Delaware offers more than 7,000 deer stand hunting days to individuals who desire to hunt deer on public lands. The shotgun deer stand lottery is held the first week of October. Applicants are notified of the results within two weeks of the drawing.

To participate in the lottery, hunters must complete the application contained on the Delaware DNR Web page. Applicants have the choice of up to three hunting locations and three hunting dates. However, they must keep in mind that the lottery is based upon date preference. The areas and dates available for hunting are listed in the application.

Each hunter may only submit one application. Additional applications will be deleted, possibly resulting in the applicant's expulsion from the lottery. For additional information about the lottery or completing this application, contact the Wildlife section at (302) 739-5297.

— Delaware Dept. of Natural Resources

DELAWARE SNAPSHOT

Deer Population: 30,000, 33rd in U.S.
Average Harvest: 10,802, 37th in U.S.
Forested Land: 398,000 acres
Harvest Calculation Method: Mandatory registration
Does State Predict Annual Harvest? No
How Close is Annual Prediction? NA
Gun-Hunters: 17,000
Bow-Hunters: 6,900
Muzzleloading Hunters: 8,500
Hunter Education: Required for persons born after Jan. 1, 1967. Bow-hunter education is not required.
Orange Required for Gun-Hunting? Yes

FLORIDA
Sunshine State

Harvest Ranking: #22

For more information, contact:
Fish & Game Commission
620 S. Meridian Farris Bryant Blvd.
Tallahassee, FL 32399
(850) 488-3641   www.state.fl.us/gfc

HISTORY OF FLORIDA'S WHITETAIL HARVEST

Year	Firearms	Bow	Total
1972	NA	NA	58,500
1973	NA	NA	57,122
1974	NA	NA	54,102
1975	NA	NA	54,380
1976	NA	NA	60,805
1977	NA	NA	85,744
1978	NA	NA	NA
1979	NA	NA	54,765
1980	NA	NA	72,039
1981	NA	NA	66,489
1982	NA	NA	64,557
1983	NA	NA	77,146
1984	NA	NA	73,895
1985	NA	NA	80,947
1986	NA	NA	89,212
1987	NA	NA	105,917
1988	NA	NA	107,240
1989	NA	NA	85,753
1990	NA	NA	79,170
1991	NA	NA	81,255
1992	NA	NA	81,942
1993	NA	NA	104,178
1994	NA	NA	84,408
1995	NA	NA	81,891
1996	NA	NA	78,446
1997	NA	NA	80,000
1998	NA	NA	80,000
1999	NA	NA	80,000
2000	93,319	18,317	111,636
2001	117,000	23,000	140,000
2002	109,536	8,579	118,115

Florida Harbors Big Bucks

Several Florida hunters bagged trophy bucks during the 2000-2001 season. Among the biggest was a Jefferson County buck killed by Carl Joiner. His buck scored 149 5/8 inches.

Two other bucks entered into Florida's big-buck registry included a 138-inch 8-pointer taken by Tom Price in Clay County, and a 136-inch 11-pointer taken by Mark Johnson in Calhoun County.

FLORIDA WHITETAIL RECORDS

- **Record harvest:** 140,000 (2001)
- **Record low harvest:** 48,900 (1971)
- **Bow-hunting record:** 23,000 (2001)
- **Gun-hunting record:** 117,000 (2001)

- **Season to remember:** 2001. Florida hunters kill an estimated 140,000 deer, surpassing the 1999 harvest by about 60,000.

Florida Offers Hunter Safety Classes Online

The Florida Fish and Wildlife Conservation Commission's hunter safety class now is available online as well as on compact disc. Hunters can take most of the classroom instruction without leaving home before taking part in a field day that includes live-firing instruction on a shooting range to earn certification.

The interactive Internet course was developed in cooperation with seven southeastern states as a means of increasing accessibility to hunter safety programs. Field days are offered throughout Florida. Internet users can click on the "course schedules" link, then the appropriate region for information regarding field days in their areas. This alternative-delivery format is in addition to the traditional courses scheduled in all of Florida's counties.

The course has many activities and questions, including a 50-question test that students must complete. After completing the online course, students must print out the final report form with test results and have it notarized. Then they can enroll in one of the scheduled field days.

— Florida Fish & Wildlife Conservation Commission

FLORIDA SNAPSHOT

Deer Population: 820,000, 14th in U.S.
Average Harvest: 105,950, 22nd in U.S.
Forested Land: 16.55 million acres
Harvest Calculation Method: Surveys and voluntary registration
Does State Predict Annual Harvest? No
How Close is Annual Prediction? NA
Gun-Hunters: 117,509
Bow-Hunters: 27,878
Muzzleloading Hunters: 19,949
Hunter Education: Required for persons born on or after June 1, 1975. Bow-hunter education is not required.
Orange Required for Gun-Hunting? Yes

GEORGIA
Peach State

Harvest Ranking: #5

For more information, contact:
Wildlife Resources
2070 U.S. Hwy. 278 SE
Social Circle, GA 30025
(770) 414-3333   www.dnr.state.ga.us

HISTORY OF GEORGIA'S WHITETAIL HARVEST

Year	Firearm	Bow	Total
1981-82	NA	NA	134,000
1982-83	NA	NA	144,000
1983-84	NA	NA	164,000
1984-85	NA	NA	177,000
1985-86	NA	NA	189,600
1986-87	NA	NA	226,000
1987-88	NA	NA	280,536
1988-89	NA	NA	300,624
1989-90	NA	NA	293,167
1990-91	NA	NA	351,652
1991-92	265,352	15,708	281,060
1992-93	284,412	21,841	306,253
1993-94	309,522	37,331	346,853
1994-95	345,869	35,687	381,556
1995-96	355,267	36,328	391,595
1996-97	351,990	49,368	401,358
1997-98	350,000	45,000	395,000
1998-99	383,000	44,000	427,000
1999-2000	380,000	46,000	426,000
2000-2001	401,400	44,600	446,000
2001-2002	372,200	37,800	410,000

Understanding Doe Productivity

A healthy herd of 50 mature does will out-produce an unhealthy herd of 100 mature does. For example:

✓ 50 healthy does give birth to two fawns each.

✓ 95 percent of the fawns survive, meaning the herd increases by 95 deer.

On the other hand:

✓ 100 unhealthy does give birth to one fawn each.

✓ 50 percent of the fawns survive, meaning the herd, at best, increases by 50 deer. Healthy does will reproduce every year until they die. "Barren does" occur mostly in poor-health herds.

GEORGIA WHITETAIL RECORDS

- **Record harvest:** 446,000 (2000-01)
- **Record low harvest:** 134,000 (1981-82)
- **Bow-hunting record:** 49,368 (1996-97)
- **Gun-hunting record:** 401,100 (2000-2001)

- **Season to remember:** 1993-94. Georgia bow-hunters experience a banner season, killing 37,331 deer — 15,490 more deer than the previous year.

Hunters Help Feed Hungry

Hunters for the Hungry is a program that began in 1993 in an effort to improve the image of hunters and to provide a much-needed product to those in need. Protein is one of the items least-frequently donated to food banks. Hunters for the Hungry has been the most consistent source of protein for the Atlanta Community Food Bank. Since the program's inception, hunters have donated more than 100,000 pounds of venison to feed thousands of hungry Georgians.

To participate, hunters donate harvested deer at a designated collection site during the times indicated. The deer are processed into ground venison and distributed to those in need by the Atlanta Community Food Bank and other food banks across Georgia.

Hunters who drop off a field-dressed deer at a designated collection site will receive a T-shirt and will have their name entered into a drawing for a deer rifle. Last season, 829 deer were collected. That amounted to approximately 24,800 pounds of venison that fed more than 99,000 people.

— *Georgia Wildlife Resources Division*

GEORGIA SNAPSHOT

Deer Population: 1.3 million, 6th in U.S.

Average Harvest: 420,800, 5th in U.S.

Forested Land: 24.1 million acres

Harvest Calculation Method: Surveys

Does State Predict Annual Harvest? No

How Close is Annual Prediction? NA

Gun-Hunters: 279,382

Bow-Hunters: 96,844

Muzzleloading Hunters: 42,259

Hunter Education: Required for persons born after Jan. 1, 1961. Bow-hunter education is not required.

Orange Required for Gun-Hunting? Yes

IDAHO
Gem State
Harvest Ranking: #34

For more information, contact:
Fish & Game Department
Box 25
Boise, ID 83707
(208) 334-3717
www.state.id.us/fishgame/fishgame.html

HISTORY OF IDAHO'S DEER HARVEST

Year	Firearm	Bow	Total
1981	NA	NA	50,580
1982	NA	NA	48,670
1983	NA	NA	50,600
1984	NA	NA	42,600
1985	NA	NA	48,950
1986	NA	NA	59,800
1987	NA	NA	66,400
1988	NA	NA	82,200
1989	NA	NA	95,200
1990	NA	NA	72,100
1991	16,721	364	17,085
1992	NA	NA	23,633
1993	23,251	303	23,554
1994	29,760	595	30,355
1995	28,180	320	28,500
1996	NA	NA	22,600
1997	37,450	1,100	38,550
1998	38,162	880	39,042
1999	17,070	310	17,380
2000	15,850	390	16,240
2001	15,850	450	16,300
2002	15,160	340	15,500

Editor's note — The figures before 1991 include white-tailed deer and mule deer.

Feeding Often Harms Whitetails

Although well-meaning individuals attempt to help deer by providing supplemental foods in winter, such efforts can be detrimental. Eye and respiratory infections are common at feeding sites, and the change from natural to supplemental feed often causes diarrhea in fawns.

Research shows that animals in good condition can survive winter with little nutrition. Supplemental feeding is virtually irrelevant to survival, and it is not an adequate way to make up for habitat loss. There is no substitute for healthy habitat.

IDAHO WHITETAIL RECORDS

- **Record harvest:** 39,042 (1998)
- **Record low harvest:** 15,500 (2002)
- **Bow-hunting record:** 1,100 (1997)
- **Gun-hunting record:** 37,450 (1997)

- **Season to remember:** 1991. For the first time in state history, Idaho recognizes white-tailed deer separately. Of the 17,085 deer killed, 97.9 percent were taken by gun-hunters.

Idaho Requires Bow-Hunter Education Permit

The Bowhunter Education Program was mandated by the state legislature in 1993, effective January 1, 1994. It requires all bowhunters who have never hunted in an Idaho archery-only season, regardless of age, to complete a bow-hunter education course, or show proof of having successfully completed a state-approved course in this or another state.

The program is taught by trained, certified volunteer instructors. The course averages 14 hours of classroom training, combined with a field exercise.

The program content includes learning to recognize equipment and personal limitation, when and where to shoot, becoming a responsible bow-hunter, how to locate the animal (after the shot), tree stand safety and much more.

The program is taught using the National Bowhunter Education Foundation's curriculum and materials. The cost for the program is the same as for the hunter education program. For more information or to register for a bow-hunter education class, contact your nearest DNR regional office.

— *Idaho Department of Natural Resources*

IDAHO SNAPSHOT
Deer Population: 255,000, 24th in U.S.
Average Harvest: 20,892, 34th in U.S.
Forested Land: 21.6 million acres
Harvest Calculation Method: Surveys
Does State Predict Annual Harvest? No
How Close is Annual Prediction? NA
Gun-Hunters: 130,000
Bow-Hunters: 12,800
Muzzleloading Hunters: 3,300
Hunter Education: Required for persons born after Jan. 1, 1975. Bow-hunter education is required for first-time bow-hunters.
Required for Gun-Hunting? No

ILLINOIS
Prairie State

Harvest Ranking: #19

For more information, contact:
Department of Conservation
524 S. Second St.
Springfield, IL 62701
(217) 782-7305   www.dnr.state.il.us

HISTORY OF ILLINOIS' WHITETAIL HARVEST

Year	Firearm	Bow	Total
1958	2,493	NA	2,493
1959	2,604	NA	2,604
1960	2,438	NA	2,438
1961	4,313	NA	4,313
1962	6,289	NA	6,289
1963	6,785	NA	6,785
1964	9,975	NA	9,975
1965	7,651	NA	7,651
1966	7,357	NA	7,357
1967	6,588	NA	6,588
1968	8,202	NA	8,202
1969	8,345	NA	8,345
1970	8,889	590	9,479
1971	10,359	566	10,925
1972	10,100	552	10,652
1973	12,902	960	13,862
1974	12,853	1,425	14,278
1975	15,614	1,608	17,222
1976	15,308	1,600	16,908
1977	16,231	2,810	19,041
1979	20,058	1,074	21,132
1980	20,825	1,463	22,288
1981	20,800	1,766	22,566
1982	22,657	2,205	24,862
1983	26,112	2,554	28,666
1984	29,212	3,023	32,235
1985	31,769	3,746	35,515
1986	36,056	4,357	40,413
1987	42,932	6,646	49,578
1988	47,786	7,820	55,606
1989	56,143	10,000	66,143
1990	NA	NA	81,000
1991	83,191	18,099	101,290
1992	84,537	19,564	104,101
1993	92,276	23,215	115,491
1994	97,723	25,607	123,330
1995	107,742	34,491	142,233
1996	97,498	35,239	132,737
1997	96,511	36,763	133,274
1998	99,008	36,280	135,288
1999	95,222	41,310	136,532
2000	106,433	42,630	149,063
2001	101,566	42,900	144,460
2002	102,336	48,012	150,348

ILLINOIS WHITETAIL RECORDS

- **Record harvest:** 150,348 (2002)
- **Record low harvest:** 1,709 (1957)
- **Bow-hunting record:** 48,012 (2002)
- **Gun-hunting record:** 107,742 (1995)

- **Season to remember:** 2000. Illinois hunters kill 149,063 deer, surpassing the previous record of 142,233, set in 1995. That figure is especially amazing considering that 20 years earlier, the harvest was only 22,288.

CWD Appears in Illinois Whitetails

In October 2002, a landowner noticed a doe behaving strangely on his property. He killed the deer, then reported it to the Illinois Department of Natural Resources.

The doe was the first case of chronic wasting disease discovered in Illinois.

The DNR subsequently tested about 4,100 deer across 36 counties for the fatal brain disease during Illinois' shotgun seasons and discovered six more CWD-positive deer.

All of the CWD-positive deer were found in McHenry, Boone and Winnebago counties in the northern part of the state.

Early in 2003, sharpshooters were employed to kill 400 more deer in the affected counties. Five more CWD-positive deer were killed during the shoot.

Two other deer that were acting strangely were also killed and identified as having CWD. Illinois' CWD-positive deer total stood at 14 as of Summer 2003.

To combat CWD, Illinois has banned deer feeding and the importation of cervid carcasses. The state plans to test 4,000 to 5,000 hunter-killed deer for CWD this fall.

ILLINOIS SNAPSHOT

Deer Population: 700,000, 15th in U.S.
Average Harvest: 143,138, 19th in U.S.
Forested Land: 4.3 million acres
Harvest Calculation Method: Mandatory registration
Does State Predict Annual Harvest? Yes
How Close is Annual Prediction? 5%
Gun-Hunters: 190,000
Bow-Hunters: 110,000
Muzzleloading Hunters: 7,050
Hunter Education: Required for persons born after Jan. 1, 1980. Bow-hunter education is not required.
Orange Required for Gun-Hunting? Yes

INDIANA
Hoosier State

Harvest Ranking: #23

For more information, contact:
Division of Wildlife
553 E. Miller Drive
Bloomington, IN 47401
(317) 232-4080   www.state.in.us/dnr

HISTORY OF INDIANA'S WHITETAIL HARVEST

Year	Firearm	Bow	Total
1951	NA	NA	1,590
1953	NA	NA	83
1955	NA	NA	149
1957	NA	NA	NA
1959	NA	NA	800
1961	NA	NA	2,293
1963	NA	NA	4,634
1965	NA	NA	4,155
1967	NA	NA	6,560
1969	NA	NA	7,323
32-YEAR HISTORY			
1971	NA	NA	5,099
1972	NA	NA	NA
1973	NA	NA	8,244
1974	NA	NA	9,461
1975	NA	NA	8,758
1976	NA	NA	11,344
1977	NA	NA	12,476
1978	NA	NA	9,896
1979	NA	NA	13,718
1980	NA	NA	19,780
1981	12,600	5,527	18,127
1982	16,267	4,651	20,918
1983	21,244	3,988	25,232
1984	21,944	5,640	27,584
1985	25,768	6,371	32,139
1986	33,837	9,621	43,458
1987	38,937	12,841	51,778
1988	46567	13,667	60,234
1989	62,901	16,417	79,318
1990	70,928	17,775	88,703
1991	77,102	21,581	98,683
1992	73,396	21,918	95,314
1993	77,226	23,988	101,214
1994	89,037	23,379	112,416
1995	92,496	25,233	117,729
1996	99,886	23,200	123,086
1997	84,637	20,300	104,937
1998	82,101	18,360	100,461
1999	79,384	20,234	99,618
2000	76,313	22,412	98,725
2001	79,047	24,116	103,163
2002	85,156	19,272	104,428

INDIANA WHITETAIL RECORDS

- **Record harvest:** 123,086 (1996)
- **Record low harvest:** 68 (1954)
- **Bow-hunting record:** 25,233 (1995)
- **Gun-hunting record:** 99,886 (1996)

- **Season to remember:** 1996. Indiana hunters break the firearms and overall harvest records, killing 123,086 whitetails. Amazingly, just eight years earlier, Indiana hunters killed just 60,234 deer — less than half as many as in 1996.

Indiana Strives to Reduce Deer-Vehicle Collisions

Through safety measures and heightened awareness, deer-vehicle accident rates in Indiana were reduced from 203 collisions per billion miles traveled in 1989 to 174 in 1994. However, officials still aren't satisfied.

Those officials hope to reduce the number of deer-vehicle collisions per billion miles driven as reported to the police from 174 in 1994 to 170 in the near future.

They hope to accomplish this objective through a variety of methods, including monitoring deer-vehicle accidents by county and using data when setting population trend goals.

Also, they plan to reduce deer population levels where necessary by continuing to liberalize the harvest of antlerless deer and by continuing to develop new strategies for increasing antlerless deer harvests.

Officials will continue the Deer Damage Control Permit program to put additional pressure on localized areas of high deer density.

— *Indiana Dept. of Natural Resources*

INDIANA SNAPSHOT

Deer Population: 450,000, 18th in U.S.
Average Harvest: 101,279, 23rd in U.S.
Forested Land: 4.4 million acres
Harvest Calculation Method: Mandatory registration
Does State Predict Annual Harvest? No
How Close is Annual Prediction? NA
Gun-Hunters: 211,767
Bow-Hunters: 122,617
Muzzleloading Hunters: 93,015
Hunter Education: Required for persons born after Dec. 31, 1986. Bow-hunter education is not required.
Orange Required for Gun-Hunting? Yes

IOWA
Hawkeye State

Harvest Ranking: #20

For more information, contact:
Department of Natural Resources
Wallace State Office Bldg.
Des Moines, IA 50319-0034
(515) 281-4687 www.state.ia.us/wildlife/

HISTORY OF IOWA'S WHITETAIL HARVEST

Year	Firearm	Bow	Total
1954	2,413	10	2,423
1955	3,006	58	3,064
1956	2,561	117	2,678
1957	2,667	138	2,805
1958	2,729	162	2,891
1959	2,476	255	2,731
1960	3,992	277	4,269
1961	4,997	367	5,364
1962	5,299	404	5,703
1963	6,612	538	7,151
1964	9,024	670	9,694
1965	7,910	710	8,620
1966	10,742	579	11,321
1967	10,392	791	11,183
1968	12,941	830	13,771
1969	10,731	851	11,582
1970	12,743	1,037	13,780
1971	10,459	1,232	11,691
1972	10,485	1,328	11,813
1973	12,208	1,822	14,030
1974	15,817	2,173	17,990
1975	18,948	2,219	21,167
1976	14,257	2,350	16,607
1977	12,788	2,400	15,188
1978	15,168	2,957	18,125
1979	16,149	3,305	19,454
1980	18,857	3,803	22,660
1981	21,578	4,368	25,946
1982	21,741	4,720	26,461
1983	30,375	5,244	35,619
1984	33,756	5,599	39,355
1985	38,414	5,805	44,219
1986	52,807	9,895	62,702
1987	66,036	9,722	75,758
1988	83,184	9,897	93,756
1989	87,300	11,857	99,712
1990	87,856	10,146	98,002
1991	74,828	8,807	83,635
1992	68,227	8,814	77,684
1993	67,139	9,291	76,430
1994	75,191	12,040	87,231
1995	83,884	13,372	97,256
1996	90,000	16,000	106,000
1997	104,091	14,313	118,404
1998	102,000	13,000	115,000
1999 (estimated)	NA	NA	115,000
2000	107,934	15,266	123,200
2001	112,161	18,798	130,959
2002	117,401	20,042	137,443

IOWA WHITETAIL RECORDS

- **Record harvest:** 137,443 (2002)
- **Record low harvest:** 2,423 (1954)
- **Bow-hunting record:** 20,042 (2002)
- **Gun-hunting record:** 117,401 (2002)

- **Season to remember:** 2002. Iowa hunters kill a record 137,443 whitetails. Just 17 years earlier, Hawkeye hunters killed only 44,219.

A Historic Look At Iowa's Deer Herd

When settlers arrived in what is now Iowa in the early 1800s, white-tailed deer were plentiful. At first, clearing of the land boosted deer populations, but as settlers increasingly harvested deer for food and hides, deer numbers plummeted. By 1880, deer were scarce, and in 1898, the deer season was closed.

Deer began repopulating the state through translocation, releases and escapes from captive herds and from natural immigration. In 1936, the state conservatively estimated it contained 500 to 700 whitetails.

By 1950, deer were reported in most counties and the statewide estimate was more than 10,000 deer. As deer became concentrated, Iowa reported its first cases of crop damage, and the first modern deer season was held in 1953. That year, hunters killed 4,000 deer.

The current deer population is approximately 350,000 deer, with hunters harvesting more than 100,000 deer annually in recent years.

– Iowa Dept. of Natural Resources

IOWA SNAPSHOT

Deer Population: 350,000, 21st in U.S.
Average Harvest: 124,320, 20th in U.S.
Forested Land: 2 million acres
Harvest Calculation Method: Surveys
Does State Predict Annual Harvest? Yes
How Close is Annual Prediction? 5%
Gun-Hunters: 173,497
Bow-Hunters: 45,787
Muzzleloading Hunters: 23,862
Hunter Education: Required for persons born after Jan. 1, 1967. Bow-hunter education is not required.
Orange Required for Gun-Hunting? Yes

KANSAS
Sunflower State

Harvest Ranking: #24

For more information, contact:
Department of Wildlife
Box 1525
Emporia, KS 66801
(620) 672-5911   www.kdwp.state.ks.us

HISTORY OF KANSAS' WHITETAIL HARVEST

Year	Firearm	Bow	Total
1965	1,340	164	1,504
1966	2,139	376	2,515
1967	1,542	434	1,976
1968	1,648	614	2,262
1969	1,668	583	2,251
1970	2,418	793	3,211
1971	2,569	578	3,147
1972	2,318	664	2,982
1973	3,220	892	4,112
1974	4,347	1,130	5,477
1975	4,352	1,136	5,488
1976	3,955	1,114	5,069
1977	3,766	1,174	4,940
1978	4,942	1,738	6,680
1979	5,810	2,259	8,069
1980	7,296	3,007	10,303
1981	9,413	2,939	12,352
1982	11,446	3,441	14,887
1983	13,640	3,918	17,558
1984	19,446	4,167	23,613
1985	21,296	4,230	25,526
1986	24,123	4,358	28,481
1987	31,664	4,329	35,993
1988	35,236	5,118	40,354
1989	34,000	5,550	39,550
1990	40,800	5,000	45,800
1991	41,803	NA	41,803
1992	31,750	NA	31,750
1993	33,590	NA	33,590
1994	36,040	7,800	43,840
1995	39,390	7,200	46,590
1996	43,550	8,500	52,050
1997	53,440	9,700	63,140
1998	73,100	8,000	81,100
1999	84,230	11,770	96,000
2000	NA	NA	108,000
2001	88,856	9,259	98,115
2002	77,000	10,000	87,000

KANSAS SNAPSHOT

Deer Population: 250,000, 25th in U.S.
Average Harvest: 94,043, 24th in U.S.
Forested Land: 1.36 million acres
Gun-Hunters: 74,126
Bow-Hunters: 21,508
Muzzleloading Hunters: 4,909
Hunter Education: Required for persons born after July 1, 1957. Bow-hunter education is not required.
Orange Required for Gun-Hunting? Yes

P&Y and B&C Directory

P&Y and B&C Scorers
Robert Barbee, Pratt, (620) 672-5911
Tommie Berger, Sylvan Grove, (785) 658-2465
Tom E. Bowman, Pratt, (785) 461-5739
Bill Hlavachick, Pratt, (620) 672-2084
Ron Little, Topeka, (785) 273-6740
Mike McFadden, Lawrence, (785) 295-2530
Tom Mosher, Emporia, (620) 342-0658
David Rogers, El Dorado, (316) 321-1496
Scott Showalter, Garden City, (620) 275-9426
Keith Sexson, Pratt, (620) 672-5911
Steve Sorenson, Valley Center, (316) 755-2239
Mark Steffen, Hutchinson, (620) 662-2121
Tom Swan, Wichita, (316) 683-8069
Charlie Swank, Great Bend, (620) 793-3066
Marvin Whitehead, Fredonia, (620) 378-3251

P&Y Only
Lloyd Fox, Emporia, (620) 342-0658
Matt Gideon, St. Francis, (785) 332-2763
Michael Gilbert, Garden City, (620) 275-4755
Blake Grabast, Osborne, (785) 346-5771
Wally Hayward, Kansas City, (913) 788-5164
Gary Hunsicker, Topeka, (785) 246-4033
Dale/Connie Larson, Olsburg, (785) 468-3640
Lynn Leonard, Sublette, (620) 675-8318
Stan Mangas, Onaga, (785) 889-4447
Drew McCartney, Gorham, (785) 637-5421
Toddy Murray, Buhler, (620) 543-2249
Michael Murphy, Sylvia, (620) 486-2962
Michael Sohm, Great Bend, (620) 793-9222
Odie Sudbeck, Seneca, (785) 336-3144
Daniel Willems, Windom, (620) 489-6462
Greg Wright, Wichita, (316) 681-3171

KANSAS WHITETAIL RECORDS

•**Record harvest:** 108,000 (2000)
•**Record low harvest:** 1,504 (1965)
•**Bow-hunting record:** 11,770 (1999)
•**Gun-hunting record:** 92,500 (2001)

•**Season to remember:** 1999. Kansas bow-hunters kill 11,770 deer, doubling the archery harvest from just 10 years earlier.

KENTUCKY
Bluegrass State
Harvest Ranking: #21

For more information, contact:
Department of Wildlife
#1 Game Farm Road
Frankfort, KY 40601
(800) 858-1549   www.state.ky.us

HISTORY OF KENTUCKY'S WHITETAIL HARVEST

Year	Firearm	Bow	Total
1976	3,476	NA	3,476
1977	5,682	NA	5,682
1978	6,012	421	6,433
1979	7,442	620	8,062
1980	7,988	1,714	9,702
1981	13,134	1,849	14,983
1982	15,804	2,165	17,969
1983	16,027	2,705	18,732
1984	20,344	2,668	23,012
1985	26,024	4,051	30,075
1986	34,657	4,863	39,520
1987	54,372	6,000	60,372
1988	57,553	6,707	64,260
1989	62,667	7,482	70,149
1990	66,151	7,767	73,918
1991	84,918	8,016	92,934
1992	73,664	8,274	81,938
1993	64,598	8,680	73,278
1994	93,444	12,672	106,116
1995	98,033	12,900	110,933
1996	98,430	13,010	111,440
1997	NA	NA	109,496
1998	94,299	9,771	104,070
1999	83,309	11,920	95,229
2000	138,821	18,500	157,321
2001	90,278	13,006	103,284
2002	102,141	12,941	115,082

Kentucky's Top Deer Counties

Where's the best place to hunt deer in Kentucky? Well, if sheer numbers are what you're after, it's hard to beat Owen, Crittenden, Lawrence, Shelby and Christian counties.

In 2000, Owen County hunters bagged a state-high 3,098 whitetails, including 1,374 bucks. In Crittenden County, hunters bagged 2,597 deer (1,069 bucks). Rounding out the Top 5 were Lawrence, 2,368, (993); Shelby, 2,057, (938); and Christian, 2,027, (911).

KENTUCKY WHITETAIL RECORDS

- **Record harvest:** 157,321 (2000)
- **Record low harvest:** 3,476 (1976)
- **Bow-hunting record:** 18,500 (2000)
- **Gun-hunting record:** 138,821 (2000)

- **Season to remember:** 2001. Kentucky hunters kill 103,284 deer. Although that harvest is the eighth-highest in state history, it's about 35 percent lower than the record-breaking 2000 harvest.

Kentucky DNR Urges Citizens to Treat Public Lands With Respect

Kentucky's wildlife-management areas are a gift to the citizens of the commonwealth provided by those who purchase hunting and fishing licenses and register boats. License fees allow the Kentucky DNR to buy land so everyone has a place to enjoy the outdoors, not just hunters and anglers. Thousands of acres of Kentucky's natural areas are available for hunting, fishing, bird watching, hiking or a simple picnic, thanks to sportsmen's dollars.

Unfortunately, some people don't value these gifts. They use public lands to dump household trash, leftover debris from construction or remodeling projects, old tires, old appliances and other unsightly junk. Or, they use signs for target practice or tear them down, vandalize picnic areas or drive their vehicles off road where they aren't allowed.

Concerned citizens may help stymie this kind of activity on WMAs. If you see dumping, vehicles off maintained roads, shooting of signs or any other form of destructive activities, call (800) 25ALERT to report it.

— *Kentucky Department of Wildlife*

KENTUCKY SNAPSHOT

Deer Population: 611,191, 16th in U.S.
Average Harvest: 114,997, 21st in U.S.
Forested Land: 12.7 million acres
Harvest Calculation Method: Mandatory registration
Does State Predict Annual Harvest? Yes
How Close is Annual Prediction? 5%
Gun-Hunters: 199,500
Bow-Hunters: 72,450
Muzzleloading Hunters: 89,890
Hunter Education: Required for persons born after Jan. 1, 1975. Bow-hunter education is also required.
Orange Required for Gun-Hunting? Yes

LOUISIANA
Pelican State

Harvest Ranking: #10

For more information, contact:
Department of Wildlife
Box 98000
Baton Rouge, LA 70898
(225) 765-2887 www.wlf.state.la.us

HISTORY OF LOUISIANA'S WHITETAIL HARVEST

Year	Firearm	Bow	Total
1961-62	NA	NA	NA
1962-63	NA	NA	NA
1963-64	24,000	NA	24,000
1964-65	23,000	NA	23,000
1965-66	26,000	NA	26,000
1966-67	32,500	NA	32,500
1967-68	36,000	NA	36,000
1968-69	50,000	NA	50,000
1969-70	53,000	NA	53,000
1970-71	53,500	NA	53,500
1971-72	61,000	NA	61,000
1972-73	65,000	NA	65,000
1973-74	74,500	NA	74,500
1974-75	82,000	NA	82,000
1975-76	77,000	NA	77,000
1976-77	84,500	NA	84,500
1977-78	82,500	NA	82,500
1978-79	85,000	NA	85,000
1979-80	90,000	5,000	95,000
1980-81	105,500	5,000	110,500
1981-82	115,000	5,500	120,500
1982-83	132,000	5,500	137,500
1983-84	131,000	6,000	137,000
1984-85	128,000	6,500	134,500
1985-86	139,000	7,500	146,500
1986-87	149,000	8,750	157,750
1987-88	164,000	9,500	173,500
1988-89	161,000	10,500	171,500
1989-90	162,000	11,000	173,000
1990-91	176,200	18,200	194,300
1991-92	186,400	17,700	204,100
1992-93	192,300	22,600	214,900
1993-94	193,000	20,100	213,100
1994-95	210,200	27,200	237,400
1995-96	208,500	26,200	234,700
1996-97	220,000	25,000	245,000
1997-98	243,400	24,200	267,600
1998-99	222,300	21,100	243,400
1999-00	246,900	20,500	267,400
2000-01	256,000	20,000	276,000
2001-02	193,800	18,400	212,200
2002-03	219,189	20,811	240,000

LOUISIANA WHITETAIL RECORDS

- **Record harvest:** 276,000 (2000-01)
- **Record low harvest:** 16,500 (1960-61)
- **Bow-hunting record:** 27,200 (1994-95)
- **Gun-hunting record:** 256,000 (2000-01)

- **Season to remember:** 2000-01. Louisiana bow- and gun-hunters kill an estimated 276,000 whitetails, breaking the previous record harvest of 267,600, set in 1997-98.

Antler Restrictions Proposed

The Louisiana Wildlife and Fisheries Commission has included an experimental deer season with antler restrictions in its proposal for future seasons.

It is proposed that during future deer hunting seasons, only bucks with six or more points, or spikes having both spikes three inches or less, would be considered legal bucks. An exception would be made for the special youth deer hunt (either sex) in early November, when any buck would be legal. A legal "point" is a projection that is at least one inch long, and the length is longer than the width. The beam tip counts as a legal point.

Violation of any of the provisions of the rules and regulations of this experimental season would be a Class Two violation. The fine for a first offense of a Class Two violation is a fine of up to $350, up to 60 days in jail, or both.

This experimental season is part of the proposal that the commission will vote to ratify. Pictures of legal and illegal deer, as well as point measuring, are available in the News and Events section of the LDWF Web site.

— Louisiana Dept. of Wildlife & Fisheries

LOUISIANA SNAPSHOT

Deer Population: 1 million, 7th in U.S.
Average Harvest: 247,800, 10th in U.S.
Forested Land: 13.86 million acres
Harvest Calculation Method: Surveys
Does State Predict Annual Harvest? Yes
How Close is Annual Prediction? 10%
Gun-Hunters: 182,529
Bow-Hunters: 51,342
Muzzleloading Hunters: 51,494
Hunter Education: Required for persons born after Sept. 1, 1969. Bow-hunter education is not required.
Orange Required for Gun-Hunting? Yes

MAINE
Pine Tree State
Harvest Ranking: #33

For more information, contact:
Department of Inland Fisheries and Wildlife
284 State St., State House Station 41
Augusta, ME 04333
(207) 287-2571   www.state.me.us/ifw

HISTORY OF MAINE'S DEER HARVEST

Year	Firearm	Bow	Total
1919	5,784	NA	5,784
1929	11,708	NA	11,708
1939	19,187	NA	19,187
1949	35,051	NA	35,051
1959	41,720	15	41,735
1969	30,388	21	30,409

32-YEAR HISTORY

Year	Firearm	Bow	Total
1971	18,873	30	18,903
1972	28,664	34	28,698
1973	24,681	39	24,720
1974	34,602	65	34,667
1975	34,625	50	34,675
1976	29,918	47	29,965
1977	31,354	76	31,430
1978	28,905	97	29,002
1979	26,720	101	26,821
1980	37,148	107	37,255
1981	32,027	140	32,167
1982	28,709	125	28,834
1983	23,699	100	23,799
1984	19,225	133	19,358
1985	21,242	182	21,424
1986	19,290	302	19,592
1987	23,435	294	23,729
1988	27,754	302	28,056
1989	29,844	416	30,260
1990	25,658	319	25,977
1991	26,236	500	26,736
1992	28,126	694	28,820
1993	26,608	682	27,402
1994	23,967	716	24,683
1995	26,233	1,151	27,384
1996	27,601	774	28,375
1997	30,149	1,003	31,152
1998	26,996	1,245	28,241
1999	29,361	2,112	31,473
2000	34,724	2,161	36,885
2001	25,558	2,211	27,769
2002	35,571	2,029	37,600

MAINE WHITETAIL RECORDS

- **Record harvest:** 41,735 (1959)
- **Record low harvest:** 5,784 (1919)
- **Bow-hunting record:** 2,211 (2001)
- **Gun-hunting record:** 41,730 (1951)

- **Season to remember:** 1999. After decades of relatively low deer harvests, Maine bow-hunters kill a record 2,112 whitetails.

Video Cautions Against Winter Feeding

The Maine Department of Inland Fisheries and Wildlife has produced a video explaining why deer should not be supplementally fed in winter. *What You Should Know About Supplemental Feeding* acknowledges that most people are well intentioned, but don't realize that by feeding deer, they increase disease, deer losses to predators, depredation by dogs, motor vehicle accidents and browsing on shrubs in suburban areas.

The video promotes improving the amount and quality of wintering habitat as the best way to ensure viable, healthy deer populations and points out ways people can protect and maintain this critical habitat.

The video can be purchased by calling (207) 287-8000 or online at www.mefish-wildlife.com.

MAINE SNAPSHOT

Deer Population: 342,000, 22nd in U.S.
Average Harvest: 32,394, 33rd in U.S.
Forested Land: 17.5 million acres
Harvest Calculation Method: Mandatory registration
Does State Predict Annual Harvest? Yes
How Close is Annual Prediction? 5%
Gun-Hunters: 175,200
Bow-Hunters: 9,250
Muzzleloading Hunters: 11,000
Hunter Education: Required for all first-time hunters. Bow-hunter education is also required.
Orange Required for Gun-Hunting? Yes

MARYLAND
Old Line State

Harvest Ranking: #26

For more information, contact:
Division of Wildlife
4220 Steele Neck Road
Vienna, MD 21869
(410) 260-8200 www.dnr.state.md.us

HISTORY OF MARYLAND'S WHITETAIL HARVEST

Year	Firearm	Bow	Total
1983	16,239	2,181	18,420
1984	17,324	2,501	19,825
1985	17,241	2,549	19,790
1986	22,411	3,404	25,815
1987	24,846	4,216	29,062
1988	27,625	5,983	33,608
1989	38,305	7,988	46,293
1990	37,712	8,605	46,317
1991	36,169	10,454	46,623
1992	39,858	11,240	51,098
1993	39,429	11,251	51,234
1994	39,547	11,324	50,871
1995	49,237	12,397	61,634
1996	39,048	13,588	52,636
1997	52,600	12,919	65,519
1998	57,270	16,300	93,570
1999	59,963	16,214	76,177
2000	66,535	18,241	84,776
2001	65,431	18,356	83,787
2002	75,026	19,088	94,114

Maryland Recognizes Outstanding Bucks

Each year, the Maryland Bowhunters Society and the DNR co-sponsor the *Maryland Trophy Deer Contest*. This contest recognizes hunters who have killed big bucks and promotes quality deer management in Maryland.

The contest is open only for deer taken legally in Maryland. A possession tag is required. Deer taken with crop damage permits and road-killed deer are not eligible.

For more information, contact the Maryland Department of Natural Resources at the address or phone number listed at the top of this page.

MARYLAND WHITETAIL RECORDS

- **Record harvest:** 94,114 (2002)
- **Record low harvest:** 18,420 (1983)
- **Bow-hunting record:** 19,088 (2002)
- **Gun-hunting record:** 75,026 (2002)

- **Season to remember:** 2002. Maryland hunters kill a record 94,114 deer, breaking state record kill numbers for both bow and gun-hunting.

Maryland Earmarks $1 Per Deer License For Venison Program

The Maryland Department of Natural Resources used a little creativity to come up with a way to control its burgeoning deer population and find a reliable funding source for its venison-donation program.

In 2002, Tim Lambert, of the Maryland Sportsmen's Association, along with State Senator John Astle and Paul Peditto, director of the Wildlife and Heritage Service of the MDNR, successfully pushed for a $12 increase in the state's deer hunting license. It was the first deer license increase since 1989.

The bill met little opposition in the legislature because $1 from the increase was earmarked to fund the state's venison-donation program. The MDNR said the license increase would raise about $100,000 for the venison-donation program.

— *C.J. Winand*

MARYLAND SNAPSHOT

Deer Population: 224,000, 27th in U.S.
Average Harvest: 86,485, 26th in U.S.
Forested Land: 2.7 million acres
Harvest Calculation Method: Mandatory registration

Does State Predict Annual Harvest? No
How Close is Annual Prediction? NA

Gun-Hunters: 69,400
Bow-Hunters: 35,770
Muzzleloading Hunters: 37,200

Hunter Education: Required for persons born after July 1, 1977. Bow-hunter education is not required.

Orange Required for Gun-Hunting? Yes

MASSACHUSETTS
Bay State

Harvest Ranking: #38

For more information, contact:
Massachusetts Wildlife
Westborough, MA 01581
(617) 727-1614
www.state.ma.us/dfwele

HISTORY OF MASSACHUSETTS' DEER HARVEST

Year	Firearm	Bow	Total
1990	5,829	1,061	6,890
1991	8,085	1,378	9,463
1992	8,470	1,570	10,040
1993	6,514	1,387	8,345
1994	7,545	1,587	9,132
1995	9,158	1,901	11,059
1996	7,029	1,687	8,714
1997	8,473	1,813	10,286
1998	7,501	1,803	9,304
1999	7,042	2,466	9,508
2000	8,297	2,765	11,096
2001	6,915	2,914	9,930
2002	9,434	2,819	12,264

Program Encourages Women To Enjoy the Outdoors

In an effort to attract more women to outdoor sports, Massachusetts holds several "Becoming an Outdoors Woman" programs each year.

These programs focus on outdoor skills — skills traditionally passed from father to son — but valuable to anyone wishing to enjoy outdoor pursuits. A sampling of workshop offerings can include fishing, shooting, kayaking, orienteering, reading the woods, archery, pond and stream adventures, nature photography and game cooking. Designed primarily for women, it is an opportunity for anyone 18 or older who wants an opportunity to learn outdoor skills. The program is co-sponsored by the Massachusetts Sportsmen's Council.

For more information, contact the Massachusetts Division of Wildlife at the address/phone number listed at the top of this page, or visit www.magnet.state.ma.us

MASSACHUSETTS DEER RECORDS

- Record harvest: 12,264 (2002)
- Record low harvest: 6,708 (1989)
- Bow-hunting record: 2,914 (2001)
- Gun-hunting record: 9,434 (2002)

- Season to remember: 2002. Massachusetts bow- and gun-hunters kill a record 12,264 whitetails, about 25 percent of which were bow-kills.

State Bans Deer Imports

Massachusetts has joined with other northeastern states to prohibit the importation of all species of deer. This is a precautionary measure to prevent the spread of chronic wasting disease into wild or farm-raised deer. The importation prohibition takes effect immediately and applies to European red deer, sika deer, fallow deer and reindeer, all species commonly raised commercially. The farming or importation of white-tailed deer, elk or moose was not permitted prior to the newly-enacted restrictions.

Massachusetts' action follows deer-importation bans in New York and Vermont, as well as a resolution passed by the Association of Northeastern U.S. Fish & Wildlife Agency Directors. CWD is a relatively new disease and is not fully understood.

CWD has been diagnosed in captive deer and elk herds in Colorado, Wyoming, Nebraska, Montana, Oklahoma, South Dakota, Wisconsin and Minnesota and the Canadian province of Saskatchewan. It has been confirmed in wild deer populations in Colorado, Wyoming, Nebraska, Wisconsin, New Mexico and Illinois. There are no known cases of the disease in Massachusetts.

— *Massachusetts Dept. of Fish and Game*

MASSACHUSETTS SNAPSHOT

Deer Population: 90,000, 31st in U.S.

Average Harvest: 10,420, 38th in U.S.

Forested Land: 3.2 million acres

Harvest Calculation Method: Mandatory registration

Does State Predict Annual Harvest? No

How Close is Annual Prediction? NA

Gun-Hunters: 61,500

Bow-Hunters: 25,500

Muzzleloading Hunters: 18,150

Hunter Education: Required for first-time hunters and hunters ages 15 to 18. Bow-hunter education is not required.

Orange Required for Gun-Hunting? Yes

MICHIGAN
Wolverine State
Harvest Ranking: #1

For more information, contact:
Department of Natural Resources
Box 30028
Lansing, MI 48909
www.dnr.state.mi.us

HISTORY OF MICHIGAN'S WHITETAIL HARVEST

Year	Firearm	Bow	Total
1899	NA	NA	12,000
1911	NA	NA	12,000
1920	NA	NA	25,000
1929	NA	NA	28,710
1939	44,770	6	44,776
1949	77,750	780	78,530
1959	115,400	1,840	117,240
1969	106,698	2,582	109,280

32-YEAR HISTORY

Year	Firearms	Bow	Total
1971	62,076	3,354	65,430
1972	55,796	3,694	59,490
1973	66,359	4,631	70,990
1974	92,111	7,969	100,080
1975	106,800	8,790	115,590
1976	107,625	10,365	117,990
1977	137,110	21,250	158,360
1978	145,710	25,140	170,850
1979	119,790	25,640	145,430
1980	137,380	28,110	165,490
1981	175,090	33,320	208,410
1982	163,520	38,420	201,940
1983	127,770	30,640	158,410
1984	131,280	32,630	163,910
1985	197,370	42,050	239,420
1986	219,260	57,960	277,220
1987	265,860	72,820	338,680
1988	311,770	72,020	383,790
1989	355,410	97,080	452,490
1990	338,890	93,800	432,690
1991	318,460	115,880	434,340
1992	274,650	99,990	374,640
1993	232,820	98,160	330,980
1994	251,420	112,490	363,910
1995	346,830	132,130	478,960
1996	319,289	100,000	419,289
1997	282,000	100,000	382,000
1998	329,000	121,000	450,000
1999	402,280	142,615	544,895
2000	412,775	128,926	541,701
2001	343,788	119,918	463,706
2002	358,440	117,775	476,215

MICHIGAN WHITETAIL RECORDS

- **Record harvest:** 544,895 (1999)
- **Record low harvest:** 8,000 (1916)
- **Bow-hunting record:** 142,615 (1999)
- **Gun-hunting record:** 412,775 (2000)

- **Season to remember:** 1999. Michigan hunters break several state records, including the all-time harvest. The overall harvest is second only to Wisconsin's 2000 harvest of 618,274 whitetails.

Michigan DNR Supports Quality Deer Management

The Michigan DNR supports the voluntary implementation of quality seer management on private lands in Michigan. QDM is an approach that restricts the buck harvest and sustains the antlerless harvest to produce a more balanced sex ratio in the herd and a population in balance with the habitat.

This year four proposals for mandatory restrictions on buck harvest have been received. Public meeting dates in the proposed area have been scheduled, and a formal survey of a sample of landowners and hunters in the affected area will be conducted this fall.

When a clear majority (66 percent) of both hunters and landowners support implementation, the proposed regulations will be submitted for approval by the Natural Resources Commission. If approved, the proposed regulations will take effect in the 2003 deer hunting seasons for a five-year period. Collection of biological data from 100 bucks and 200 antlerless deer each year is required to determine whether the regulations are having the desired impact. The biological and social aspects of the regulations will be re-evaluated in the fourth year of the experiment.

— Michigan Dept. of Natural Resources

MICHIGAN SNAPSHOT

Deer Population: 1.9 million, 2nd in U.S.

Average Harvest: 495,303, 1st in U.S.

Forested Land: 18.25 million acres

Harvest Calculation Method: Surveys

Does State Predict Annual Harvest? No

How Close is Annual Prediction? NA

Gun-Hunters: 721,980

Bow-Hunters: 351,077

Muzzleloading Hunters: 174,505

Hunter Education: Required for persons born after Jan. 1, 1969. Bow-hunter education is not required.

Orange Required for Gun-Hunting? Yes

MINNESOTA
Gopher State
Harvest Ranking: #13

For more information, contact:
Department of Natural Resources
Box 7, 500 Lafayette Road
St. Paul, MN 55155
(651) 296-4506   www.dnr.state.mn.us

HISTORY OF MINNESOTA'S WHITETAIL HARVEST

Year	Firearm	Bow	Total
1918	9,000	NA	9,000
1928	27,300	NA	27,300
1938	44,500	NA	44,500
1948	61,600	NA	61,600
1958	75,000	403	75,403
1968	103,000	819	103,819
1978	57,800	2,608	60,408
1988	138,900	8,262	147,162

33-YEAR HISTORY

Year	Firearms	Bow	Total
1970	50,000	453	50,453
1971	closed	1,279	1,279
1972	73,400	1,601	75,001
1973	67,100	1,935	69,035
1974	65,000	2,176	67,176
1975	63,600	2,265	65,865
1976	36,200	1,167	37,367
1977	58,100	2,609	60,709
1978	57,800	2,608	60,408
1979	55,400	2,578	57,978
1980	77,100	3,641	80,741
1981	108,100	5,535	113,635
1982	107,000	5,566	112,566
1983	NA	5,977	NA
1984	132,000	6,390	138,390
1985	138,000	7,575	145,575
1986	129,800	7,610	137,410
1987	135,000	7,535	142,535
1988	138,900	8,262	147,162
1989	129,600	9,307	138,907
1990	166,600	11,106	177,706
1991	206,300	12,964	219,264
1992	230,064	13,004	243,068
1993	188,109	13,722	202,928
1994	180,008	13,818	193,826
1995	200,645	14,521	215,166
1996	142,979	14,338	157,317
1997	130,069	13,258	143,327
1998	146,548	12,306	158,854
1999	166,487	13,000	179,487
2000	193,754	15,746	209,500
2001	201,557	15,895	217,452
2002	207,306	14,744	222,050

MINNESOTA WHITETAIL RECORDS

- **Record harvest:** 243,068 (1992)
- **Record low harvest:** 1,279 (1971)
- **Bow-hunting record:** 15,895 (2001)
- **Gun-hunting record:** 230,064 (1992)

- **Season to remember:** 1928. In an era when most states' deer herds were all but nonexistent, Minnesota hunters kill 27,300 whitetails.

Minnesota Tests 4,462 Deer for Chronic Wasting Disease

In response to the discovery of chronic wasting disease in neighboring South Dakota and Wisconsin, and nearby Illinois, Minnesota tested 4,462 wild, hunter-killed deer for CWD in 2002. No cases of CWD were reported.

However, two CWD-positive captive elk were identified within the state's borders earlier in the year. In August 2002, an Aitkin County elk tested positive for CWD, and a captive Stearns County elk was diagnosed with CWD soon after.

Archers, landowners and sharpshooters quickly moved in to kill 69 wild deer near the Aitkin County game farm where the CWD-positive elk lived, but no evidence of the fatal disease was found in those wild deer.

Members of the Minnesota Department of Natural Resources, tribal staff and volunteers collected hunter-killed deer from 17 permit areas around the state. Veterinarians also collected more than 500 deer from concerned hunters, but no deer were diagnosed with CWD.

In 2003, Minnesota plans to test 12,000 whitetails for CWD.

—Joe Shead

MINNESOTA SNAPSHOT

Deer Population: 960,000, 10th in U.S.

Average Harvest: 197,469, 13th in U.S.

Forested Land: 16.7 million acres

Harvest Calculation Method: Mandatory registration

Does State Predict Annual Harvest? No

How Close is Annual Prediction? NA

Gun-Hunters: 460,300

Bow-Hunters: 70,218

Muzzleloading Hunters: 11,037

Hunter Education: Required for persons born after Jan. 1, 1980. Bow-hunter education is not required.

Orange Required for Gun-Hunting? Yes

MISSISSIPPI
Magnolia State

Harvest Ranking: #7

For more information, contact:
Department of Conservation
Southport Mall, Box 451
Jackson, MS 39205
(800) 546-4868   www.mdwfp.com

HISTORY OF MISSISSIPPI'S WHITETAIL HARVEST

Year	Firearm	Bow	Total
1971	580	39	619
1972	816	53	869
1973	919	57	976
1974	NA	NA	NA
1975	NA	NA	NA
1976	2,529	975	3,504
1977	NA	NA	NA
1978	NA	NA	NA
1979	NA	NA	NA
1980	184,163	17,437	201,600
1981	196,856	14,860	211,716
1982	227,432	16,222	243,654
1983	176,400	19,747	196,147
1984	209,574	17,815	227,389
1985	216,959	18,120	235,079
1986	237,075	19,209	256,284
1987	240,337	24,662	264,999
1988	236,012	28,744	264,756
1989	236,012	28,744	262,386
1990	218,347	29,982	249,572
1991	243,175	33,940	277,714
1992	260,093	40,886	300,980
1993	229,425	32,971	262,409
1994	262,342	47,345	309,687
1995	286,293	48,669	334,962
1996	289,399	44,574	333,973
1997	284,190	48,119	332,309
1998	256,692	38,406	295,098
2000	243,000	33,000	276,000
2001	306,248	43,000	321,000

Ample Land and Deer Make Mississippi a Hunting Leader

Mississippi has more than 800,000 acres of public hunting lands held in 38 intensively managed wildlife management areas. Mississippi also has one of the country's largest deer populations, making the state a prime hunting destination.

MISSISSIPPI WHITETAIL RECORDS

- **Record harvest:** 334,962 (1995-96)
- **Record low harvest:** 619 (1971)
- **Bow-hunting record:** 48,669 (1995-96)
- **Gun-hunting record:** 289,399 (1996-97)

- **Season to remember:** 1995-96. Mississippi bow- and gun-hunters kill a record 334,962 deer. Only 19 years earlier, the harvest was 3,504 — almost 99 percent less.

Quality Food Sources Bring Big Bucks

Last fall began with exceptional habitat conditions created by above-normal rainfall throughout the summer growing season. Fall was abnormally wet and produced a challenge to farmers attempting to harvest cotton and soybeans. Many supplemental plantings of cereal grains and clovers were inundated with rainfall during the September-October planting period, a time when moisture is normally limited. As a result, native browse was plentiful and high in quality while supplemental plantings were sparse and not as attractive to deer.

Acorn production was outstanding during 2002-2003. The majority of the state experienced a second year of good production from most oak species. A banner acorn year normally causes poor hunter success because deer are not concentrated around isolated producing trees.

Poor deer movement resulted in low hunter success and the regular complaint that deer populations had been excessively reduced by continued antlerless seasons. The cumulative effects of the fall conditions were minimal food plot use by deer, poor hunting success around mast trees and decreased movement by deer because native foods were plentiful.

— *Mississippi Wildlife, Fisheries & Parks*

MISSISSIPPI SNAPSHOT

Deer Population: 1.5 million, 5th in U.S.

Average Harvest: 311,676, 7th in U.S.

Forested Land: 17 million acres

Harvest Calculation Method: Surveys

Does State Predict Annual Harvest? No

How Close is Annual Prediction? NA

Gun-Hunters: 182,000

Bow-Hunters: 49,500

Muzzleloading Hunters: 49,000

Hunter Education: Required for persons born after Jan. 1, 1972. Bow-hunter education is not required.

Orange Required for Gun-Hunting? Yes

MISSOURI
Show-Me State
Harvest Ranking: #11

For more information, contact:
Department of Conservation
Box 180
Jefferson City, MO 65102-0180
(573) 751-4115
www.conservation.state.mo.us

HISTORY OF MISSOURI'S WHITETAIL HARVEST

Year	Firearm	Bow	Total
1944	583	NA	583
1948	1,432	NA	1,432
1952	7,466	2	7,468
1956	7,864	33	7,897
1960	17,418	263	17,681
1964	20,619	316	20,935
1968	22,090	559	22,649

33-YEAR HISTORY

Year	Firearm	Bow	Total
1970	28,400	828	29,228
1971	31,722	962	32,684
1972	30,084	1,130	31,214
1973	33,438	1,285	34,723
1974	29,262	1,437	30,699
1975	51,823	1,850	53,673
1976	40,683	1,973	42,656
1977	36,562	2,199	38,761
1978	40,261	2,781	43,042
1979	53,164	3,327	56,491
1980	49,426	3,661	53,087
1981	50,183	3,495	53,678
1982	55,852	4,191	60,043
1983	57,801	4,626	62,427
1984	71,569	5,134	76,703
1985	80,792	5,621	86,413
1986	102,879	5,832	108,711
1987	132,500	8,077	140,577
1988	139,726	10,183	149,909
1989	157,506	10,970	168,476
1990	161,857	11,118	172,975
1991	149,112	14,096	164,384
1992	150,873	15,029	166,929
1993	156,704	14,696	172,120
1994	164,624	17,136	181,760
1995	187,406	20,077	207,483
1996	190,770	23,566	214,336
1997	196,283	20,915	217,198
1998	207,764	20,000	227,764
1999	193,720	23,414	217,134
2000	220,495	23,558	244,053
2001	234,752	26,165	257,910
2002	249,858	29,587	279,445

MISSOURI WHITETAIL RECORDS

- **Record harvest:** 279,445 (2002)
- **Record low harvest:** 583 (1944)
- **Bow-hunting record:** 29,587 (2002)
- **Gun-hunting record:** 249,858 (2002)

- **Season to remember:** 2002. Missouri bow- and gun-hunters kill 279,445 deer, surpassing the previous record set in 2001. Nearly 272,00 more deer were taken than in 1952, 50 years ago.

Billions Spent Enjoying Missouri's Wildlife in 2001

According to a survey from the U.S. Fish and Wildlife Service, 489,000 hunters; 1.2 million anglers; and 2.3 million wildlife watchers, feeders and photographers partook of their respective activities in Missouri in 2001.

Participants in these activities spent $1.99 billion in Missouri that year.

The survey also revealed that 738,000 wildlife watchers, feeders and photographers came to Missouri from out of state to enjoy these activities within the state's borders.

The survey also indicated that nationally, 13 million people hunted, spending $20.6 billion; 34 million people fished, spending $35.6 billion; and 66 million people watched, fed or photographed wildlife, spending $40 billion.

All told, 39 percent of Americans participated in these activities in 2001. Although the number was down slightly from the USFWS's 1991 survey, these expenditures accounted for 1.1 percent of the U.S. gross domestic product.

— *U.S Fish and Wildlife Service*

MISSOURI SNAPSHOT

Deer Population: 850,000, 13th in U.S.
Average Harvest: 245,261, 11th in U.S.
Forested Land: 14 million acres
Harvest Calculation Method: Mandatory registration
Does State Predict Annual Harvest? Yes
How Close is Annual Prediction? 10%
Gun-Hunters: 435,448
Bow-Hunters: 96,982
Muzzleloading Hunters: 15,500
Hunter Education: Required for persons born after Jan. 1, 1967. Bow-hunter education is not required.
Orange Required for Gun-Hunting? Yes

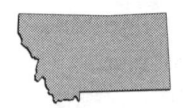

MONTANA
Treasure State

Harvest Ranking: #29

For more information, contact:
Department of Fish and Wildlife
1420 E. Sixth Ave.
Helena, MT 59620
(406) 444-2535   www.fwp.state.mt.us

HISTORY OF MONTANA'S ANNUAL DEER HARVEST

Year	Firearm	Bow	Total
1984	NA	NA	56,760
1985	NA	NA	43,019
1986	NA	NA	44,733
1987	NA	NA	40,675
1988	NA	NA	43,971
1989	NA	NA	44,261
1990	NA	NA	49,419
1991	NA	NA	56,789
1992	58,565	2,067	60,632
1993	60,369	2,038	62,407
1994	67,577	1,857	69,434
1995	60,907	1,636	62,543
1996	76,487	1,800	78,287
1997	70,000	1,600	71,600
1998	84,445	1,500	85,945
1999	41,798	3,031	44,809
2000	45,242	6,212	51,454
2001	36,208	2,559	38,767

*Totals before 1999 include mule deer harvest figures.

Montana Harbors Big Whitetails

Montana has a reputation as a top-notch elk hunting state, but its deer hunting opportunities are what lure most hunters.

Known for record-class whitetails and mule deer, Montana attracts more than 160,000 deer hunters annually. In fact, 70 percent of all big-game hunters in Montana hunt strictly for deer.

Including elk hunters and small-game hunters, Montana hunters spend more than $215 million each year to hunt the Treasure State. That's an average of $954 per hunter.

In 1996, Montana hunters spent more than $116 million on hunting equipment, according to a survey by the United States Fish & Wildlife Service.

MONTANA WHITETAIL RECORDS

- **Record harvest:** 85,945 (1998)
- **Record low harvest:** 38,767 (2001)
- **Bow-hunting record:** 6,212 (2000)
- **Gun-hunting record:** 84,445 (1998)

- **Season to remember:** 1999. For the first time in state history, Montana segregates mule deer and whitetail harvest figures. Montana hunters kill 44,809 whitetails.

Spring Rains May Stabilize State Deer Population

Wildlife officials said spring rains may help stabilize mule deer populations that suffered significant fawn losses over winter in parts of south-central and eastern Montana.

More than two decades of deer research in Montana shows that fawn survival depends on precipitation during late spring and early summer. Dry summers with little forage make it difficult for fawns to build the fat they need to survive winter. Older adult females also tend to be vulnerable if they are in poorer condition going into the winter.

While the total number of mule deer is at or above the long-term average in many of the areas surveyed, there were higher than average fawn losses in portions of FWP Regions 3, 4, 5, 6 and 7 that may lead to population declines if drought continues in these areas.

Overall, June's snow and rain is likely to improve forage in early summer, hopefully improving mule deer survival this winter. The question that concerns biologists is whether specific areas in the state with low over-winter fawn survival will receive enough precipitation this summer to turn the situation around.

— Montana Dept. of Fish and Wildlife

MONTANA SNAPSHOT

Deer Population: 400,000, 19th in U.S.

Average Harvest: 58,515, 29th in U.S.

Forested Land: 22.5 million acres

Harvest Calculation Method: Surveys and automobile checks

Does State Predict Annual Harvest? Yes

How Close is Annual Prediction? 20%

Gun-Hunters: 157,090

Bow-Hunters: 27,011

Muzzleloading Hunters: 2,020

Hunter Education: Required for persons age 12-17. Bow-hunter education is required for all first-time bow-hunters.

Orange Required for Gun-Hunting? Yes

NEBRASKA
Cornhusker State

Harvest Ranking: #31

For more information, contact:
Nebraska Game and Parks
Box 508
Bassett, NE 68714-0508
(402) 471-0641   www.ngpc.state.ne.us

HISTORY OF NEBRASKA'S WHITETAIL HARVEST

Year	Firearm	Bow	Total
1945	2	0	2
1949	0	0	0
1952	7	0	7
1955	189	0	189
1958	340	103	443
1961	1,443	198	1,641
1964	5,138	326	5,464
1969	5,440	524	5,964

33-YEAR HISTORY

Year	Firearms	Bow	Total
1970	6,460	654	7,114
1971	6,343	662	7,005
1972	5,635	624	6,259
1973	7,090	865	7,955
1974	7,894	1,032	8,926
1975	8,404	1,155	9,559
1976	7,595	831	8,426
1977	5,921	769	6,690
1978	6,164	958	7,122
1979	7,899	1,151	9,050
1980	9,939	1,639	11,578
1981	11,364	2,025	13,389
1982	12,957	2,049	15,006
1983	15,980	2,781	18,761
1984	19,679	2,471	22,150
1985	20,930	2,593	23,523
1986	22,859	2,291	25,150
1987	24,266	2,812	27,078
1988	24,938	2,951	27,889
1989	24,359	2,847	27,206
1990	21,973	2,716	24,689
1991	20,820	2,931	23,751
1992	20,125	3,141	23,266
1993	23,377	3,282	26,683
1994	26,050	3,830	29,880
1995	26,000	4,000	34,160
1996	30,400	4,500	34,560
1997	41,700	3,900	45,600
1998	38,085	3,887	41,972
1999	37,263	4,254	41,490
2000	39,200	4,300	43,500
2001	55,377	4,141	59,518
2002	46,000	7,600	53,600

NEBRASKA WHITETAIL RECORDS

- **Record harvest:** 59,518 (2001)
- **Record low harvest:** 0 (1949)
- **Bow-hunting record:** 7,600 (2002)
- **Gun-hunting record:** 55,377 (2001)

- **Season to remember:** 1949. With Nebraska's modern deer season in its infancy, the state's hunters experienced a trying season, failing to kill any deer.

Nebraska Has Deer Network

The Deer Network, a new program offered by the Nebraska Game and Parks Commission, will help connect landowners with too many deer on their land to hunters who can help control the deer herd.

During the winter, deer often congregate in areas where food is easily accessible. In many cases, especially in Nebraska's ranch country, the easiest food source is stacked hay. When deer get into haystacks, they can make a mess and leave the feed unusable for livestock.

Hunting can do two things for landowners. It will reduce the number of deer, but the hunting pressure also helps by dispersing the deer herd. The Commission hopes The Deer Network will help get more hunters and landowners together during the remainder of the archery and muzzle-loader deer hunting seasons.

Landowners in the Panhandle who have large herds of antelope wintering on their property can also subscribe to the Deer Network, making their names available to hunters with late-season antelope permits.

— *Nebraska Game & Parks Commission*

NEBRASKA SNAPSHOT

Deer Population: 300,000, 23rd in U.S.
Average Harvest: 48,016, 31st in U.S.
Forested Land: 426,000 acres
Harvest Calculation Method: Mandatory registration
Does State Predict Annual Harvest? No
How Close is Annual Prediction? NA
Gun-Hunters: 86,400
Bow-Hunters: 15,760
Muzzloading Hunters: 17,800
Hunter Education: Required for persons born after Jan. 1, 1977. Bow-hunter education is required.
Orange Required for Gun-Hunting? Yes

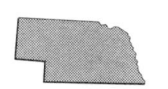

NEW HAMPSHIRE
Granite State
Harvest Ranking: #39

For more information, contact:
New Hampshire Fish & Game
Region 1, Rt. 2, Box 241
Lancaster, NH 03584
(603) 271-3422
www.wildlife.state.nh.us

HISTORY OF NEW HAMPSHIRE'S DEER HARVEST

Year	Firearm	Bow	Total
1922	1,896	NA	1,896
1932	1,687	NA	1,687
1942	4,844	NA	4,844
1952	6,932	NA	6,932
1962	7,917	5	7,922

33-YEAR HISTORY

Year	Firearm	Bow	Total
1970	7,214	17	7,231
1971	7,263	12	7,275
1972	6,923	20	6,943
1973	5,440	22	5,462
1974	6,875	20	6,895
1975	8,308	24	8,332
1976	9,076	14	9,090
1977	6,877	62	6,939
1978	5,545	57	5,602
1979	4,939	42	4,981
1980	5,353	31	5,384
1981	6,028	125	6,153
1982	4,577	97	4,674
1983	3,156	124	3,280
1984	4,169	120	4,289
1985	5,523	148	5,671
1986	6,557	263	6,820
1987	5,864	257	6,121
1988	5,900	225	6,125
1989	6,749	489	7,238
1990	6,466	482	7,872
1991	8,060	732	8,792
1992	9,013	1,202	10,215
1993	9,012	877	9,889
1994	7,478	901	8,379
1995	9,627	1,580	11,207
1996	8,901	1,462	10,363
1997	10,042	1,758	11,800
1998	8,236	1,549	9,785
1999	8,722	1,981	10,703
2000	8,889	1,970	10,859
2001	7,566	1,577	9,143
2002	9,235	1,854	11,089

NEW HAMPSHIRE DEER RECORDS

- **Record harvest:** 14,186 (1967)
- **Record low harvest:** 1,402 (1923)
- **Bow-hunting record:** 1,981 (1999)
- **Gun-hunting record:** 14,153 (1967)

- **Season to remember:** 1962. Five deer fall to New Hampshire bow-hunters — the first modern bow-killed deer in the state. By 1995, bow-hunters were killing about 15 percent of the state's total harvest.

State Lowers Restrictions On Hunter-Killed Cervid Imports

The New Hampshire Department of Agriculture continues to reinforce its ban on imported cervid meat, but is now allowing exemptions on some antlers, hides and capes.

As personal trophies, hunters are allowed to import a maximum of two sets of antlers/racks (with or without the skull cap) as their personal trophy. A larger number of antler/racks may be imported provided the quantity to be imported corresponds to the number authorized by a valid hunting license. For example, if the hunting license authorizes three elk to be hunted, then the hunter may import three sets of elk antlers.

However, if the head still contains the brain or if there is still excess meat on the trophy, then the hide or cape would be prohibited. The concerns are with large amounts of blood and tissue. Small amounts of soft tissue adhering to the hide or cape would not pose a significant risk (as seen with field-dressed trophies). Customs Border Protection inspectors at the port of arrival will inspect the trophy condition. If found to contain excess meat and soft tissue, it may be refused entry.

—New Hampshire Fish & Game Department

NEW HAMPSHIRE SNAPSHOT

Deer Population: 75,000, 32nd in U.S.
Average Harvest: 10,316, 39th in U.S.
Forested Land: 4.98 million acres
Harvest Calculation Method: Mandatory registration
Does State Predict Annual Harvest? No
How Close is Annual Prediction? NA
Gun-Hunters: 68,833
Bow-Hunters: 22,353
Muzzleloading Hunters: 30,564
Hunter Education: Required for persons born after 1971. Bow-hunter education is not required.
Orange Required for Gun-Hunting? No

NEW JERSEY
Garden State

Harvest Ranking: #27

For more information, contact:
Division of Fish & Wildlife
Box 418
Port Republic, NJ 08241
(609) 748-2044 www.state.nj.us/dep/fgw

HISTORY OF NEW JERSEY'S WHITETAIL HARVEST

Year	Firearm	Bow	Total
1909	86	NA	86
1919	353	NA	353
1929	1,331	NA	1,331
1939	2,336	NA	2,336
1949	3,618	9	3,627
1959	9,612	1,230	10,842
1969	7,121	1,356	8,477

32-YEAR HISTORY

Year	Firearm	Bow	Total
1971	6,111	1,434	7,545
1972	9,557	1,464	11,021
1973	9,629	1,689	11,318
1974	11,429	1,717	13,146
1975	10,675	2,013	12,688
1976	10,908	2,110	13,018
1977	11,828	2,591	14,419
1978	13,177	2,641	15,818
1979	13,843	2,263	16,106
1980	16,030	5,161	21,191
1981	16,291	5,846	22,137
1982	16,817	6,928	23,745
1983	16,403	6,902	23,305
1984	17,920	7,699	25,619
1985	21,480	7,971	29,451
1986	23,590	10,187	33,777
1987	27,415	11,813	39,228
1988	33,140	12,760	45,900
1989	34,812	13,714	48,526
1990	34,372	13,850	48,222
1991	29,936	15,480	45,416
1992	31,257	16,418	47,675
1993	32,936	17,006	49,942
1994	32,602	18,840	51,442
1995	39,176	20,593	59,769
1996	36,709	19,995	56,704
1997	39,290	20,261	59,551
1998	39,039	20,975	60,014
1999	50,266	25,132	75,398
2000	52,602	24,842	77,444
2001	45,153	23,516	68,669
2002	41,474	21,557	63,031

NEW JERSEY WHITETAIL RECORDS

- **Record harvest:** 77,444 (2000)
- **Record low harvest:** 86 (1909)
- **Bow-hunting record:** 25,132 (1999)
- **Gun-hunting record:** 52,602 (2000)

- **Season to remember:** 1949. New Jersey bow-hunters kill nine whitetails — the first recorded bow-kills in state history. Amazingly, by 2001, bow kills constituted more than one-third of the state's harvest.

Community-Based Deer Management Works In N.J.

White-tailed deer have reached problematic numbers in many suburban communities in New Jersey. Increased deer-vehicle collisions, damage to ornamental plantings and gardens, damage to agricultural crops and destruction of the natural forest ecosystem are some of the problems associated with high deer populations.

In an effort to limit deer populations in areas of New Jersey where sport hunting is not considered a viable management tool, the DNR has permitted alternative methods of controlling deer populations under the Community-Based Deer Management Program. The program was created in 1995 to explore alternative methods of deer population control.

Since 1995, Union County's deer reduction program has reduced the deer population in the reservation from 180 deer per square mile to 20 deer per square mile. The population can be maintained at that level by utilizing 12 volunteer sportsmen on two days per year shooting up to 50 deer annually. Agents who volunteer at least three half-days may receive 20 pounds of dressed venison. The rest of the venison is donated to the Community Food Bank of New Jersey.

— *New Jersey Division of Fish & Wildlife*

NEW JERSEY SNAPSHOT

Deer Population: 165,500, 28th in U.S.
Average Harvest: 68,911, 27th in U.S.
Forested Land: 2 million acres
Harvest Calculation Method: Mandatory registration
Does State Predict Annual Harvest? Yes
How Close is Annual Prediction? 5%
Gun-Hunters: 94,900
Bow-Hunters: 45,350
Muzzleloading Hunters: 24,240
Hunter Education: Required for first-time hunters. Bow-hunter education is also required.
Orange Required for Gun-Hunting? Yes

NEW YORK
Empire State

Harvest Ranking: #8

For more information, contact:
Department of Conservation
50 Wolf Road
Albany, NY 12233
(518) 402-8985
www.dec.state.ny.us/website/outdoors

HISTORY OF NEW YORK'S WHITETAIL HARVEST

Year	Firearm	Bow	Total
1941	18,566	NA	18,566
1951	31,049	75	31,124
1961	57,723	731	58,454

32-YEAR HISTORY

Year	Firearm	Bow	Total
1971	47,039	1,243	48,282
1972	54,041	1,596	55,637
1973	73,191	2,002	75,193
1974	100,097	3,206	103,303
1975	99,835	3,288	103,323
1976	86,421	3,794	90,215
1977	79,035	4,169	83,204
1978	81,749	3,810	85,559
1979	90,691	3,368	94,059
1980	131,606	4,649	136,255
1981	161,593	3,792	165,385
1982	178,825	6,175	185,000
1983	161,640	5,466	167,106
1984	124,244	5,400	129,644
1985	142,802	9,705	152,507
1986	168,366	9,705	178,071
1987	192,867	11,325	204,192
1988	181,186	11,644	192,830
1989	167,558	12,770	180,328
1990	175,544	14,664	190,208
1991	192,812	19,008	211,820
1992	212,988	18,947	231,935
1993	200,240	20,048	220,288
1994	146,255	19,428	165,683
1995	166,430	21,854	188,284
1996	180,082	22,683	202,765
1997	194,684	22,152	216,836
1998	205,074	25,684	230,758
1999	225,524	30,435	255,959
2000	276,867	29,812	306,679
2001	252,939	28,931	281,870
2002	274,961	33,255	308,216

New York Hunters Share Venison

In 2001, New York deer hunters again proved their generosity, donating almost 30,000 pounds of ground venison to state food pantries.

NEW YORK WHITETAIL RECORDS

- **Record harvest:** 308,216 (2002)
- **Record low harvest:** 15,136 (1945)
- **Bow-hunting record:** 33,255 (2002)
- **Gun-hunting record:** 276,867 (2000)

- **Season to remember:** 2002. New York hunters kill 308,216 deer, setting a new state record. A record bow-kill of 33,255 helps break the record.

New York Breaks Record for Donated Venison

Deer can be donated, processed and distributed to help feed the hungry throughout New York State. Because donated deer must be professionally processed, the Venison Donation Coalition has coordinated a program where legally tagged and properly field dressed deer can be taken to participating processors at no cost to the hunter or farmer.

Meat cutters are recruited for participation and paid to process the donated deer. The venison is processed and packaged according to the Environmental Conservation Law and the meat is picked up by Food Banks for delivery to soup kitchens, food pantries and needy families throughout New York.

The venison-donation program, through the Venison Donation Coalition, expanded last year and New York hunters donated more than 85,000 pounds of ground venison to charitable institutions during its fourth year of operation.

—*N.Y. Dept. of Environmental Conservation*

NEW YORK SNAPSHOT

Deer Population: 975,000, 9th in U.S.

Average Harvest: 276,696, 8th in U.S.

Forested Land: 18.7 million acres

Harvest Calculation Method: Mandatory registration

Does State Predict Annual Harvest? Yes

How Close is Annual Prediction? 3%

Gun-Hunters: 719,696

Bow-Hunters: 177,762

Muzzleloading Hunters: 80,356

Hunter Education: Required for all first-time hunters. Bow-hunter education is also required.

Orange Required for Gun-Hunting? Yes

NORTH CAROLINA
Tar Heel State

Harvest Ranking: #18

For more information, contact:
North Carolina Wildlife
512 N. Salisbury St.
Raleigh, NC 27604-1188
(919) 733-3393
www.state.nc.us/Wildlife

HISTORY OF NORTH CAROLINA'S DEER HARVEST

Year	Firearm	Bow	Total
1949	NA	NA	14,616
1951	NA	NA	17,739
1952	NA	NA	15,572
1953	NA	NA	18,598
1954	NA	NA	20,084
1955	NA	NA	20,114
1962	NA	NA	28,808
1964	NA	NA	39,793
1967	NA	NA	38,688

28-YEAR HISTORY

Year	Firearm	Bow	Total
1970	NA	NA	38,405
1972	NA	NA	47,469
1974	NA	NA	53,079
1976	22,645	539	23,184
1977	28,182	679	28,861
1978	29,193	781	29,974
1979	29,246	841	30,087
1980	27,792	1,142	28,934
1981	33,644	1,400	35,044
1982	35,840	2,092	37,932
1983	45,316	2,543	47,859
1984	47,565	2,355	49,920
1985	52,315	2,759	55,074
1986	59,767	2,924	62,691
1987	74,767	3,498	78,265
1988	79,694	3,405	83,099
1989	85,030	4,660	148,208
1992	NA	NA	217,743
1993	107,669	8,727	118,638
1994	116,462	8,235	124,697
1995	202,000	14,000	216,000
1996	177,500	13,500	191,000
1997	181,000	14,000	195,000
1998	110,352	8,095	132,372
1999	116,023	8,258	124,281
2000	198,920	13,560	212,480
2001	134,501	8,268	143,122
2002	111,120	7,054	118,174

NORTH CAROLINA DEER RECORDS

- **Record harvest:** 217,743 (1992)
- **Record low harvest:** 14,616 (1949)
- **Bow-hunting record:** 14,000 (1995, 1997)
- **Gun-hunting record:** 202,000 (1995)

- **Season to remember:** 2000. North Carolina hunters kill 212,480 deer — 88,119 more than the previous year. However, the harvest dropped to 143,122 in 2001.

Get a Jump on Fall Hunting By Taking A Summer Class

With school out and most extra-curriculars idle, summer is the perfect time for young hunters to take a hunting safety class.

North Carolina requires first-time hunters to complete a 10-hour hunter education course. The Wildlife Resources Commission offers these courses free throughout the year, although many participants don't register until fall, when hunting is on their minds. The result can be crowded classes that may not fit easily into busy schedules.

Many don't realize that the classes are also offered in summer. Most fall courses take place on Saturday and Sunday or on three consecutive week nights, which can interfere with homework, school events or other commitments. And parents shuttling their kids to after-school activities can find themselves making additional trips.

Most that have taken the summer course have found it to be much more convenient.

— *N.C. Wildlife Resources Commission*

NORTH CAROLINA SNAPSHOT

Deer Population: 1 million, 7th in U.S.
Average Harvest: 146,086, 18th in U.S.
Forested Land: 19.3 million acres
Harvest Calculation Method: Surveys and mandatory registration
Does State Predict Annual Harvest? No
How Close is Annual Prediction? NA
Gun-Hunters: 178,571
Bow-Hunters: 45,450
Muzzleloading Hunters: 60,600
Hunter Education: Required for first-time hunters. Bow-hunter education is not required.
Orange Required for Gun-Hunting? Yes

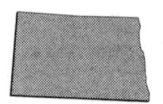

NORTH DAKOTA
Peace Garden State
Harvest Ranking: #28

For more information, contact:
North Dakota Game Department
100 N. Bismarck Expy.
Bismarck, ND 58501
(701) 328-6300
www.state.nd.us/gnf

HISTORY OF NORTH DAKOTA'S DEER HARVEST

Year	Firearm	Bow	Total
1941	NA	NA	2,665
1950	NA	NA	13,933
1954	NA	NA	22,705
1958	NA	NA	9,828
1962	NA	NA	23,429
1966	NA	NA	26,469
1967	NA	NA	26,524

33-YEAR HISTORY

Year	Firearm	Bow	Total
1970	NA	NA	22,882
1971	NA	NA	28,673
1972	NA	NA	25,424
1973	NA	NA	27,780
1974	NA	NA	23,445
1975	NA	NA	20,666
1976	NA	NA	19,969
1977	NA	NA	17,201
1978	NA	NA	17,120
1979	NA	NA	18,118
1980	NA	NA	24,179
1981	NA	NA	27,006
1982	NA	NA	31,210
1983	NA	NA	35,709
1984	NA	NA	41,582
1985	NA	NA	43,074
1986	NA	NA	60,122
1987	NA	NA	47,157
1988	NA	NA	41,190
1989	47,025	2,934	49,959
1990	42,347	2,862	45,209
1991	46,980	3,299	50,279
1992	54,144	3,996	58,142
1993	58,246	4,006	62,252
1994	56,462	3,946	60,408
1995	66,686	4,078	70,764
1996	65,303	4,861	70,164
1997	52,971	2,894	55,865
1998	55,405	3,200	58,605
1999	55,980	3,400	59,380
2000	63,275	3,300	66,575
2001	81,000	NA	NA
2002	83,625	4,700	88,325

NORTH DAKOTA DEER RECORDS

- **Record harvest:** 88,325 (2002)
- **Record low harvest:** 2,665 (1941)
- **Bow-hunting record:** 4,861 (1996)
- **Gun-hunting record:** 83,625 (2002)

- **Season to remember:** 2002. North Dakota hunters kill a record 88,325 deer. The record is accomplished on the strength of an 83,625-deer rifle harvest, beating the 2000 number by more than 20,000 deer.

North Dakota Heightens CWD Testing Efforts

Samples from 470 deer and 25 elk killed during the 2002 North Dakota hunting season tested negative for chronic wasting disease. In February, producers in the state completed five years of mandatory surveillance on farmed elk and deer, also finding no signs of the disease.

North Dakota Game and Fish Department wildlife managers will continue to scrutinize the state's wild elk, whitetail and mule deer for CWD. The Department's long-term goal is to sample wild deer and elk from all over the state, which could take several years.

In 2002, biologists removed lymph nodes, tonsils and brain stems for CWD testing from hunter-harvested deer and elk, sending samples to a laboratory in Wyoming. The majority of deer used in testing were from hunting units in eastern and western North Dakota. The deer were obtained from participating meat processors within selected units. This year, the state might try adding drop-off stations in order to collect even more samples, along with expanding sample areas.

— North Dakota Game & Fish Department

NORTH DAKOTA SNAPSHOT

Deer Population: 243,750, 26th in U.S.

Average Harvest: 65,750, 28th in U.S.

Forested Land: 722,000 acres

Harvest Calculation Method: Surveys

Does State Predict Annual Harvest? Yes

How Close is Annual Prediction? 5%

Gun-Hunters: 80,000

Bow-Hunters: 11,000

Muzzleloading Hunters: 1,700

Hunter Education: Required for all persons born after Dec. 31, 1961. Bow-hunter education is not required.

Orange Required for Gun-Hunting? Yes

OHIO
Buckeye State
Harvest Ranking: #17

For more information, contact:
Division of Wildlife
1840 Belcher Drive
Columbus, OH 43224
(614) 265-6300   www.dnr.state.oh.us

HISTORY OF OHIO'S WHITETAIL HARVEST

Year	Firearm	Bow	Total
1952	NA	NA	450
1954	NA	NA	closed
1956	NA	NA	3,911
1958	NA	NA	4,415
1960	NA	NA	2,584
1962	NA	NA	2,114
1964	NA	NA	1,326
1966	NA	NA	1,073
1968	NA	NA	1,396

32-YEAR HISTORY

Year	Firearm	Bow	Total
1971	NA	NA	3,831
1972	NA	NA	5,074
1973	NA	NA	7,594
1974	NA	NA	10,747
1975	NA	NA	14,972
1976	NA	NA	23,431
1977	NA	NA	22,319
1978	NA	NA	22,967
1979	NA	NA	34,874
1980	NA	NA	40,499
1981	NA	NA	47,634
1982	NA	NA	52,885
1983	NA	NA	59,812
1984	NA	NA	66,860
1985	NA	NA	64,263
1986	NA	NA	67,626
1987	NA	NA	79,355
1988	NA	NA	100,674
1989	NA	NA	91,236
1990	80,109	12,087	92,196
1991	94,342	17,109	111,451
1992	97,676	19,577	117,253
1993	104,540	23,160	138,752
1994	141,137	29,390	170,527
1995	149,413	27,299	179,543
1996	130,237	26,305	158,000
1997	125,504	26,639	153,159
1998	92,722	25,548	118,270
1999	96,701	29,319	126,020
2000	115,291	34,333	149,624
2001	116,092	34,340	150,432
2002	155,210	48,904	204,114

OHIO WHITETAIL RECORDS

- **Record harvest:** 204,114 (2002)
- **Record low harvest:** 406 (1965)
- **Bow-hunting record:** 48,904 (2002)
- **Gun-hunting record:** 155,210 (2002)

- **Season to remember:** 2002. Ohio hunters kill a record 204,114 deer, beating both their gun and bow harvest records.

Special Disabled Deer Hunt Held in Morgan County

Approximately 40 outdoor enthusiasts with disabilities have the opportunity to hunt deer, participate in field activities and create lasting memories and friendships in fall during Ohio's annual Wheelin' Sportsmen deer hunt. The event, scheduled for early November in Morgan County, is a joint effort between the National Wild Turkey Federation, American Electric Power and the Ohio Department of Natural Resources Division of Wildlife.

The NWTF-developed program is open to applicants with any type of physically challenging disability. Each disabled hunter is paired with an experienced guide who offers whatever assistance may be needed in the field. The special program is dedicated to providing all people with disabilities the opportunity to enjoy the great outdoors.

Interested applicants can mail their name, address and phone number to Wheelin' Sportsmen, American Electric Power, 59 West Main St., McConnelsville, OH 43756. The 40 available openings will be filled on a first-come, first-served basis and successful applicants will be notified in early September.

— *Ohio Department of Natural Resources*

OHIO SNAPSHOT

Deer Population: 475,000, 17th in U.S.

Average Harvest: 149,692, 17th in U.S.

Forested Land: 7.9 million acres

Harvest Calculation Method: Mandatory registration

Does State Predict Annual Harvest? Yes

How Close is Annual Prediction? 10%

Gun-Hunters: 481,000

Bow-Hunters: 287,700

Muzzleloading Hunters: 111,500

Hunter Education: Required for first-time hunters. Bow-hunter education is not required.

Orange Required for Gun-Hunting? Yes

OKLAHOMA
Sooner State
Harvest Ranking: #25

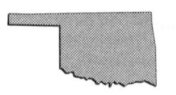

Fore more information, contact:
Department of Wildlife
1801 N. Lincoln, Box 53465
Oklahoma City, OK 73105
(405) 521-3851   www.state.ok.us

HISTORY OF OKLAHOMA'S DEER HARVEST

Year	Firearms	Bow	Total
1964	3,368	140	3,508
1965	4,090	213	4,303
1966	4,925	275	5,200
1967	4,976	259	5,235
1968	5,490	260	5,750
1969	6,069	304	6,373

32-YEAR HISTORY

Year	Firearms	Bow	Total
1971	6,587	465	7,052
1972	7,714	508	8,222
1973	7,140	427	7,567
1974	7,821	489	8,310
1975	9,028	649	9,677
1976	10,544	1,004	11,548
1977	10,192	680	10,872
1978	13,080	1,028	14,108
1979	13,023	1,185	14,208
1980	12,800	1,497	14,297
1981	11,446	1,964	13,410
1982	17,006	2,249	19,255
1983	19,222	2,698	21,920
1984	20,041	2,568	23,609
1985	16,664	3,523	20,187
1986	25,096	3,320	28,416
1987	29,239	4,115	33,354
1988	34,436	4,414	38,850
1989	33,752	4,589	38,341
1990	38,545	5,525	44,070
1991	40,197	7,079	47,286
1992	42,620	7,792	50,412
1993	49,978	7,853	57,831
1994	51,145	9,054	60,199
1995	56,770	9,116	65,886
1996	52,826	11,430	64,256
1997	60,277	10,930	71,207
1998	67,788	12,220	80,008
1999	70,967	11,757	82,724
2000	87,663	14,272	101,935
2001	75,711	9,964	85,675
2002	84,303	14,278	98,581

OKLAHOMA WHITETAIL RECORDS

- **Record harvest:** 101,935 (2000)
- **Record low harvest:** 3,508 (1964)
- **Bow-hunting record:** 14,278 (2002)
- **Gun-hunting record:** 87,663 (2000)

- **Season to remember:** 1990. Oklahoma deer and deer hunting show amazing progress. Although the harvest of 44,070 deer pales compared to more recent harvests, it's huge compared to the harvest from 20 years earlier, when Oklahoma hunters killed only 7,226 deer.

Cy Curtis Award Recognizes Trophy Bucks

The Cy Curtis Award was established in 1975 to recognize trophy deer killed in Oklahoma. The award was named after Cy Curtis Award — the man most responsible for the restoration of white-tailed deer to the state.

All deer legally killed in Oklahoma after 1972 are eligible for scoring. Official scoring of trophies can be done any time following a 60-day drying period. Measurements must be taken by an employee of the Oklahoma Department of Wildlife Conservation, or by a measurer certified by the Boone & Crockett or Pope & Young clubs. Sportsmen who harvest deer that meet minimum entry requirements (135 for typicals and 150 for nontypicals) are awarded a certificate and their names are entered in the state record book.

For more information on the Cy Curtis Program, contact the Wildlife Department's Game Division at (405) 521-2739.

— *Oklahoma Dept. of Wildlife*

OKLAHOMA SNAPSHOT

Deer Population: 397,000, 20th in U.S.
Average Harvest: 89,785, 25th in U.S.
Forested Land: 7.54 million acres
Harvest Calculation Method: Mandatory registration
Does State Predict Annual Harvest? Yes
How Close is Annual Prediction? 5%
Gun-Hunters: 163,671
Bow-Hunters: 86,893
Muzzleloading Hunters: 106,978
Hunter Education: Required for all persons born after Jan. 1, 1972. Bow-hunter education is not required.
Orange Required for Gun-Hunting? Yes

OREGON
Beaver State
Harvest Ranking: #43

For more information, contact:
Department of Fish and Wildlife
400 Public Service Bldg.
Salem, OR 97310
(503) 872-5268   www.dfw.state.or.us

HISTORY OF OREGON'S WHITETAIL HARVEST

Year	Firearm	Bow	Total
1992	422	NA	422
1993	594	NA	594
1994	707	NA	707
1995	667	NA	667
1996	893	NA	893
1997	800	NA	800
1998	NA	NA	611
1999	1,011	NA	1,011
2000	1,013	NA	1,013
2001	1,457	NA	1,457

Editor's Note — *White-tailed deer are rare in Oregon. In fact, the 1992 season was the first time the Oregon Dept. of Wildlife distinguished between mule deer and whitetails in harvest totals. The estimated deer population in the "Oregon Snapshot" on this page includes mostly mule deer and blacktails.*

Oregon Whitetails Are Isolated

Oregon is home to a sizable black-tailed deer population, but some whitetails live in the Umpqua River Basin near Roseburg, on a series of Columbia River islands. Efforts are being made to increase these small herds. Therefore, all of western Oregon is closed to whitetail hunting.

The Idaho whitetail strain is also found in Oregon. These deer thrive in areas with heavy shrub patches and thick riparian vegetation.

Mule deer are native to eastern Oregon. Explorers in the early 1800s reported a scarcity of big game, but 20 years later gold miners found abundant mule deer herds. This century has seen similar fluctuations. Between 1926 and 1933, Oregon's muley population ranged from 39,000 to 75,000.

OREGON WHITETAIL RECORDS

- **Record harvest:** 1,457 (2002)
- **Record low harvest:** 422 (1992)
- **Bow-hunting record:** Not available
- **Gun-hunting record:** 1,457 (2002)

- **Season to remember:** 1996. Despite having relatively few whitetails, Oregon gun- and bow-hunters kill 893 whitetails.

Exotic Species May Threaten Native Deer

Disease, critical as it is, does not pose the only risk to wild deer and elk in Oregon. Captive-reared exotic sika deer, fallow deer and mouflon sheep have already been found ranging free in Oregon. All have come from escapes or releases from private facilities.

Where free-ranging herds of exotic wildlife do occur, these animals have often shown an amazing ability to out-compete native wildlife for food and living space. This increased competition can cause lower native fawn and calf survival.

Some exotic deer and elk have the potential to crossbreed with native wildlife. European red deer have interbred with wild native elk in Colorado, Montana and Wyoming. In Scotland, where red deer are native, the species has interbred with introduced sika deer from Asia to the point where some scientists believe pure red deer no longer exist in that country. This cannot be allowed to happen in Oregon.

— *Oregon Department of Fish and Wildlife*

OREGON SNAPSHOT

Deer Population: 647,600, (Includes other species)
Average Harvest: 978, 43rd in U.S.
Forested Land: 27.99 million acres
Harvest Calculation Method: Surveys and camp checks
Does State Predict Annual Harvest? No
How Close is Annual Prediction? NA
Gun-Hunters: 208,943
Bow-Hunters: 25,829
Muzzleloading Hunters: 3,030
Hunter Education: Required for persons under the age of 18. Bow-hunter education is not required.
Orange Required for Gun-Hunting? No

PENNSYLVANIA
Keystone State
Harvest Ranking: #3

For more information, contact:
Game Commission
2001 Elmerton Ave.
Harrisburg, PA 17110
(717) 787-4250
www.pgc.state.pa.us

HISTORY OF PENNSYLVANIA'S DEER HARVEST

Year	Firearm	Bow	Total
1949	130,723	0	130,723
1954	40,870	55	40,925
1959	88,845	1,327	90,172
1963	83,028	1,388	84,416
1967	141,164	3,251	144,415

32-YEAR HISTORY

Year	Firearm	Bow	Total
1971	101,458	2,769	104,227
1972	104,270	2,945	107,215
1973	123,239	3,652	126,891
1974	121,743	3,909	125,652
1975	133,134	5,061	138,195
1976	118,385	3,648	122,033
1977	141,400	4,678	146,078
1978	116,188	5,053	121,241
1979	110,562	4,232	114,794
1980	129,703	5,774	135,477
1981	142,592	5,938	148,530
1982	130,958	7,264	138,222
1983	130,071	6,222	136,293
1984	133,606	6,574	140,180
1985	154,060	7,368	161,428
1986	148,562	8,570	157,132
1987	164,055	8,901	172,956
1988	185,565	9,834	195,399
1989	184,856	10,951	195,807
1990	396,529	19,032	415,561
1991	365,267	22,748	388,015
1992	335,439	25,785	361,224
1993	359,224	49,409	408,557
1994	345,184	49,897	395,081
1995	375,961	54,622	430,583
1996	294,674	56,323	350,997
1997	342,556	54,460	397,016
1998	317,774	59,715	377,489
1999	306,521	72,401	378,992
2000	426,078	78,522	504,600
2001	411,963	74,051	486,014
2002	447,881	69,648	517,529

PENNSYLVANIA DEER RECORDS

- **Record harvest:** 517,529 (2002)
- **Record low harvest:** 40,925 (1954)
- **Bow-hunting record:** 78,522 (2000)
- **Gun-hunting record:** 447,881 (2002)

- **Season to remember:** 2002. Pennsylvania hunters kill a state record 517,529 whitetails. The harvest ranks as the largest in the country and is the fourth-highest harvest ever compiled by a state in a season.

Pennsylvania Hunters Have Exciting Season

The 2002 season marked the first year in which Pennsylvania hunters had to make sure their deer complied with statewide antler restrictions before they shot.

Legal bucks had to have at least 4 points on a side. Hunters who mistakenly killed a sublegal buck paid a $25 fine and were allowed to keep the carcass, minus the antlers.

2002 was also the second year in which the buck and doe seasons ran concurrently. Hunters killed a record 447,881 deer during the state's 2002 firearms season.

Hunters reported seeing a large number of bigger bucks during 2002, and many hunters brought home trophies. The Pennsylvania Game Commission estimates that the harvest of 2½-year-old bucks will double during the 2003 season, as many of this year's 2½-year-old bucks didn't meet antler requirements last year and were protected.

— Pennsylvania Game Commission

PENNSYLVANIA SNAPSHOT

Deer Population: 1.5 million, 5th in U.S.
Average Harvest: 452,925, 3rd in U.S.
Forested Land: 16.97 million acres
Harvest Calculation Method: Harvest cards mailed to hunters
Does State Predict Annual Harvest? Yes
How Close is Annual Prediction? 10%
Gun-Hunters: 1,060,728
Bow-Hunters: 282,700
Muzzleloading Hunters: 136,600
Hunter Education: Required for all first-time hunters. Bow-hunter education is not required.
Orange Required for Gun-Hunting? Yes

RHODE ISLAND
Ocean State
Harvest Ranking: # 42

For more information, contact:
Department of Environ. Mgmt.
83 Park St.
Providence, RI 02903
(401) 222-6822 www.state.ri.us/dem

HISTORY OF RHODE ISLAND'S DEER HARVEST

Year	Firearm	Bow	Total
1973	46	56	102
1974	62	48	110
1975	57	54	111
1976	61	50	111
1977	95	62	157
1978	91	78	169
1979	103	93	196
1980	145	72	217
1981	155	88	243
1982	112	104	216
1983	123	99	222
1984	139	109	248
1985	144	112	256
1986	299	126	425
1987	252	179	431
1988	323	125	448
1989	466	169	635
1990	701	238	943
1991	857	291	1,148
1992	1,052	417	1,474
1993	945	378	1,323
1994	1,157	252	1,409
1995	1,351	415	1,766
1996	1,689	474	2,163
1997	1,542	243	1,785
1998	1,222	382	1,532
1999	1,661	390	2,043
2000	1,819	488	2,307
2001	1,582	470	2,052
2002	1,506	525	2,031

Small State, Big Opportunities

Rhode Island is home to more than 46,000 acres of state management area land. Maps of these areas are available from the Division of Fish and Wildlife.

Deer hunting in the Simmons Mill Pond management area is only allowed during the archery season. Camping is prohibited, except in portions of the Arcadia and George Washington management areas.

RHODE ISLAND DEER RECORDS

- **Record harvest:** 2,307 (2000)
- **Record low harvest:** 102 (1973)
- **Bow-hunting record:** 525 (2002)
- **Gun-hunting record:** 1,819 (2000)

- **Season to remember:** 1986. Although the harvest is miniscule when compared to those of other states, Rhode Island's deer hunters kill 425 deer — 40 percent more than the previous year.

Rhode Island Offers Hunter Ethics and Landowner Relations Course

Rhode Island now offers a course on hunting ethics and landowner relations.

The course is comprised of home study, classroom work, a written examination and proficiency testing with firearms and/or bow and arrow.

The program is intended to foster positive relations between hunters and landowners and to promote ethical hunting practices. Individuals who successfully complete the course will receive a course completion card, proficiency card and have their name included on a list that is made available to farmers and nursery owners.

To take the course, you must be at least 18 years old, submit an application, consent to a background check, have a five-year record that is free of fish and wildlife violations, complete a basic hunter education course, complete a basic bowhunter education course and possess a current Rhode Island hunting license.

— *Craig Mandli*

RHODE ISLAND SNAPSHOT

Deer Population: 11,000, 34th in U.S.
Average Harvest: 1,993, 42nd in U.S.
Forested Land: 401,000 acres
Harvest Calculation Method: Mandatory registration
Does State Predict Annual Harvest? No
How Close is Annual Prediction? NA
Gun-Hunters: 5,465
Bow-Hunters: 3,143
Muzzleloading Hunters: 5,754
Hunter Education: Required for first-time hunters. Bow-hunter education is not required.
Orange Required for Gun-Hunting? Yes

SOUTH CAROLINA
Palmetto State

Harvest Ranking: #9

For more information, contact:
Department of Natural Resources
Box 167
Columbia, SC 29202
(803) 734-3888
http://water.dnr.state.sc.us/

HISTORY OF SOUTH CAROLINA'S DEER HARVEST

Year	Firearm	Bow	Total
1973	NA	NA	23,703
1974	NA	NA	26,727
1975	NA	NA	29,133
1976	NA	NA	33,749
1977	NA	NA	36,363
1978	NA	NA	39,721
1979	NA	NA	43,569
1980	NA	NA	44,698
1981	NA	NA	56,410
1982	NA	NA	54,321
1983	NA	NA	57,927
1984	NA	NA	60,182
1985	NA	NA	62,699
1986	NA	NA	69,289
1987	NA	NA	86,208
1988	NA	NA	98,182
1989	NA	NA	107,081
1990	NA	NA	125,171
1991	NA	NA	130,848
1992	NA	NA	126,839
1993	NA	NA	142,795
1994	NA	NA	138,964
1995	NA	NA	142,527
1996	NA	NA	155,654
1997	NA	NA	165,000
1998	NA	NA	150,000
1999	284,701	16,299	301,000
2000	278,700	16,000	294,700
2001	289,647	19,181	308,828
2002	300,598	19,322	319,920

South Carolina Has Early Season

Deer hunting in South Carolina is characterized by two distinct season frameworks. The Coastal Plain encompasses 28 counties where the deer season begins on Aug. 15, Sept. 1 or Sept. 15, and continues until Jan. 1. In this region, which encompasses about two-thirds of the state, baiting and dog-hunting are legal.

South Carolina's upstate areas have different season dates and hunting laws.

SOUTH CAROLINA DEER RECORDS

- **Record harvest:** 319,920 (2002)
- **Record low harvest:** 18,894 (1972)
- **Bow-hunting record:** 19,322 (2002)
- **Gun-hunting record:** 300,598 (2002)

- **Season to remember:** 1972. Although the 18,894-deer harvest is miniscule by today's standards, the 1972 season began a series of almost-always increasing deer harvests, which eventually broke the 300,000 mark in 1999.

South Carolina Hunters Help Stop Spread of CWD

Although chronic wasting disease has not been detected in South Carolina, resident hunters who travel to other states to hunt deer and elk may be able to help prevent the introduction of this disease into the Palmetto State by properly handling the carcasses of deer or elk harvested where CWD has been diagnosed.

Many states are imposing restrictions on the importation of certain carcass parts from deer harvested in states or parts of states where chronic wasting disease has been diagnosed, and the Department of Natural Resources is asking resident hunters who travel to other states to voluntarily restrict the importation of certain carcass parts into South Carolina. These recommendations will not keep hunters from importing harvested game because most game taken elsewhere is processed in the state where it was harvested.

Currently, deer hunting generates more than $200 million annually for South Carolina's economy.

— *S. C. Dept. of Natural Resources*

SOUTH CAROLINA SNAPSHOT

Deer Population: 1 million, 7th in U.S.

Average Harvest: 274,890, 9th in U.S.

Forested Land: 12.3 million acres

Harvest Calculation Method: Surveys and voluntary registration

Does State Predict Annual Harvest? Yes

How Close is Annual Prediction? 10%

Gun-Hunters: 175,813

Bow-Hunters: 42,218

Muzzleloading Hunters: 30,704

Hunter Education: Required for all persons born after June 30, 1979. Bow-hunter education is not required.

Orange Required for Gun-Hunting? Yes

SOUTH DAKOTA
Coyote State
Harvest Ranking: #30

For more information, contact:
Division of Wildlife
Bldg. 445 E. Capital
Pierre, SD 57501
(605) 773-3485
www.state.sd.us/gfp/index.htm

HISTORY OF SOUTH DAKOTA'S DEER HARVEST

Year	Firearm	Bow	Total
1985	43,989	2,738	46,727
1986	40,798	1,953	42,751
1987	32,018	2,456	34,474
1988	33,265	2,327	35,592
1989	42,947	3,081	46,028

12-YEAR HISTORY

Year	Firearm	Bow	Total
1991	39,915	2,686	42,601
1992	41,959	2,964	44,923
1993	45,431	2,963	48,394
1994	47,142	2,325	49,467
1995	39,868	2,625	42,493
1996	39,936	3,107	43,043
1997	47,503	2,440	49,943
1998	43,000	2,800	45,800
1999	43,214	2,700	45,914
2000	39,600	2,600	42,200
2001	45,340	3,418	48,758
2002	58,367	4,224	62,591

South Dakota Holds Successful Youth Hunt

South Dakota's 1999 antlerless deer hunt for youths was a big hit — more than 54 percent of participants tagged a deer.

Nearly 2,500 young hunters participated, and they killed 1,339 deer.

The state's most successful hunt occurred in the special buck unit in the West River region. Only 730 tags were issued for the hunt, but 506 hunters killed bucks — a 69 percent success ratio.

Overall, state bow-hunters had a successful season. More than 22 percent of archers harvested a deer in 1999.

SOUTH DAKOTA DEER RECORDS

- **Record harvest:** 62,591 (2002)
- **Record low harvest:** 34,474 (1987)
- **Bow-hunting record:** 4,224 (2002)
- **Gun-hunting record:** 58,367 (2002)

- **Season to remember:** 2002. South Dakota hunters bag a record 62,591 deer, breaking records in both gun and bow harvests.

State Resident Antlerless Deer Permit Fees Reduced

Fees for resident one-tag and two-tag antlerless deer and antelope licenses have been reduced by the Game, Fish and Parks Commission.

More antlerless deer harvest is needed in South Dakota. If the current large deer population is allowed to increase even more, the chances that deer will cause damage to crops and stored livestock feed on farms and ranches in a severe winter will also increase. By harvesting does, not only is the deer population decreased directly, but also the potential for population growth is reduced.

To help achieve this, often the number of antlerless licenses available is increased. However, those licenses need to be purchased and filled by hunters. To make these licenses more attractive to hunters and hopefully increase harvest, the GFP Commission has reduced antlerless license fees.

Fees have been reduced from $20 to $15 for a resident one-tag antlerless deer or antelope license. Two-tag antlerless licenses have been reduced from $30 to $25.

—*South Dakota Dept. of Game, Fish & Parks*

SOUTH DAKOTA SNAPSHOT

Deer Population: 153,000, 29th in U.S.
Average Harvest: 49,053, 30th in U.S.
Forested Land: 1.7 million acres
Harvest Calculation Method: Surveys
Does State Predict Annual Harvest? Yes
How Close is Annual Prediction? 10%
Gun-Hunters: 72,600
Bow-Hunters: 11,900
Muzzleloading Hunters: 1,800
Hunter Education: Required for all persons under age 16. Bow-hunter education is required.
Orange Required for Gun-Hunting? Yes

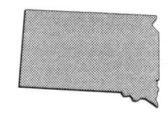

TENNESSEE
Volunteer State
Harvest Ranking: #17

For more information, contact:
Tennessee Wildlife Resources
Box 407
Nashville, TN 37204
(888) 814-8972
www.state.tn.us/twra

HISTORY OF TENNESSEE WHITETAIL HARVEST

Year	Firearm	Bow	Total
1971	6,202	365	6,567
1972	7,354	499	7,853
1973	10,937	474	11,411
1974	12,624	685	13,309
1975	13,897	993	14,890
1976	16,374	1,739	18,113
1977	19,527	1,770	21,297
1978	22,819	2,465	25,284
1979	25,970	2,570	28,540
1980	27,196	3,457	30,653
1981	28,885	3,407	32,292
1982	35,726	4,644	40,370
1983	42,528	6,347	48,875
1984	49,493	5,883	55,376
1985	53,118	7,278	60,396
1986	69,044	8,578	77,622
1987	86,777	12,040	98,817
1988	81,469	10,796	92,265
1989	95,475	13,287	108,762
1990	97,172	16,061	113,233
1991	105,832	15,764	121,596
1992	106,168	19,728	125,896
1993	118,946	19,596	138,542
1994	111,598	20,832	132,430
1995	124,179	20,953	145,132
1996	127,129	22,501	149,630
1997	126,233	24,108	150,341
1998	135,261	20,414	155,675
1999	122,497	21,000	143,497
2000	129,580	19,900	149,480
2001	134,765	21,591	156,356
2002	150,537	18,272	168,809

Tennessee WMAs Offer Fantastic Opportunities

Aside from thousands of acres of public land, Tennessee offers deer hunters 93 refuges and wildlife management areas spread throughout the state. These WMAs are managed by the Tennessee Wildlife Resources Agency and vary in size from 53 to 625,000 acres.

All WMAs are open to public hunting and trapping.

TENNESSEE DEER RECORDS

- **Record harvest:** 168,809 (2002)
- **Record low harvest:** 6,567 (1971)
- **Bow-hunting record:** 24,108 (1997)
- **Gun-hunting record:** 150,537 (2002)

- **Season to remember:** 2002. Tennessee hunters kill a record 168,809 deer on the strength of 150,537 gun kills — by far a state record.

Lifetime Sportsman Licenses Now Available

The lifetime sportsman license is available to any individual who has resided in Tennessee continuously for 12 consecutive months immediately preceding the purchase of the license. Applicants under the age of three must have at least one parent or designated guardian who was a resident of Tennessee at the time of the child's birth and has continued to reside in Tennessee since birth. The lifetime sportsman license entitles the holder to all the hunting and fishing privileges afforded holders of an annual sportsman license.

This license is good for the life of the holder, even if the license holder moves out of state. The actual license will be mailed to the youngster when they reach the age the license will be needed to hunt or fish. Revenue from the sale of the lifetime sportsman license will be set aside in a permanent trust fund from which only the interest will be used to finance programs designed to manage wildlife and preserve the heritage of hunting and fishing in Tennessee. The fee for a lifetime sportsman license must be paid in full in either cash, check or credit card.

— *Tennessee Wildlife Resources*

TENNESSEE SNAPSHOT

Deer Population: 990,000, 8th in U.S.
Average Harvest: 154,763, 17th in U.S.
Forested Land: 13.6 million acres
Harvest Calculation Method: Mandatory registration
Does State Predict Annual Harvest? No
How Close is Annual Prediction? NA
Gun-Hunters: 209,684
Bow-Hunters: 99,000
Muzzleloading Hunters: 99,000
Hunter Education: Required for persons born after Jan. 1, 1969. Bow-hunter education is not required.
Orange Required for Gun-Hunting? Yes

TEXAS
Lone Star State

Harvest Ranking: #6

For more information, contact:
Texas Parks & Wildlife
4200 Smith School Road
Austin, TX 78744
(800) 895-4248   www.tpwd.state.tx.us

HISTORY OF TEXAS' ANNUAL WHITETAIL HARVEST

Year	Firearm	Bow	Total
1980	253,993	6,390	260,383
1981	292,525	7,527	300,052
1982	328,678	8,943	337,621
1983	309,409	8,935	318,344
1984	361,811	11,451	373,262
1985	370,732	12,767	383,499
1986	431,002	14,117	445,119
1987	489,368	15,585	504,953
1988	458,576	16,392	474,968
1989	460,896	16,595	477,491
1990	413,910	15,622	429,532
1991	459,083	14,964	474,047
1992	453,361	15,532	468,893
1993	438,934	13,575	452,509
1994	408,780	12,643	421,423
1995	436,975	13,518	450,593
1996	320,819	13,000	333,819
1997	357,832	13,500	371,332
1998	NA	NA	392,573
1999	431,927	6,700	438,627
2000	NA	NA	424,000
2001	383,215	10,452	395,160
2002	420,432	16,517	436,949

Big Bucks Abound in South Texas Brush Country

Texas is comprised of 10 ecological areas: the Edward Plateau, South Texas Plains, Cross Timbers, Gulf Prairies, Marshes, Post Oak Savannah, Blackland Prairies, Rolling Plains, High Plains and Piney Woods.

The South Texas Plains is also known as "Brush Country," and is a level to rolling plain extending south and west from San Antonio to the Gulf of Mexico and the Rio Grande. This area is known for large-antlered bucks.

TEXAS DEER RECORDS

- **Record harvest:** 504,953 (1987)
- **Record low harvest:** 260,383 (1980)
- **Bow-hunting record:** 16,595 (1989)
- **Gun-hunting record:** 489,368 (1987)
- **Season to remember:** 1989. Texas bow-hunters kill a record 16,595 whitetails. In the following years, however, bow harvests steadily declined. In 1999, Texas bow-hunters killed only 6,700 deer.

Study Shows Ranches Are Being Subdivided

Texas rural lands are being splintered into "ranchettes," endangering wildlife and the family farmers who make their living off the land, according to a joint study by American Farmland Trust and the Texas Cooperative Extension of the Texas A&M University System.

The study shows that mid-sized farms and ranches are disappearing fastest from the Texas landscape. Every year, the state loses about 250,000 acres of mid-sized properties. In the rapidly fragmenting portions of the state, these farms and ranches are most often broken into smaller ownerships.

The study found that there is a strong correlation between rural land fragmentation and degraded wildlife habitat. Loss of large blocks of contiguous grassland habitat is a major factor in the decline of bobwhite quail, as well as other grassland birds and mammals.

The study was funded by The Meadows Foundation and Houston Endowment, Inc. An analysis of the study's implications and a map of the top 10 percent of Texas counties struggling with fragmentation can be found on American Farmland Trust's Web site.

— *Texas Parks & Wildlife*

TEXAS SNAPSHOT

Deer Population: 3,543,000, 1st in U.S.
Average Harvest: 417,462, 6th in U.S.
Forested Land: 19.2 million acres
Harvest Calculation Method: Surveys
Does State Predict Annual Harvest? No
How Close is Annual Prediction? NA
Gun-Hunters: 561,415
Bow-Hunters: 38,500
Muzzleloading Hunters: 65,650
Hunter Education: Required for all persons born on or after Sept. 1, 1979. Bow-hunter education is not required.
Orange Required for Gun-Hunting? No

VERMONT
Green Mountain State

Harvest Ranking: #35

For more information, contact:
Vermont Dept. of Fish and Wildlife
103 S. Main St.
Waterbury, VT 05671
(802) 241-3701   www.anr.state.vt.us

HISTORY OF VERMONT'S WHITETAIL HARVEST

Year	Firearm	Bow	Total
1899	90	NA	90
1909	4,597	NA	4,597
1919	4,092	NA	4,092
1929	1,438	NA	1,438
1939	2,589	NA	2,589
1949	5,983	NA	5,983
1959	11,268	232	11,500
1969	20,753	1,547	22,300

32-YEAR HISTORY

Year	Firearm	Bow	Total
1971	7,760	604	8,364
1972	8,980	1,073	10,053
1973	8,560	1,040	9,600
1974	11,254	1,580	12,834
1975	9,939	1,606	11,545
1976	10,278	1,200	11,478
1977	10,029	2,094	12,123
1978	7,087	1,688	8,775
1979	14,936	1,587	16,523
1980	24,675	1,257	25,932
1981	19,077	1,169	20,246
1982	9,148	798	9,946
1983	6,092	538	6,630
1984	12,418	630	13,048
1985	13,150	727	13,877
1986	11,943	810	12,753
1987	8,046	958	9,004
1988	6,451	627	7,078
1989	8,030	1,202	9,232
1990	7,930	1,053	8,983
1991	9,993	1,591	11,584
1992	11,215	3,245	14,460
1993	10,043	2,999	13,333
1994	9,177	3,276	12,903
1995	12,769	5,046	18,116
1996	13,632	4,990	18,622
1997	14,836	5,000	19,836
1998	12,000	4,562	16,562
1999	14,487	5,296	19,783
2000	15,975	4,523	20,498
2001	11,340	3,633	14,973
2002	13,140	3,492	16,632

VERMONT DEER RECORDS

- **Record harvest:** 25,932 (1980)
- **Record low harvest:** 90 (1899)
- **Bow-hunting record:** 5,296 (1999)
- **Gun-hunting record:** 24,675 (1980)

- **Season to remember:** 1983. Three years after Vermont hunters killed a record 25,932 whitetails, the overall harvest bottoms out at 6,630 — the lowest since 1949.

Seasoned Hunters Pass on the Tradition to Youth

Ask any seasoned hunter how they started hunting and you are likely to hear about an older person who provided the initial spark while they were a kid. It may have been a dad or grandfather, uncle or friend. It really doesn't matter — the results are always the same — our hunting tradition is typically passed from one generation to the next as something valuable to be treasured, treated with respect and passed on again. And that's exactly what Vermont's youth deer hunting weekend is all about.

Vermont's youth deer hunting weekend is held the weekend before the opening weekend of the November deer hunting season. Young resident hunters who qualify can obtain youth deer hunting tag applications from license agents.

Anyone under 16 years of age who has successfully completed a hunter education course, and who has at least one parent or guardian who is a legal resident of Vermont may get a youth deer hunting tag. The hunter safety course certificate must be shown when the application is presented to the license agent. The parent or guardian must also sign the application.

— Vermont Agency of Natural Resources

VERMONT SNAPSHOT

Deer Population: 150,000, 30th in U.S.
Average Harvest: 17,690, 35th in U.S.
Forested Land: 4.5 million acres
Harvest Calculation Method: Mandatory registration
Does State Predict Annual Harvest? No
How Close is Annual Prediction? NA
Gun-Hunters: 94,908
Bow-Hunters: 40,764
Muzzleloading Hunters: 29,944
Hunter Education: Required for first-time hunters. Bow-hunter education also required.
Orange Required for Gun-Hunting? No

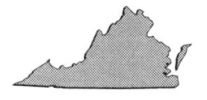

VIRGINIA
Old Dominion
Harvest Ranking: #15

For more information, contact:
Department of Game & Fisheries
Box 11104
Richmond, VA 23230
(804) 367-1000   www.dgif.state.va.us

HISTORY OF VIRGINIA'S WHITETAIL HARVEST

Year	Firearms	Bow	Total
1935	NA	NA	1,158
1945	NA	NA	4,545
1955	NA	NA	14,227
1965	NA	NA	27,983

32-YEAR HISTORY

Year	Firearms	Bow	Total
1971	NA	NA	42,369
1972	NA	NA	48,775
1973	NA	NA	60,789
1974	NA	NA	61,989
1975	NA	NA	63,443
1976	NA	NA	63,671
1977	NA	NA	67,059
1978	NA	NA	72,545
1979	NA	NA	69,940
1980	NA	NA	75,208
1981	NA	NA	78,388
1982	NA	NA	88,540
1983	NA	NA	85,739
1984	NA	NA	84,432
1985	NA	NA	101,425
1986	NA	NA	121,801
1987	NA	NA	119,309
1988	NA	NA	114,562
1989	NA	NA	135,094
1990	NA	NA	160,411
1991	NA	NA	179,344
1992	NA	NA	200,446
1993	185,222	15,900	201,122
1994	190,673	18,700	209,373
1995	202,277	16,199	218,476
1996	193,134	15,974	209,108
1997	182,881	15,074	197,995
1998	164,449	14,578	179,027
1999	173,619	15,370	190,043
2000	168,527	17,210	187,114
2001	196,392	18,191	214,583
2002	195,325	18,593	213,918

Editor's note — Virginia has one of the most popular "Hunters for the Hungry" programs in the nation. For more information, contact Hunters for the Hungry, Box 304, Dept. DDH, Big Island, VA 24526.

VIRGINIA DEER RECORDS

- **Record harvest:** 218,476 (1995)
- **Record low harvest:** 1,158 (1935)
- **Bow-hunting record:** 18,700 (1994)
- **Gun-hunting record:** 202,277 (1995)

- **Season to remember:** 2001. Virginia bow- and gun-hunters combine to harvest 214,583 deer — a 14 percent increase from 2000.

Hunters Help Less Fortunate With Donations

Governor Mark R. Warner signed legislation enabling hunters in Virginia to voluntarily contribute to those in need. Sponsored by Lieutenant Governor Tim Kaine, House Bill 1874, introduced by Delegate Vic Thomas, and Senate Bill 808, introduced by Senator Ken Stolle, allow for the voluntary donation of $2 to the Hunters for the Hungry program when hunters purchase their hunting licenses.

Each $2 donation from a hunter in Virginia will enable Hunters for the Hungry to provide 13 additional servings of venison. The legislation was proposed and named in honor of David Horne, the founder of Virginia Hunters for the Hungry, who passed away in 2002. Hunters for the Hungry is a 501(c)(3) non-profit association that provides donated venison to people in need across Virginia. The group was established in 1991 and, since then, has provided more than 6.6 million servings of venison.

Successful hunters can also donate surplus deer to Hunters for the Hungry.

— *Virginia Dept. of Game & Inland Fisheries*

VIRGINIA SNAPSHOT

Deer Population: 950,000, 11th in U.S.
Average Harvest: 196,937, 15th in U.S.
Forested Land: 15.8 million acres
Harvest Calculation Method: Mandatory registration
Does State Predict Annual Harvest? Yes
How Close is Annual Prediction? 35%
Gun-Hunters: 282,816
Bow-Hunters: 58,513
Muzzleloading Hunters: 103,015
Hunter Education: Required for all persons born after June 30, 1979. Bow-hunter education is not required.
Orange Required for Gun-Hunting? Yes

WASHINGTON
Evergreen State
Harvest Ranking: #32

For more information, contact:
Department of Fish & Wildlife
600 Capitol Way N.
Olympia, WA 98501
(360) 902-2200   www.wa.gov/wdfw

HISTORY OF WASHINGTON'S ANNUAL DEER HARVEST

Year	Firearms	Bow	Total
1974	49,792	808	50,600
1984	38,416	1,790	40,206

12-YEAR HISTORY

Year	Firearms	Bow	Total
1991	52,745	4,367	57,112
1992	50,441	4,856	55,297
1993	31,892	3,789	35,681
1994	42,054	4,948	47,002
1995	34,469	3,296	37,765
1996	35,970	3,472	39,442
1997	29,775	2,366	32,141
1998	27,578	2,675	30,253
1999	32,556	3,204	35,760
2000	37,565	3,411	40,976
2001	37,253	3,758	41,011
2002 (estimated)	35,880	3,620	39,500

Editor's note — *Washington is one of several states that has limited numbers of white-tailed deer. The above harvest figures are for all species, including blacktails, whitetails and mule deer.*

Washington Harbors Whitetails, Blacktails and Mule Deer

Mule deer and whitetail populations in southeast Washington are at high levels, except for the very southern and mountainous part of the Blue Mountains. In fact, since 1992, whitetail populations have steadily increased in the Spokane area.

In 1991, the state had a record whitetail harvest of about 18,000. Since then, the harvest has leveled off at about 10,000 deer annually. That's an excellent figure considering most deer hunters target blacktails and mule deer.

WASHINGTON DEER RECORDS

- **Record harvest:** 66,000 (1979)
- **Record low harvest:** 30,253 (1998)
- **Bow-hunting record:** 4,948 (1994)
- **Gun-hunting record:** 64,888 (1979)

- **Season to remember:** 1994. Washington bowhunters kill a record 4,948 deer. Although this number is low compared to other states' archery kills, it's amazing, considering Washington archers killed just 808 deer in 1974.

New Partnership Stresses Outdoor Education

Recreational license purchasers can contribute to youth outdoor education programs under a pilot program recently undertaken by the Washington Department of Fish and Wildlife and the Washington Wildlife Federation's newly formed coalition of outdoor groups.

Each hunter who purchases a state recreational license online will be able to make a voluntary, tax-deductible contribution of a dollar or more toward the youth programs. Those buying licenses in person or by telephone will be able to make similar donations.

The donated funds will be used for outdoor education activities at schools, sport shows, fairs and other events, offering skills training and hands-on fishing, shell fishing, hunting and target-shooting experiences.

The pilot outdoor education partnership is being undertaken as part of WDFW's "Go Play Outside" initiative, aimed at encouraging participation in outdoor recreation activities.

Donations from license purchasers are expected to raise approximately $50,000 annually. All donations, except for an administrative fee, will go directly to the Washington Wildlife Federation for outdoor education programs.

— *Washington Dept. of Fish & Wildlife*

WASHINGTON SNAPSHOT

Deer Population: 380,000 (includes other species)
Average Harvest: 37,500, 32nd in U.S.
Forested Land: 20.5 million acres
Gun-Hunters: 129,987
Bow-Hunters: 17,136
Muzzleloading Hunters: 6,804
Hunter Education: Required for all persons born after Jan. 1, 1972. Bow-hunter education is not required.
Orange Required for Gun-Hunting? Yes

WEST VIRGINIA
Mountain State

Harvest Ranking: #12

For more information, contact:
W. Va. Wildlife Resources
State Capital, Bldg. 3
Charleston, WV 25305
(304) 367-2720 www.wvwildlife.com

HISTORY OF WEST VIRGINIA'S WHITETAIL HARVEST

Year	Firearms	Bow	Total
1939	897	NA	897
1949	6,466	6	6,472
1959	19,588	90	19,678
1969	13,620	470	14,090

32-YEAR HISTORY

Year	Firearms	Bow	Total
1971	15,905	714	16,619
1972	20,960	1,443	22,403
1973	24,179	1,684	25,863
1974	27,821	2,119	29,940
1975	32,368	2,968	35,336
1976	38,712	2,323	41,035
1977	37,987	2,531	40,518
1978	40,096	4,350	44,446
1979	49,625	5,461	55,086
1980	47,022	7,144	54,166
1981	65,505	9,003	74,508
1982	74,642	13,454	88,096
1983	78,605	11,235	89,840
1984	94,132	12,578	106,710
1985	71,183	13,416	84,599
1986	101,404	17,207	118,611
1987	109,367	19,742	129,109
1988	112,155	16,537	128,692
1989	129,350	16,217	145,567
1990	148,233	21,715	169,948
1991	149,536	27,448	176,984
1992	177,265	28,659	205,924
1993	142,589	26,425	169,014
1994	120,954	24,448	145,402
1995	173,553	28,072	201,625
1996	157,275	29,637	186,912
1997	200,859	34,446	235,305
1998	165,609	28,430	194,039
1999	197,339	33,942	231,281
2000	162,184	30,752	192,936
2001	182,155	33,622	215,777
2002	218,212	37,144	255,356

WEST VIRGINIA DEER RECORDS

- **Record harvest:** 255,356 (2002)
- **Record low harvest:** 897 (1939)
- **Bow-hunting record:** 37,144 (2002)
- **Gun-hunting record:** 218,212 (2002)

- **Season to remember:** 1984. West Virginia hunters kill 106,710 deer, breaking the 100,000 mark for the first time in state history.

Mountain State Counties Reject Sunday Hunting

West Virginia hunters received a blow in Spring 2001, when 35 of the state's counties rejected allowing Sunday hunting.

Barbour, Berkeley, Braxton, Calhoun, Doddridge, Fayette, Gilmer, Grant, Greenbrier, Hampshire, Harrison, Jackson, Lewis, Marion, Mason, Mercer, Mineral, Monongalia, Monroe, Morgan, Nicholas, Pendelton, Pleasants, Pocohontas, Preston, Raleigh, Randolf, Ritchie, Roane, Summers, Taylor, Tucker, Tyler, Upshur and Wood counties rejected the proposal. Furthermore, the Sunday hunting issue cannot reappear on the ballot in these counties for two years.

Tradition runs deep in West Virginia, and no hunting on Sundays is one such tradition. However, West Virginia remains one of the few states in the nation in which Sunday hunting is not allowed.

—*U.S. Sportsmen's Alliance*

WEST VIRGINIA SNAPSHOT

Deer Population: 890,000, 12th in U.S.
Average Harvest: 217,878, 12th in U.S.
Forested Land: 12.1 million acres
Harvest Calculation Method: Mandatory registration
Does State Predict Annual Harvest? Yes
How Close is Annual Prediction? 20%
Gun-Hunters: 290,000
Bow-Hunters: 153,793
Muzzleloading Hunters: 74,736
Hunter Education: Required for all persons born after Jan. 1, 1975. Bow-hunter education is not required.
Orange Required for Gun-Hunting? Yes

WISCONSIN
Badger State
Harvest Ranking: #2

For more information, contact:
Department of Natural Resources
101 S. Webster St.
Madison, WI 53707
(608) 266-2621 http://www.dnr.state.wi.us

HISTORY OF WISCONSIN'S WHITETAIL HARVEST

Year	Firearms	Bow	Total
1897	2,500	--	2,500
1907	4,750	--	4,750
1917	18,000	--	18,000
1928	17,000	--	17,000
1937	14,835	0	14,835
1947	53,520	368	53,888
1957	68,138	1,753	68,138
1967	128,527	7,592	136,119

32-YEAR HISTORY

Year	Firearms	Bow	Total
1971	70,835	6,522	77,357
1972	74,827	7,087	81,914
1973	82,105	8,456	90,561
1974	100,405	12,514	112,919
1975	117,378	13,588	130,966
1976	122,509	13,636	136,145
1977	131,910	16,790	148,700
1978	150,845	18,113	168,958
1979	125,570	16,018	141,588
1980	139,624	20,954	160,578
1981	166,673	29,083	195,756
1982	182,715	30,850	213,565
1983	197,600	32,876	230,476
1984	255,240	38,891	294,131
1985	274,302	40,744	315,046
1986	259,240	40,490	299,730
1987	250,530	42,651	293,181
1988	263,424	42,393	305,817
1989	310,192	46,394	356,586
1990	350,040	49,291	399,331
1991	352,328	67,005	419,333
1992	288,906	60,479	349,385
1993	217,584	53,008	270,592
1994	307,629	66,254	373,883
1995	397,942	69,158	467,100
1996	388,211	72,313	460,524
1997	292,513	66,792	359,305
1998	332,314	75,301	407,615
1999	402,179	91,937	494,116
2000	528,494	86,899	618,274
2001	361,264	83,120	446,957
2002	317,983	54,093	372,076

WISCONSIN DEER RECORDS
- **Record harvest:** 618,274 (2000)
- **Record low harvest:** 2,500 (1897)
- **Bow-hunting record:** 91,937 (1999)
- **Gun-hunting record:** 528,494 (2000)

- **Season to remember:** 2000. Wisconsin becomes the first state ever to surpass 600,000 deer harvested in one year.

Badger State Hunters Donate Venison

In 2002, Wisconsin hunters donated 5,646 deer to food pantries.

Eighty-six processors participated in the venison-donation program, which produced more than 250,000 pounds of ground venison to help feed needy people in the state.

For the first time in 2002, Wisconsin hunters could volunteer to donate $1 or more to the Wisconsin Deer Donation Program when they purchased their hunting licenses. Nearly 5,000 hunters donated money to the program when purchasing their licenses, contributing $18,075.16 to help pay for the processing costs.

Wisconsin is Home to Experienced Bow-Hunters

According to a 2001 survey by the Wisconsin Department of Natural Resources, Wisconsin bow-hunters averaged more than 17 years of experience. The survey also revealed that an average Wisconsin bow-hunter is 42.3 years old.

— *Wisconsin Dept. of Natural Resources*

WISCONSIN SNAPSHOT

Deer Population: 1.6 million, 3rd in U.S.

Average Harvest: 467,808, 2nd in U.S.

Forested Land: 15.5 million acres

Harvest Calculation Method: Mandatory registration

Does State Predict Annual Harvest? Yes

How Close is Annual Prediction? 5%

Gun-Hunters: 694,712

Bow-Hunters: 258,230

Muzzleloading Hunters: 8,250

Hunter Education: Required for all persons born after Jan. 1, 1973. Bow-hunter education is not required.

Orange Required for Gun-Hunting? Yes

WYOMING
Equality State

Harvest Rating: #40

For more information, contact:
Wyoming Game and Fish
5400 Bishop Blvd.
Cheyenne, WY 82002
(307) 777-4600   http://gf.state.wy.us/

HISTORY OF WYOMING'S DEER HARVEST

Year	Firearm	Bow	Total
1971	7,806	NA	7,806
1972	4,306	NA	4,306
1973	9,174	NA	9,174
1974	12,832	NA	12,832
1975	14,001	NA	14,001
1976	11,298	NA	11,298
1977	11,049	NA	11,049
1978	7,796	NA	7,796
1979	7,452	NA	7,452
1980	7,014	NA	7,014
1981	7,286	NA	7,286
1982	7,608	NA	7,608
1983	8,498	NA	8,498
1984	9,888	NA	9,888
1985	9,267	NA	9,267
1986	7,983	254	8,237
1987	5,628	192	5,820
1988	7,005	174	7,179
1989	8,903	197	9,100
1990	9,535	147	9,632
1991	10,240	139	10,379
1992	14,533	216	14,749
1993	12,623	1,322	13,945
1994	8,249	228	8,477
1995	6,959	175	7,134
1996	6,857	232	7,089
1997	6,889	200	7,089
1998	6,842	194	7,036
1999	6,883	196	7,079
2000	10,833	290	11,103
2001	9,125	292	9,417
2002	9,057	159	9,216

Wyoming Recognizes Wildlife Stewards

As a part of the annual Wyoming Hunting and Fishing Heritage Expo, awards are presented to youth, adults, landowners and companies who have demonstrated stewardship important to preservation of the hunting and fishing heritage.

Youth organization leaders, teachers, shooting organization members, adult instructors or anyone with knowledge about deserving individuals can nominate them for awards.

The youth awards are Hunting Skills and Stewardship. Wyoming students between 14 and 19 who are ethical hunters and anglers, good role models and wildlife stewards qualify.

The Wildlife Stewardship Award is presented to an adult who has demonstrated outstanding stewardship of fish and wildlife resource and is a recognized role model for ethical hunting or other related outdoor activities.

— *Wyoming Game and Fish*

Wyoming Hunters Enjoy High Success Rates

Nonresident deer hunters in Wyoming have a 60.4 percent success rate. Although that's largely because nonresident hunters rely heavily on guides and outfitters, it's also testament to Wyoming's often-underestimated hunting opportunities.

WYOMING DEER RECORDS

- **Record harvest:** 14,749 (1992)
- **Record low harvest:** 4,306 (1972)
- **Bow-hunting record:** 1,322 (1993)
- **Gun-hunting record:** 14,533 (1992)
- **Season to remember:** 1993. Wyoming bow-hunters shatter the standing archery harvest, killing 1,322 deer. Since that year, Wyoming's highest archery occurred in 2000, when bow-hunters killed 290 deer — only 22 percent of the 1993 harvest.

WYOMING SNAPSHOT

Deer Population: 65,000 (includes other species)

Average Harvest: 8,770, 40th in U.S.

Forested Land: 9.97 million acres

Harvest Calculation Method: Surveys

Does State Predict Annual Harvest? Yes

How Close is Annual Prediction? 10%

Gun-Hunters: 53,940

Bow-Hunters: 6,790

Muzzleloading Hunters: 7,700

Hunter Education: Required for all persons born after Jan. 1, 1966. Bow-hunter education is not required.

Orange Required for Gun-Hunting? Yes

WHITETAILS CAN CLEAR a 7-foot fence from a standing start and an 8-foot fence with a running start, but they prefer to go under or through fences.

8
Whitetail Facts
Insights Into Deer Behavior

1. A fawn spends up to 12 hours a day lying motionless, hiding from predators. Even when a deer matures and has the strength and agility to escape danger by fleeing, the instinct to sit tight is strong. Often, deer stay in their beds, letting hunters and other predators pass by unaware.

2. Although whitetails can easily clear a 7-foot fence from a standing start, or an 8-foot fence from a running start, they generally choose to go under or through a fence. Fence lines serve as natural travel routes for deer. Often deer trails run parallel with fences for great distances. Tufts of hair on the barbs indicate favorite crossings.

3. Do deer look up? Yes! For this reason, it's important to be well camouflaged, even when you're hunting from a tree stand. Generally, deer spend most of their time looking for danger at ground level, but they do look up.

4. Deer are strong swimmers and frequently cross large streams and lakes. They have been observed swimming between offshore islands several miles apart. They will take to the water to throw hounds off their trail, and they will also partially submerge themselves to escape biting insects or simply to cool off in hot weather.

5. As the rut intensifies and does approach estrus, bucks begin to chase does. Does run to prevent bucks from catching up. Sometimes a buck will trot along, nose to the ground, following a doe's scent trail for a mile or more before losing interest. At other times, bucks make short dashes in pursuit of does at close distances. When a doe is in estrus, she will not run from a buck.

6. Often a doe in estrus urinates in front of a buck, who then sniffs or tastes the urine to determine the doe's breeding status. After doing so, a buck often performs a lip curl, or flehmen. The response lasts about five to 10 seconds. He curls back his upper lip and inhales while holding his neck and chin upward at a 45-degree angle, apparently deciding whether to pursue the doe.

7. White-tailed bucks are more social than does, and two or three adult bucks often travel together as a group, except during the rut. There is little need for overt aggression between bucks within this group, as subordinate members avoid dominant members. Often, bucks pause to groom each other.

8. Fights between equally large, dominant bucks are uncommon. Generally, fights are avoided through aggressive posturing of the dominant male and submissive behavior of the subordinate animal. When neither animal accepts a subordinate role, intense bouts of shoving and neck twisting occur. Fights usually last 15 to 30 seconds.

9. The white underside of the tail is a danger signal to other deer, but when a buck runs, he commonly clamps his tail down tight to his rump, apparently to

WHITE-TAILED FAWNS may spend 12 hours a day in their beds, hiding from predators. Even when deer mature, they prefer to hold tight to avoid danger.

attract less attention to himself.

10. Because they can utilize the woody portions of many shrubs and trees, deer are considered browsers. Their diet, however, includes a variety of foods including grasses, sedges, fruits, nuts, acorns, forbs and mushrooms. Their favorite foods are acorns, apples, alfalfa, corn, soybeans and honeysuckle.

11. Whitetails obtain minerals from a variety of sources, including mineral or salt blocks put out for cattle, natural mineral licks in bottomlands and along roadsides after winter salting operations. Deer will even lick their shed antlers for their mineral content.

12. The insulative qualities of a deer's coat prevents snow that falls on them from melting, and the covering of snow acts as additional insulation. Deer that bed down in a snowstorm usually remain bedded, if undisturbed, until the storm passes, even if it lasts for several days. Deer can literally be buried by snow and yet be perfectly warm.

WHITETAIL CLASSROOM

✓ **NEBRASKA'S HEAVIEST** recorded white-tailed deer weighed 287 pounds field dressed and had an estimated live weight of 355 pounds.

✓ **ALBINO DEER** are entirely white, except for their pink eyes, nose and inner ears. Albinos produce no pigment, thus the white coloration. The pink color is blood vessels as seen through thin skin. In the eyes, we see blood vessels behind the lenses, seen through unpigmented irises. Melanistic deer have the opposite abnormality: they produce too much pigment, which results in a dark brown or even black color. Melanism is even rarer than albinism.

✓ **EVER WONDER WHY** Canadian deer are so much larger than deer from southern locales? The reason has to due with winter survival. Northern deer have large bodies, which reduces the ratio of body mass to surface area. As a result, deer are better able to maintain a constant body temperature, as the effect of heat loss through surface area is lessened. This is also why other Northern species, such as polar bears, grow so large.

— *Compiled by Joe Shead*

Peak-Rut Predictor

It's no secret the rut offers some of the best deer hunting of the year. Testosterone-charged bucks let down their guard as they pursue does, making them more vulnerable to hunters. They are also more visible, and often move all day long.

To cash in on increased buck activity, it helps to have an idea when various stages of the rut will kick in. *Deer & Deer Hunting* Northern field editor Charles Alsheimer and Vermont biologist Wayne Laroche have long studied the moon's effect on the rut. Through their research, they have discovered patterns that help them reliably predict when rutting activities will occur.

Alsheimer and Laroche have broken the rut into three phases: seeking, chasing and tending. During the seeking phase, bucks actively seek estrous does. They move into the wind, scent-checking does. At this time they travel widely and are susceptible to deer calls and rattling.

The chase phase begins as does near estrus. Does run from bucks, but allow them to follow. Bucks attempt to corner does until ultimately the doe enters estrus and is ready to breed.

Tending begins when a doe readily allows the buck to tag along as she reaches estrus. This phase only lasts about 24 hours while the doe is in estrus. The buck will travel and bed with the doe and breed her until she is no longer in estrus.

These three phases blend together gradually. However, it is important to note that many factors interfere with the rut.

Heavy rain or snow suppresses rutting activity, as does warm temperatures. If deer are heavily pressured by hunters, they may go nocturnal, which also interferes with rutting activity. Another common rut suppressor is skewed buck-to-doe ratios. The rut predictor works most reliably in herds in which the buck-to-doe ratio is balanced. As the ratio becomes skewed toward does, young bucks will do more breeding, as there are too many does for the mature bucks to sire. Skewed doe-to-buck ratios draw out the rut, and activity is generally less intense.

In 2003, the rutting moon occurs Nov. 9. In the North (north of 40 degrees north latitude), seeking activity should peak around Nov. 14. Peak chasing should occur around Nov. 19, and peak tending should occur around Nov. 21.

In the South, seeking should peak about Dec. 12. Chasing activity should peak around Dec. 17, and tending should peak about Dec. 19.

For more detailed information on peak rut predictions, consult the *Deer & Deer Hunting* Whitetail Calendar. To order, call (800) 258-0929.

Deer Hunting Guide to Full-Moon Dates* 2003-2004

Month	Date	Day
August	12	Tuesday
September	10	Wednesday
October	10	Friday
November	9	Sunday
December	8	Monday
January	7	Wednesday
February	6	Friday

*Based on Central Standard Time

Plan Your Hunts by the 'Rutting Moon'

In most areas, the rut usually peaks in late October or early November.

Many deer biologists and hunting experts believe it's possible to accurately predict the peak times for deer activity during the rut. Three in-depth research articles on this topic were published in the August, September and October 1997 issues of *Deer & Deer Hunting*. These articles revealed a new theory on the moon's influence on deer activity.

The dates on this page are nearest to the full-moon phases for the rutting months. This guide will help

YEAR	RUTTING MOON
2003	Nov. 9
2004	Oct. 28
2005	Oct. 17
2006	Nov. 5

you plan this year's hunts, enabling you to be in the woods when deer are most active.

For an in-depth look at how the moon influences deer behavior, check out Charles Alsheimer's book, *Whitetails by the Moon*.

To order, call (888) 457-2873, or visit www.deeranddeerhunting.com.

Standard Time Differences Across North America

City, State	Time
Akron, Ohio	12:00 p.m.
Albuquerque, N.M.	10:00 a.m.
Atlanta, Ga.	12:00 p.m.
Austin, Texas	11:00 a.m.
Bismarck, N.D.	11:00 a.m.
Boise, Idaho	10:00 a.m.
Buffalo, N.Y.	12:00 p.m.
Butte, Mont.	10:00 a.m.
Charleston, S.C.	12:00 p.m.
Chattanooga, Tenn.	12:00 p.m.
Cheyenne, Wy.	10:00 a.m.
Chicago, Ill.	11:00 a.m.
Colorado Springs, Colo.	10:00 a.m.
Dallas, Texas	11:00 a.m.
Detroit, Mich.	12:00 p.m.
Duluth, Minn.	11:00 a.m.
Erie, Pa.	12:00 p.m.
Evansville, Ind.	11:00 a.m.
Fort Wayne, Ind.*	12:00 p.m.
Frankfort, Ky.	12:00 p.m.
Halifax, Nova Scotia	1:00 p.m.
Hartford, Conn.	12:00 p.m.
Jacksonville, Fla.	12:00 p.m.
Juneau, Alaska	8:00 a.m.
Kansas City, Mo.	11:00 a.m.
Lincoln, Neb.	11:00 a.m.
Little Rock, Ark.	11:00 a.m.
Los Angeles, Calif.	9:00 a.m.
Milwaukee, Wis.	11:00 a.m.
Mobile, Ala.	11:00 a.m.
Montreal, Quebec	12:00 p.m.
New Orleans, La.	11:00 a.m.
Norfolk, Va.	12:00 p.m.
Oklahoma City, Okla.	11:00 a.m.
Phoenix, Ariz.	10:00 a.m.
Pierre, S.D.	11:00 a.m.
Portland, Me.	12:00 p.m.
Portland, Ore.	9:00 a.m.
Reno, Nev.*	9:00 a.m.
St. John's, Newfoundland	1:30 p.m.
Salt Lake City, Utah	10:00 a.m.
Santa Fe, N.M.	10:00 a.m.
Savannah, Ga.	12:00 p.m.
Seattle, Wash.	9:00 a.m.
Sioux Falls, S.D.	11:00 a.m.
Toledo, Ohio	12:00 p.m.
Toronto, Ontario	12:00 p.m.

Sunrise and Sunset Times

Calculated for Milwaukee, Wis. (Central Time)
Corrected for Daylight Saving Time

Month	2003 Sunrise	2003 Sunset	2004 Sunrise	2004 Sunset
October				
01	6:49 a.m.	6:34 p.m.	6:50 a.m.	6:32 p.m.
02	6:50 a.m.	6:32 p.m.	6:51 a.m.	6:30 p.m.
03	6:51 a.m.	6:30 p.m.	6:52 a.m.	6:29 p.m.
04	6:52 a.m.	6:28 p.m.	6:53 a.m.	6:27 p.m.
05	6:53 a.m.	6:27 p.m.	6:54 a.m.	6:25 p.m.
06	6:54 a.m.	6:25 p.m.	6:55 a.m.	6:23 p.m.
07	6:56 a.m.	6:23 p.m.	6:56 a.m.	6:22 p.m.
08	6:57 a.m.	6:21 p.m.	6:58 a.m.	6:20 p.m.
09	6:58 a.m.	6:20 p.m.	6:59 a.m.	6:18 p.m.
10	6:59 a.m.	6:18 p.m.	7:00 a.m.	6:17 p.m.
11	7:00 a.m.	6:16 p.m.	7:01 a.m.	6:15 p.m.
12	7:01 a.m.	6:15 p.m.	7:02 a.m.	6:13 p.m.
13	7:03 a.m.	6:13 p.m.	7:04 a.m.	6:12 p.m.
14	7:04 a.m.	6:11 p.m.	7:05 a.m.	6:10 p.m.
15	7:05 a.m.	6:10 p.m.	7:06 a.m.	6:08 p.m.
16	7:06 a.m.	6:08 p.m.	7:07 a.m.	6:07 p.m.
17	7:07 a.m.	6:06 p.m.	7:08 a.m.	6:05 p.m.
18	7:09 a.m.	6:05 p.m.	7:10 a.m.	6:04 p.m.
19	7:10 a.m.	6:03 p.m.	7:11 a.m.	6:02 p.m.
20	7:11 a.m.	6:02 p.m.	7:12 a.m.	6:00 p.m.
21	7:12 a.m.	6:00 p.m.	7:13 a.m.	5:59 p.m.
22	7:13 a.m.	5:58 p.m.	7:14 a.m.	5:57 p.m.
23	7:15 a.m.	5:57 p.m.	7:16 a.m.	5:56 p.m.
24	7:16 a.m.	5:55 p.m.	7:17 a.m.	5:54 p.m.
25	7:17 a.m.	5:54 p.m.	7:18 a.m.	5:53 p.m.
26	7:18 a.m.	5:53 p.m.	7:19 a.m.	5:51 p.m.
27*	6:20 a.m.	4:51 p.m.	7:21 a.m.	5:50 p.m.
28	6:21 a.m.	4:49 p.m.	7:22 a.m.	5:49 p.m.
29	6:22 a.m.	4:48 p.m.	7:23 a.m.	5:47 p.m.
30	6:23 a.m.	4:47 p.m.	7:24 a.m.	5:46 p.m.
31*	6:25 a.m.	4:46 p.m.	6:26 a.m.	4:45 p.m.
Nov.				
01	6:26 a.m.	4:44 p.m.	6:27 a.m.	4:43 p.m.
02	6:27 a.m.	4:43 p.m.	6:28 a.m.	4:42 p.m.
03	6:29 a.m.	4:42 p.m.	6:30 a.m.	4:41 p.m.
04	6:30 a.m.	4:40 p.m.	6:31 a.m.	4:39 p.m.
05	6:31 a.m.	4:39 p.m.	6:32 a.m.	4:38 p.m.
06	6:32 a.m.	4:38 p.m.	6:33 a.m.	4:37 p.m.
07	6:34 a.m.	4:37 p.m.	6:35 a.m.	4:36 p.m.
08	6:35 a.m.	4:36 p.m.	6:36 a.m.	4:35 p.m.
09	6:36 a.m.	4:34 p.m.	6:37 a.m.	4:34 p.m.
10	6:38 a.m.	4:33 p.m.	6:39 a.m.	4:33 p.m.
11	6:39 a.m.	4:32 p.m.	6:40 a.m.	4:32 p.m.
12	6:40 a.m.	4:31 p.m.	6:41 a.m.	4:31 p.m.
13	6:41 a.m.	4:30 p.m.	6:42 a.m.	4:30 p.m.
14	6:43 a.m.	4:29 p.m.	6:44 a.m.	4:29 p.m.
15	6:44 a.m.	4:28 p.m.	6:45 a.m.	4:28 p.m.
16	6:45 a.m.	4:27 p.m.	6:46 a.m.	4:27 p.m.
17	6:46 a.m.	4:27 p.m.	6:47 a.m.	4:26 p.m.
18	6:48 a.m.	4:26 p.m.	6:49 a.m.	4:25 p.m.
19	6:49 a.m.	4:25 p.m.	6:50 a.m.	4:24 p.m.
20	6:50 a.m.	4:24 p.m.	6:51 a.m.	4:24 p.m.
21	6:51 a.m.	4:23 p.m.	6:52 a.m.	4:23 p.m.
22	6:53 a.m.	4:23 p.m.	6:54 a.m.	4:22 p.m.
23	6:54 a.m.	4:22 p.m.	6:55 a.m.	4:22 p.m.
24	6:55 a.m.	4:21 p.m.	6:56 a.m.	4:21 p.m.
25	6:56 a.m.	4:21 p.m.	6:57 a.m.	4:20 p.m.
26	6:57 a.m.	4:20 p.m.	6:58 a.m.	4:20 p.m.
27	6:59 a.m.	4:20 p.m.	7:00 a.m.	4:19 p.m.
28	7:00 a.m.	4:19 p.m.	7:01 a.m.	4:19 p.m.
29	7:01 a.m.	4:19 p.m.	7:02 a.m.	4:19 p.m.
30	7:02 a.m.	4:19 p.m.	7:03 a.m.	4:18 p.m.

Denotes end of Daylight Saving Time.
Source: United States Naval Observatory

10 Steps to Safe Venison

With the recent discovery of chronic wasting disease east of the Mississippi River, hunters everywhere are worrying about the safety of their venison. Although CWD is troubling, it should not deter you from eating venison from healthy deer. After all, the World Health Organization has officially stated there is no scientific evidence the disease can infect humans. However, the agency says no part of an infected deer or elk should be eaten by people or other animals.

Bad prions, which cause CWD, congregate in nervous tissue and lymph nodes. Therefore, boning out meat — without cutting into the brain or spine — and discarding blood vessels and internal organs is the safest way to process deer.

Any hunter can learn to process deer safely and effectively. Use these 10 tips to improve the flavor of your venison.

1 PLAY IT SAFE IN THE FIELD.
Take extra care while field-dressing your deer. For your safety, always wear rubber gloves, and be careful not to puncture the rumen or intestines. If stomach contents enter the chest cavity, rinse the cavity with cold water and pat it dry with paper towels. Wash all utensils with hot soapy water before and after field-dressing a deer.

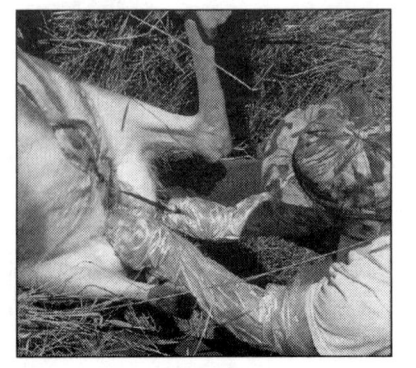

2 TAKE TIME TO SKIN YOUR DEER PROPERLY.
Some hunters remove the skin from the head down, while others prefer to start from the hind legs. Either way works well. The key is to work slowly and methodically. Pulling the hide with your hands prevents extra cuts into the meat and hide.

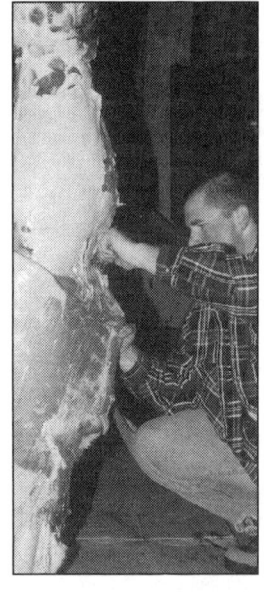

3 KEEP IT CLEAN.
After the hide is off, remove as much hair, blood, damaged tissue, gristle and fat as possible. This makes the finished product more enjoyable. Allow skinned carcass to cool. A refrigerated room

is ideal, but not necessary. Meat can hang for several days in an unrefrigerated room if the temperature is less than 35 degrees and there are no drastic temperature fluctuations. In warm weather, process the deer immediately and cool quartered sections in a refrigerator before final processing.

4 **KEEP A SHARP EDGE.** Butchering a deer requires a stiff, sharp boning knife. Keep it sharp throughout the process with frequent sharpening. Another knife, perhaps your normal hunting knife, serves for cutting through tough connective tissue, especially leg joints. Be careful when cutting around bone knuckles. Do not use your knife to pry, pound or twist through bones. One slip, and you can severely injure yourself. Instead, work slow and use your hands — not your knife — to pry meat away from bone joints.

5 **CUT YOUR OWN STEAKS.** Removing the two loin straps (or "back straps") is similar to filleting a fish. Cut down the center of the back using the tip of your knife to follow each bone of the spine. Be careful to not cut into the spinal cavity. Instead, use the tip of the knife to work the loin free on both sides. Next, grab the head of the loin with one hand and pull it free from the bones while using the knife to work it free from the rib cage. Loin straps can be cut into 1-inch-thick steaks for grilling or frying.

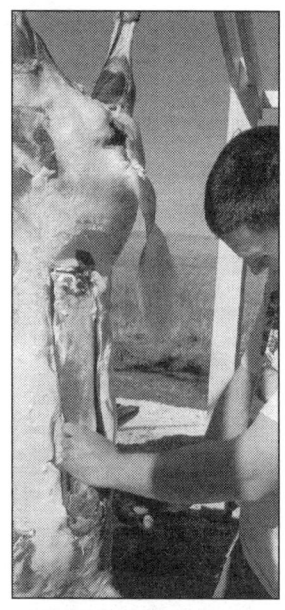

6 **DON'T BE WASTEFUL.**
Bone out the front shoulders and set the meat aside. The tendons and connective tissues of shoulder meat is perfect for ground venison or sausage meat. Meat from the neck, ribs and lower hindquarters is also good for these applications. It is very important to remove the tough, silvery connective tissue along the outside surface of all meat. This tissue gives venison an undesirable aftertaste.

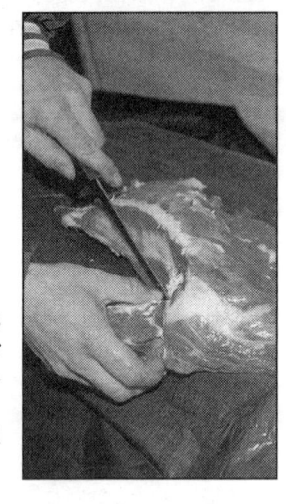

7 **AVOID MEAT SAWS.**
Although meat saws work great for cutting through bones, avoid using them at all costs. Cutting through bone means cutting through marrow. That could taint your saw blade. The hindquarter can be easily detached from the carcass by using a knife and slicing down to the hip bone. After locating the knuckle, slowly and carefully cut around the joint to "pop" it free from the skeleton. Bone out the round completely and slice it into steaks or roasts.

8 **REMOVE ALL BONES.**
Cut down the inside of the deer's leg to find the leg bone. Then use your finger to probe between the muscle bundles for the bone. Once located, cut around the leg bone to free and remove it from the meat. By removing the bones, you will save yourself the extra costs associated with freezer paper and freezer space.

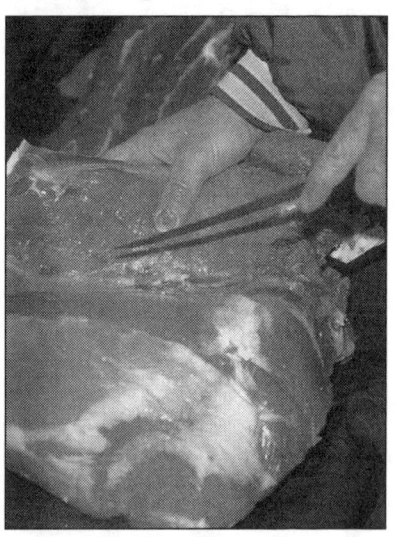

9 **BE METICULOUS.**
Venison is one the most nutritious meats available. Therefore, it's wise to utilize every scrap of meat from your deer, and that means the ribs! Meat removed from between the ribs can be

ground for sausage or burger. The more gristle and fat you remove now, the better the finished product will be.

10 **WRAP IT UP.** When all the meat is removed from the carcass, shift your operation indoors. Using clean utensils and working surfaces, package the cuts for the freezer. It's wise to double-wrap all packages, using extra care to remove all air from the packages before sealing them with tape. Two layers of wrapping paper provide better insulation and prevent the meat from getting freezer burn. Be sure to label all packages and include the date.

General Precautions
1. Do not eat the eyes, brain, spinal cord, spleen, tonsils or lymph nodes.
2. Do not eat deer that look sick.
3. If your deer is sampled for CWD, wait for the test results before eating the meat.

Field-Dressing Precautions
1. Wear rubber or latex gloves
2. Minimize contact with the brain, spinal cord, spleen and lymph nodes.
3. Do not use household knives or utensils.
4. Remove and dispose of all internal organs, including the heart and liver.
5. Clean knives and equipment of residue and disinfect with a 50/50 solution of chlorine and water. Wipe down counters and let them dry. Soak knives for one hour.

Cutting and Processing
1. Wear rubber or latex gloves
2. Minimize handling brain and spinal tissues. If you remove the antlers, use a saw designated for that purpose and dispose of the blade.
3. Do not cut through the spinal column except to remove the head.
4. Bone out the meat and remove all fat and connective tissue (the web-like membranes attached to the meat). This will also remove lymph nodes.
5. Dispose of hide, brain, spinal cord, eyes, spleen, tonsils, bones and head in a landfill or by other means available in your area.
6. Thoroughly clean and sanitize equipment and work areas with bleach water after processing.
7. Keep meat and trimmings from each deer separate.

Mossy Oak Food Plot Guide

Mossy Oak's food plot guide will help you determine the right seed and right planting time for your area. For zone boundaries and other information, visit www.mossyoakbiologic.com.

Northern Zone

To give your plants the best chance of success, plant with adequate soil moisture; typically early spring and fall planting will be the most successful. You can frost seed or plant in the spring when daytime high temperatures reach 63 to 65 degrees. Fall plantings should be planted prior to the onset of autumn rains. A good rule of thumb is to make sure your food plots are planted at least 30 to 45 days prior to the first frost. Clover Plus, Premium Perennial and Maximum are excellent choices for planting in the Northern Zone. For more details on Waterfowl Forage planting in the Northern Zone, please contact BioLogic.

Transitional Zone

For the Transitional Zone, optimum planting time for Clover Plus and Premium Perennial is early fall. This lets the plants establish a better root system to survive summer heat. However, both will do well during an early spring planting, typically 30 to 40 days before your area's last frost. These varieties provide long-term nutrition for the wildlife on your property. Excellent stands of Maximum can be established with early spring plantings or early fall plantings. Maximum is an excellent

Mossy Oak Biologic Food Plot Planting Guide

Planting	North Zone	Transitional Zone	South Zone
Maximum	spring/ late summer	early fall/early spring	early spring/ earlyfall/mid fall
Premium Perennial	frost seed/spring/ late summer	early spring/early fall	early fall/mid fall
Clover Plus	frost seed/spring/ late summer	early spring/early fall	early fall/mid fall
Green Patch	late summer/ early fall	early fall	early fall/mid fall
Full Draw	late summer/ early fall	early fall	early fall/mid fall
Bio Mass	early summer	late spring/ early summer	late spring/ early summer

choice for over-seeding existing stands of Clover Plus and Premium Perennial. Green Patch Plus and Full Draw exhibit optimum results when planted during early fall. BioMass and Waterfowl Forage should be planted when soybeans are planted locally.

Southern Zone

For the Southern Zone, Clover Plus and Premium Perennial should ideally be planted during early fall. These varieties can be planted in early spring but should be avoided for late spring plantings due to limited root growth before hot, dry conditions. Maximum is excellent for over-seeding into existing Clover Plus and Premium Perennial plots in early fall or for stand-alone plots in the early fall. BioMass is the product of choice for late spring and early summer plantings in the Southern Zone. Waterfowl Forage should only be planted in the late spring or early summer in this zone. Our central and southern Texas customers have great results planting Premium Perennial in the fall. It provides excellent fall, spring and early summer growth, but should be replanted the following fall.

Note: Many successful food plot planters mix Maximum and Premium Perennial with their current commodity blends as additional forage and are very pleased with the results. For more information on this practice call (866) 677-9625.

Web Site Addresses for Hunting Gear

Clothing
10X Products	www.10xwear.com
Gore-Tex	www.gore-tex.com
Mossy Oak	www.mossyoak.com
Realtree	www.realtreeoutdoors.com

Calls
Knight & Hale	www.knight-hale.com
Primos	www.primos.com
Woods Wise	www.woodswise.com

Bows
Darton	www.Dartonarchery.com
Browning	www.browning.com
BowTech	www.bowtecharchery.com
Golden Eagle	www.beargoldeneagle.com
Fred Bear	www.beararch.com
High Country	www.highcountryarchery.com
Hoyt USA	www.HOYTUSA.com
Barnett	www.barnettcrossbows.com
Mathews	www.mathewsinc.com
McPherson	www.mcphersonarchery.com
Parker	www.parkerbows.com
PSE	www.pse-archery.com/ddh

Broadheads
Ballistic Archery	www.steelforce.com
Barrie Archery	www.RockeyMtBroadheads.com
Innerloc	www.Innerloc.com
Muzzy Products	www.BadToTheBone.com
New Archery Products	www.newarchery.com
Satellite	www.gearchery.com

Guns and Ammo
Barnes Bullets	www.barnesbullets.com
Federal Cartridge	www.federalcartridge.com
Marlin	www.marlinfirearms.com
Hornady	www.hornady.com
Modern Muzzleloading	www.knightrifles.com
Nosler Bullets	www.nosler.com
Remington	www.remington.com
Savage	www.savagearms.com
Thompson/Center	www.tcarms.com
Weatherby	www.weatherby.com
Winchester	www.winchester.com

Tree Stands and Accessories
Aerospace America	www.aerospaceamerica.com
Bear River	www.up-north.com/bearriver
Ameristep	www.ameristep.com
API	www.apioutdoors.com
Ol'Man Treestands	www.ol-man.com
Blackwater Creek	www.blackwatercreek.com
Summit	www.summitstands.com
Warren & Sweat	www.warrenandsweat.com

*This is a partial list from the Deer & Deer Hunting links page. Visit www.deeranddeerhunting.com

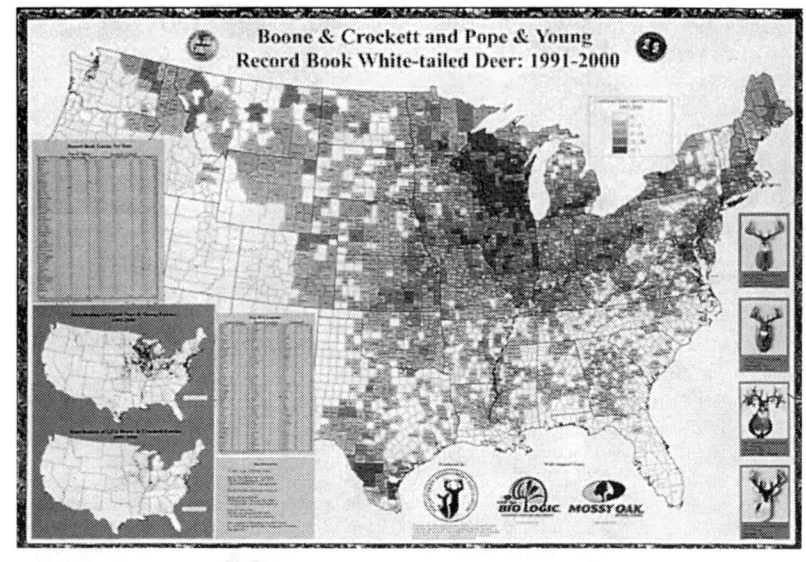

Quality Deer Management Association Offers Map of Record-Class Whitetail Kill Densities

Have you ever wondered which areas produce the most Boone and Crockett and Pope and Young bucks? Well, today, answering that question is easier than ever, thanks to detailed maps recently compiled by the Quality Deer Management Association.

The maps, created by QDMA intern Joel Helmer, reflect how many record-class bucks each county in the Unites States produced from 1991 to 2000. To illustrate concentrations of record-class buck kills during the 10-year period, each county is color-coded in shades of red, with the darkest shade indicating the most big-buck kills.

The map reveals aspects of how geography, climate and soil conditions affect deer size. For example, some of the highest concentrations of record-class bucks have been killed along the Ohio and Upper Mississippi rivers, where mineral-rich soils encourage antler growth.

The map also illustrates the fantastic hunting and big-buck potential of states like Wisconsin and Illinois, where almost every county produces high numbers of B&C and P&Y bucks.

In addition, the map lists the top 50 counties for record-class buck kills, and shows how many P&Y and B&C bucks each of those counties produced from 1991 to 2000.

To order the map, contact the Quality Deer Management Association, Box 227, Watkinsville, GA 30677, call (800) 209-DEER, visit www.qdma.com, or send an e-mail to qdma@charter.net.

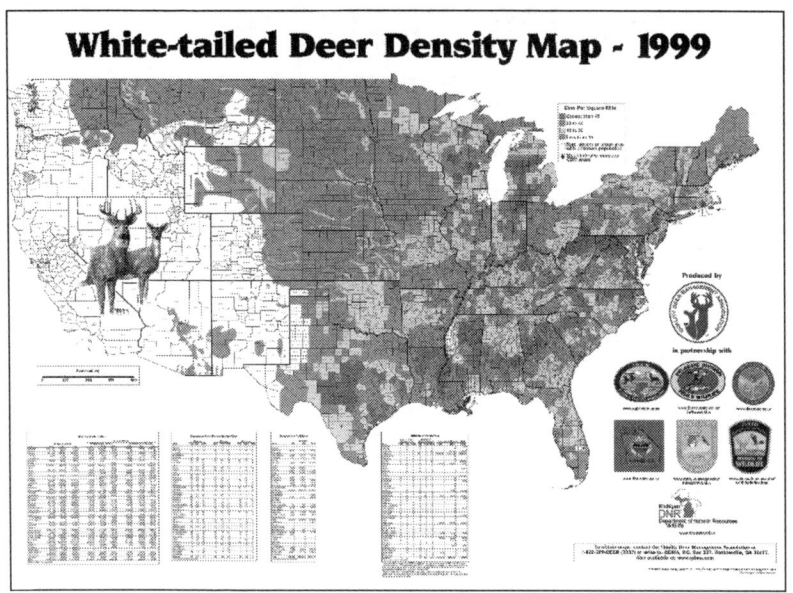

White-tailed Deer Density Map - 1999

How Many Deer Live in Your Hunting Area?

Have you ever wondered which areas of the country contain the highest deer densities?

Thanks to the Quality Deer Management Association's White-tailed Deer Density Map, you can quickly and easily access population information by county across the country.

This film-coated 28-by-40-inch color map of the United States features the most comprehensive whitetail population information ever compiled. It includes deer density by county, statewide deer population estimates, deer harvest trends by sex and age and deer/vehicle collision information. The map also features state-by-state information on QDM trends, including the amount of public support and the amount of land managed under QDM principles. The color-coded map indicates where deer are rare, and where they number less than 15, 15-30, 30-45 or greater than 45 deer per square mile.

This map is a great reference for all deer hunters, land managers, wildlife professionals or anyone with an interest in white-tailed deer. This map is an even more valuable tool when used in conjunction with the the QDMA's Boone & Crockett and Pope and Young Distribution Map.

To order the map, contact the Quality Deer Management Association, Box 227, Watkinsville, GA 30677, call (800) 209-DEER, visit www.qdma.com, or send an e-mail to qdma@charter.net.

National Hunting Organizations

American Shooting Sports Council
101 D. Street SE
Washington, DC 20003
(202) 544-1610
(202) 543-5865 fax

Archery Manufacturers Organization (AMO)
304 Brown St. E, Box 258
Comfrey, MN 56019
(866) 266-2776
(507) 877-2149 fax

Archery Hall of Fame
1555 S. 150 West
Angola, IN 46703

Archery Range and Retailers Organization
156 N. Main St., Suite D
Oregon, WI 53575
(800) 234-7499

Archery Shooters Association
Box 399
Kennesaw, GA 30144
(770) 795-0232

Becoming an Outdoors-Woman
UW-Stevens Point
College of Natural Resources
Stevens Point, WI 54481-3897
(715) 228-2070

Boone & Crockett Club
The Old Milwaukee Depot
250 Station Drive
Missoula, MT 59801
(406) 542-1888

Christian Bowhunters of America
3460 W. 13th St.
Cadillac, MI 49601
(616) 775-7744

Christian Deer Hunters Association
Box 432
Silver Lake, MN 55381
(320) 327-2266

Congressional Sportsman's Foundation
303 Pennsylvania Ave. SE
Washington, DC 20003
(202) 543-6850

Ducks Unlimited
1 Waterfowl Way
Memphis, TN 38120
(901) 758-3718

Hunter Education Association
Box 490
Wellington, CO 80549
(970) 568-7954
(970) 568-7955 fax

International Association of Fish & Wildlife Agencies
Hall of the States
444 N. Capitol St. NW, Suite 544
Washington, DC 20001
(202) 624-7890

International Bowhunters Organization
3409 E. Liberty, Box 398
Vermilion, OH 44089
(216) 967-2137

International Sportsmen's Expositions
Box 2569
Vancouver, WA 98668-2569
(800) 545-6100
(360) 693-3352 fax

Izaak Walton League of America
707 Conservation Lane
Gaithersburg, MD 20878-2983
(301) 548-0150
(301) 548-0146 fax

National Association of Sporting Goods Wholesalers
400 E. Randolph St., Suite 700
Chicago, IL 60601
(312) 565-0233
(312) 565-2654 fax

National Bowhunter Education Foundation
101½ North Front St.
Townsend, MT 59644
(406) 266-3237

National Crossbow Hunters Organization
Box 506, Verona, OH 45378
(937) 884-5017

National Field Archery Association
31407 Outer I-10
Redlands, CA 92373
(909) 794-2133
(909) 794-8512 fax

National Muzzleloading Rifle Association
Box 67, Friendship, IN 47021
(812) 667-5131
(812) 667-5137 fax

National Rifle Association
11250 Waples Mill Road
Fairfax, VA 22030-7400
(703) 267-1000

National Shooting Sports Foundation
Flintlock Ridge Office Center
11 Mile Hill Road
Newton, CT 06470-2359
(203) 426-1320

Natl. Wild Turkey Federation
770 Augusta Road, Box 530
Edgefield, SC 29824-0530
(803) 637-3106
(803) 637-0034 fax

Outdoor Writers Association of America
27 Fort Missoula Road, Suite 1
Missoula, MT 59804
(406) 728-7445

Physically Challenged Bowhunters of America
Box 57, Gorham, KS 67640
(785) 637-5421

Pope & Young Club
15 E. 2nd St., Box 548
Chatfield, MN 55923
(507) 867-4144

Quality Deer Management Association
Box 227
Watkinsville, GA 30677
(800) 209-3337

Safari Club International
4800 W. Gates Pass Road
Tucson, AZ 85745
(520) 620-1220

U.S. Fish & Wildlife Service
1849 C St. NW
Washington, DC 20240
(202) 208-4131

Wildlife Legislative Fund
801 Kingsmill Parkway
Columbus, OH 43229-1137
(614) 888-4868

Wildlife Management Institute
1101 14th St. NW, Suite 801
Washington, DC 20005
(202) 371-1808

Women's Shooting Sports Foundation
4620 Edison Ave., Suite C
Colorado Springs, CO 80915
(719) 638-1299

Deer Harvest Records

Year _____ Name of Camp _____

Month & Day	Time of Day	Hunter Name	Buck (points)	Doe	Dressed Weight	Bow or Gun	Shot Distance	Tracking Distance

Ensure A Successful Hunt

Big Bucks the Benoit Way
*Secrets from America's First Family
of Whitetail Hunting*
by Bryce Towsley

Finally, the long-awaited second book on the tried-and-true hunting strategies of the legendary Benoit family. Although tracking and woodsmanship are emphasized, hunters of all ages, no matter where they hunt, will gain the knowledge needed to bag trophy bucks.

Hardcover • 8½ x 11 • 208 pages
150 b&w photos • 16-page color section
Item# HBB • $24.95

Benoit Bucks
Whitetail Tactics for a New Generation
by Bryce Towsley

This highly anticipated follow-up volume details the "second generation" of the Benoit family, brothers Shane, Lenny, and Lane, established trophy deer hunters who are every bit as successful as their legendary father. Adventure stories recount the excitement of the chase, sharing the secret strategies that led to success-or sometimes failure-and most importantly, what was learned from those hunting experiences. Detailed accounts tie humor with solid teaching on the fundamentals of whitetail hunting.

Hardcover • 8¼x10⅞ • 224 pages
150 b&w photos • 16-page color section
Item# HBB2 • $29.99

Quality Deer Management
The Basics and Beyond
by Charles J. Alsheimer

Raise quality deer herds with bigger bucks and larger antlers through quality deer management (QDM). Learn how you can participate through land development, proper harvesting, maintaining good doe-to-buck ratios, and establishing nutritious food sources. Contains tips on land management, good forestry practices, controlling antlerless deer herds, and how to sell QDM to neighboring landowners. Even landowners of small plots can participate.

Hardcover • 8¼ x 10⅞ • 208 pages
200+ color photos
Item# QDMGT • $39.95

To order call
800-258-0929
Offer OTB3
M-F 7am - 8pm • Sat 8am - 2pm, CST

Krause Publications
Offer OTB3 • P.O. Box 5009
Iola WI 54945-5009
www.krausebooks.com

Bowhunters' Digest
Advanced Tactics, 5th Edition
edited by Kevin Michalowski

Learn advanced bowhunting tactics from more than twenty top bowhunters including Greg Miller, Bryce Towsley, M.D. Johnson, and Gary Clancy. They'll teach you how to hone your hunting and shooting skills to increase your success. Become familiar with the latest equipment and accessories and find out how to contact archery manufacturers, dealers, and other resources with the state-by-state list.

Softcover • 8½ x 11 • 256 pages
300 b&w photos
Item# BOW5 • $22.95

Legendary Deer Camps
by Robert Wegner

Travel back in time to experience deer camps of famous Americans such as William Faulkner, Aldo Leopold and Oliver Hazard Perry. Rediscover classic hunting traditions such as freedom, solitude, camaraderie, rites of initiation, story-telling and venison cuisine through a series of famous deer camp biographies and rare historical paintings and photographs. This is the second book in the *Deer and Deer Hunting* Classics Series.

Hardcover • 8¼ x 10⅞ • 208 pages
125 b&w photos • 75 color photos
Item# DERCP • $34.95

25 Years of Deer & Deer Hunting
The Original Stump Sitters Magazine
edited by Daniel E. Schmidt

For the first time ever, *Deer & Deer Hunting* magazine opens its vaults and presents a comprehensive look at the articles, photographs, and personalities that built North America's first and favorite whitetailed deer hunting magazine. Heart-warming tributes are given to the magazine's founders, and never-before-published articles provide valuable whitetail insights that cannot be found elsewhere.

Hardcover • 8¼ x 10⅞ • 208 pages
10 b&w photos • 150 color photos
Item# DDH25 • $~~29.95~~

Sale $15.00

Shipping & Handling: $4.00 first book, $2.25 each additional. Non-US addresses $20.95 first book, $5.95 each additional.
Sales Tax: CA, IA, IL, KS, NJ, PA, SD, IN, WI residents please add appropriate sales tax.

Blood-Trailing Log

Hunter: _____

Location: _____

Deer/Age: _____ Shot Distance: _____

Bow/Gun: _____ Broadhead/Bullet: _____

Pass-Through? _____ Time Allowed: _____

Trail Distance: _____ Recovery? _____

Trail details:

Indicate Shot Placement:

__ One Lung   __ Both Lungs
__ Liver   __ Heart
__ Paunch   __ Ham
__ Shoulder Blade

_____
_____
_____
_____
_____
_____
_____
_____
_____
_____
_____
_____
_____
_____
_____
_____
_____
_____
_____
_____